Polish Theatre after the Fall of Communism

Polish Theatre after the Fall of Communism:

Dionysus since '89

By

Olga Śmiechowicz

Cambridge Scholars Publishing

Polish Theatre after the Fall of Communism: Dionysus since ’89

By Olga Śmiechowicz

This book first published 2018

Cambridge Scholars Publishing

Lady Stephenson Library, Newcastle upon Tyne, NE6 2PA, UK

British Library Cataloguing in Publication Data
A catalogue record for this book is available from the British Library

ISBN (10): 1-5275-1309-2
ISBN (13): 978-1-5275-1309-9

CONTENTS

PREFACE

Poland is a country in which "theatre is for those for whom the church is not enough".[1] A country in which, despite the German occupation, roundups and public executions, theatre productions were performed in private apartments. A country in which theatre had become an organ of opposition to externally imposed authority. A country in which to take off a play would cause national protests. A country in which you simply "do not walk into a theatre unpunished…"[2]

Polish Theatre after the Fall of the Communism: Dionysus Since 89' is the first study on the latest history of the Polish theatre written in English. My work continues the narration at the point where Kazimierz Braun's: *A History of Polish Theatre 1939-1989* (published in 1996 by Greenwood Press) ended. In April 1990, during a conference "Art and Freedom" (organised by the Jagiellonian University in Krakow), Tadeusz Kantor said: "A new trend in art will not come into being as a result of Poland becoming independent. Trends in art, certain changes, transformations, revolutions come into being on entirely different bases."[3] With typical pessimism, Kantor declared the new art dead before it had even appeared in the new democratic Poland. Luckily, looking back over recent years, his argument cannot be accepted. So many art trends in Polish culture have come and gone in the last quarter century that it would be impossible to describe them in a single monograph. It is particularly noticeable in the field of theatre. This is why my primary focus is on the most talented directors: Krystian Lupa, who at the end of the twentieth century became one of the most important creators of European theatre, and his two most eminent disciples: Krzysztof Warlikowski and Jan Klata. The work of the three completely different artists made a major impact on the character of contemporary Polish theatre. Their artistic interests reflect the image of contemporary Poland: problems confronting the Poles; the literature they

---

[1] Juliusz Osterwa, creator of the Reduta Theatre.

[2] Tadeusz Kantor, creator of the Cricot 2 Theatre.

[3] Katarzyna Fazan, „Tandeta w złym, czy dobrym gatunku? Antyestetyka w polskim teatrze 20-lecia," in *20-lecie. Teatr polski po 1989*, edited by Dorota Jarząbek, 347. Kraków: Korporacja Ha! Art., 2010.

choose; what they look for in it; and the cultural codes they adopt to communicate.

Theatre in Poland has a special significance. Being always close to reality, it constitutes a live commentary on the current situation in the country. No other artistic medium has such a strong impact in Poland. Information about theatre events often appears in main news bulletins and premieres are broadly discussed by the press: *Cleansed*, directed by Krzysztof Warlikowski; an actress making offensive gestures to Krystian Lupa during a premiere performance; an attempt to removing Jan Klata from the position of managing director of the National Theatre… the massive coverage these events receive in the Polish media may suggest that they are nearly as important as health care reform.

My work on this book coincided with several anniversaries:

- 2014 marked the 25th anniversary of the fall of Communism in Poland;
- in 2015 Public Theatre in Poland celebrated its 250th birthday;
- 2015 was officially announced by UNESCO as the Year of Tadeusz Kantor (6 April marked the hundredth anniversary of his birth).

Anniversary events coincided with current issues which proved critical to the future of Polish theatre. At the beginning of March 2015, after nearly thirty years of artistic work, Krystian Lupa left the National Stary Theatre in Krakow in an atmosphere of conflict. This event dramatically ended another era in the history of Polish theatre.

Some may think that this book is written too soon, and that there has still not been enough distance to describe what has happened in Polish theatre over the past 25 years. More than once I have been tempted to write using only the *tempus imperfectum*, as all the events described seem to be in progress, still brewing. As I was born two years before the fall of Communism, I often get a feeling that in describing the past 25 years of Polish theatre I am, so to say, describing my twin.

My main objective was to show how our theatrical tradition differs from that of other European countries. When describing the most important productions of the most talented directors, I was trying to capture the energy they generate, to depict how it flows from the stage onto the audience. As is always the case with this medium, it is a challenge to render the three dimensions of a theatrical experience using flat, one-dimensional words. Having observed contemporary theatre life for many years, I have to some extent subconsciously been preparing to write this book. Notes taken during performances, and publishing reviews was completed in the final stage of my work, making detailed research of the vast archives of the Ludwik Solski Academy for the Dramatic Arts in Krakow. Working with director's copies, diaries and articles, I did my best to make sure that my book lets the creators of the productions I describe speak as well. Hence the numerous valuable quotations from interviews and texts published by directors and actors.

I took the liberty of treating the reader as someone similar to me. Someone who may have a differently tuned sensitivity, constituted by different cultural contexts, but who equally inquisitively pricks his or her synapses up to anything new and unknown. Someone who likes to look for things in the theatre where no one had previously looked. I hope, like me, that someone is in the habit of searching the Internet for information. And especially for that someone, to make the search easier, I have left the original titles of productions and the names of creators in the footnotes. I hope that having read the description of *Kalkwerk*, that someone will take advantage of the Internet to see with their own eyes Kantor's scenes which influenced Krystian Lupa's production. Similarly in the case of Krzysztof Warlikowski's theatre, we think differently about *The Taming of the Shrew* when hearing the sounds of Paweł Mykietyn's dangerously insistent music in our headphones.

The title: *Dionysus Since '89* is an erudite reference to the iconic book: *Dionysus Since '69*, edited by Edith Hall, Fiona Macintosh and Amanda Wrigley[4]. It is not, however, an "intellectual follow-up" to the book which was devoted to the reception of antiquity. I am merely adopting a suggested way of thinking introduced by the authors, in which the antique god became a prefiguration of the entire medium which is theatre. *My* Dionysus, as in the above-mentioned book, has many forms and meanings. He has the softness of a figure in a painting by Caravaggio, but also the impulsiveness of Euripides' *The Bacchae*. His heterogeneity is to me a perfect symbol of different incarnations successively adopted by Polish theatre. It may be Krystian Lupa himself, who by falling into dangerously ecstatic states during his own productions has the ability to infect his actors and audiences with them. Dionysus is an ecstatic deity, but he is also extremely dangerous…

---

[4] Edith Hall, Fiona Macintosh, Amanda Wrigley, *Dionysus Since 69: Greek Tragedy at the Dawn of the Third Millennium* (Oxford: Oxford University Press, 2004).

ACKNOWLEDGEMENTS

A fascination with Krystian Lupa's work directly influenced my decision to undertake theatre studies. Neither Professor Jacek Popiel nor I believe in coincidence. Apparently, a coincidence is in fact an unconscious necessity… How else to explain the fact that he was the first person I spoke to the first time I stepped into the Krakow Theatre Studies building? In time, he became the dearest Professor who taught us classes devoted to contemporary Polish theatre. In time, he became the dearest Supervisor, under whose kindly supervision I wrote my doctoral dissertation on the reception of Aristophanic Comedy. In some interpersonal relations the present has no end: I would thus like to express my sincere and profound gratitude to Professor Popiel for his invaluable assistance.

Heidelberg, June, 2018

CHAPTER ONE

BEFORE AND AFTER '89

If we look at the geopolitical map of Europe in the first half of the twentieth century we soon realise that Poland's position at the time could not have been worse. It was located exactly between Nazi Germany and Stalinist Russia. When the German army retreated from the Polish territories at the end of World War II, the Soviet Army took its place, bringing with it NKVD commissars who laid the foundation for Communism in Poland. The imposed political system, which firmly subordinated the state to the USSR, lasted on Polish territory until 1989.

The Communist Party assumed control over all spheres of life. All theatres were nationalised and their artistic expression tightly constricted by censorship. Theatre managements were obliged to submit a copy of each play they intended to stage to the censorship office. First of all, their "ideological content" was analysed, and particular attention devoted to those plays which might contain unwanted, anti-Soviet messages. Censorship controlled theatre brochures and posters. Even theatre critics were controlled, which resulted in the peculiar phenomenon of "controlled criticism". Artists obedient to the system were promoted, and the work of those who had the courage to speak with their own voice, independent of the current political situation, was made difficult. It was obvious that actors who were members of the party would be cast more easily. Members of the Communist Party were also appointed directors of better theatres.

In 1949, pursuant to directives from Moscow, Socialist realism was introduced in Poland as an official trend compulsory in all fields of art. What is interesting is the fact that the main task of Socialist realism was defined as presenting a reality which did not exist. It was the reality to which (according to party ideologists) the entire society should aspire. The art of acting was forced to use a debased version of the Stanislavski method, and the so-called "production novels" were introduced in the repertoires of all theatres. They were plays about the working class achieving 400 percent efficiency, and fighting the Western, capitalist enemy. It is not hard to guess that it was not top-class drama.

The theatre reality of the time was grey, sad and unimaginative. In 1952, Bertolt Brecht's Berliner Ensemble visited Poland which was an unconscious announcement of the broadly awaited "thaw". The ensemble presented: *Mother*, *The Broken Pitcher* and *Mother Courage and Her Children*. The performances provoked the harsh opposition of the party-supporting critics, but also delight and upheaval among those who dreamt of taking the risk of experimenting with new texts and forms. Influenced by the visit, Polish theatre started leaning towards "epic theatre" — it was far from the aesthetics and problems taken up by the Socialist theatre. After the death of Stalin in 1953, a significant weakening of censorship was noticeable and, most importantly, deviation from the doctrines of Socialist realism was allowed. National classics and plays by Beckett, Ionesco, Dürrenmatt and Williams, popular in the West, returned to Polish theatres. Brecht's visit blazed a trail for Western theatres. Peter Brook came to Poland with his production of Shakespeare's *Titus Andronicus* (1957), and Giorgio Strehler presented Goldoni's *Servant of Two Masters* (1958). However, construction of the Berlin Wall in 1961 reinforced the Iron Curtain: censorship was re-established and the repertoire once again limited to "Socialist" productions.

Brecht and his ensemble's visit was also pivotal in the creative development of one of Poland's greatest twentieth-century stage producers. In 1955 Konrad Swinarski made his stage debut (in the years 1955 – 56 he worked as assistant to Brecht in Berlin). In his work as theatre director Swinarski ceased offering classical interpretations of dramatic plays. His project for the staging of Shakespeare's *Hamlet* gained iconic status in Polish theatre. Swinarski planned to include the entire space of the Stary Theatre in his vision.[1] Among other things, he planned to set up an army camp on the square in front of the theatre (inspired by Velázquez' *The Surrender of Breda*), in order for spectators heading for the foyer to walk through barracks. He wanted to fit roofs of buildings surrounding the square with speakers emitting the hum of sea waves which, mixed with the sounds of the barracks, would reach inside the theatre. Swinarski was able to compile such a monumental vision with an ironically "cheap" effect — when the Ghost of Hamlet's Father appeared on stage his armour opened and visible inside it was a lit shrine with entrails. Old Hamlet was not very sensitive but, according to Swinarski, was well aware of the fact that his son never loved him and therefore tried to invoke his compassion in every

[1] The Helena Modrzejewska National Stary Theatre in Krakow remains one of the most important theatres in Poland.

possible way. (The project was unfinished — the work was interrupted by the director's tragic death in a plane crash in 1975.)

One of Swinarski's young assistants on this production was Krystian Lupa. Observers of contemporary theatre agree in pointing out Lupa as the creator closest to his theatre work. While Lupa was still studying at the Krakow Academy for Dramatic Arts, Swinarski told his actors about a very gifted student of theatre direction… but he (rightly) disagrees, and claims he managed to work out his own production style. However, Lupa adopted the basis, the deepest nuances of thinking about the art of theatre, from Swinarski.

In the same year that Swinarski made his stage debut, Tadeusz Kantor founded the Cricot 2 Theatre in Krakow (Kantor's life's work was a continuation of his artistic endeavours under the occupation, and lasted until his death in 1990). Four years later, in 1959, Jerzy Grotowski founded the Theatre of 13 Rows.[2] Grotowski creatively researched dramatic texts, and by placing them in non-traditional contexts introduced new interpretations. However, his method of working with actors proved to be most important in the history of Polish theatre. *Akropolis*, staged in 1962, was presented in the reality of a concentration camp marking the beginning of "poor theatre", which in time extracted a sequence of notions such as "bare acting" and "via negativa". These notions constituted Grotowski's method of working on productions. It was a method of intense, many hours' trainings, demanding extreme physical strength of actors. Such maximum tuning of the body was to allow them to reach the deepest areas of mind and spirituality, as well as to fully release actors' abilities. *The Constant Prince*, staged in 1965 (as well as *Apocalypsis Cum Figuris* in 1968), is considered to be one of the most important artistic expressions in the history of Polish theatre. Ryszard Cieślak, who played the title role, proved definitely that a "total act" in art is possible.

The year 1968 was not only the year of Jerzy Grotowski's *Apocalypsis Cum Figuris* premiere: on 25 November 1967, on the fiftieth anniversary of the October Revolution, Kazimierz Dejmek, hitherto an ideologically correct director of "production novels", staged Adam Mickiewicz's *Forefathers' Eve* at the National Theatre in Warsaw. It is the most important dramatic text in Polish theatre. The Party considered the production a "stab in the back" of Polish-Russian friendship and banned any publication of positive reviews. The authorities' official antipathy provoked the obvious and eager interest of the public. As a result, the production was ordered to be closed. The final performance (30 January

[2] In 1962 it changed its name to the Laboratory Theatre.

1968) developed into a national manifestation which marked the beginning of a series of protests all over the country. They were primarily initiated by students, many of whom were arrested, and many (including protesting lecturers) were expelled from universities. The Communist Party began large-scale propaganda against the Polish intelligentsia. Dejmek lost his position as manager of the National Theatre. In a gesture of solidarity, most of its actors left with him.

Student theatres, strongly involved in political and social issues,[3] emerged in 1970s Poland on a mass scale. (Obviously, the authorities did their best to limit such activity.) Repertory theatres stages abounded in outstanding productions by esteemed directors: Jerzy Jarocki, Andrzej Wajda and Jerzy Grzegorzewski. However, critics accused these artists of indifference to current issues and lack of involvement in political life. Official theatres seemed not to notice the unrest exploding in Polish society. Such were the circumstances surrounding Krystian Lupa's directing debut in 1976, still unnoticed at the time. He was bound to patiently await the right moment to turn Polish theatre upside down…

In 1980, the "Solidarity" movement was founded, which threw down the gauntlet to the Communist Party, and began enforcing changes in the management of the state (including its cultural policy). In the same year, Tadeusz Kantor staged *Wielopole, Wielopole*, one of his best plays. Social unrest and growing discontent with the situation in the country were suppressed by the introduction of martial law in December 1981. Strikes were crushed with live ammunition, and "Solidarity" was made illegal. Theatre artists, boycotting performances of the Party-controlled radio and television, also suffered repression. Such artists were savagely attacked by Communist propaganda. (Those who decided to cooperate with the authorities, on the other hand, paid the price of infamy within their circles.) Funds were drastically reduced and theatres were often banned from staging performances altogether. Censorship was reinstated. In response, underground theatre was created (as during World War II). Performances took place in private apartments and churches to which access by the Communist authorities was limited. All cultural events had heavy political undertones. In 1982, Jerzy Grotowski left Poland for good to continue his paratheatrical projects abroad. (In 1997 he was appointed to the chair of Theatre Anthropology, created specifically for him, at the Collège de France.)

---

[3] Włodzimierz Staniewski began his artistic career at the time at the Krakow STU theatre. Over time he joined Jerzy Grotowski's Laboratory Theatre, and in 1978 founded the Centre for Theatre Practices Gardzienice.

Communism lasted in Poland until 1989. Artistic circles greeted the new, democratic system with enthusiasm. However, the beginnings of capitalism negatively affected theatre funding. The state budget (which previously supported all theatres) could no longer be burdened with such a heavy load. Severe cuts were introduced and many artists lost their jobs. Profit-making productions were chosen over artistic ones. In 1990 censorship was completely abolished, but theatre had already lost its social importance. It ceased to be the carrier of banned metaphors. "Denmark is a prison" was no longer so loaded with meaning, and Lear's division of the kingdom was no longer associated by Poles with the Yalta Conference of 1945.

The death of Tadeusz Kantor on 8 December 1990 was the end of an era in Polish culture. *Today Is My Birthday*, an unfinished production which premiered one month after the death of its director, became a symbolic summary of the past century. Once again, like Konrad Swinarski, "the greatest one" was working in fringe theatre, uninterested in political issues of the day Krystian Lupa, together with a group of his devoted actors, worked at a provincial theatre until the end of the 1980s. He was often ridiculed by condescending critics. However, he patiently perfected his work and offered his audiences an intellectual retreat from politics and social involvement. With his productions he asked about the elusiveness of human sensitivity and how not to reduce existence to the level of banality. He treated a written dramatic play as a "landscape in which one can take an easy walk, stop in one's favourite spots to contemplate them, gazing at a detail — and eventually look at one's watch, conclude that it is late, get up and return home".[4] Lupa, who constructed his performances with moods and climates, was finally noticed in the late 80s. The director became well-known when he staged *The Dreamers* (1988) and *The Brothers Karamazov* (1990). During the 90s he became one of the greatest creators of Polish and European theatre. He became a teacher, a paragon, and a guru for subsequent generations of artists. From the early 90s he was head of the Directing Department at the Ludwik Solski Academy for the Dramatic Arts. A new generation in Polish theatre was composed mainly of Lupa's disciples. The best-known of them, Krzysztof Warlikowski and Jan Klata, transformed repertory theatre into an artistic theatre of risk taken by artists, directors and audiences alike. Lupa tuned their sensitivity, pushed them to experiment. What is most important, neither of them tries to copy their beloved master.

---

[4] Tomasz Kubikowski, „Pustka i forma," in *Strategie publiczne, strategie prywatne. Teatr polski 1990-2005*, edited by Tomasz Plata, 18. Izabelin: Świat literacki, 2006.

They each draw autonomous conclusions from his teaching and offer something of their own as superstructure. They depart from poetic theatre in favour of socio-political commentary and pop-culture. Their productions, reaching deep for new media, are similarly constructed to music videos. The generation of Lupa's disciples is the first one to fully function in the new political system. They produce their performances abroad and are guests on breakfast TV programmes. In Poland they have become stars of mass culture. Krystian Lupa also maintains the pace of his theatre experiments and refuses to become outdistanced. He continues to test the scope of possibilities of the great theatrical machine: "The soul lab is working at full speed".[5]

[5] Piotr Gruszczyński, *Ojcobójcy. Młodsi zdolniejsi w teatrze polskim* (Warszawa: Wydawnictwo W.A.B., 2003), 54.

CHAPTER TWO

KRYSTIAN LUPA

1. To believe in the communion of souls

Krystian Lupa was born on 7 November 1943 in Jastrzębie Zdrój, a small town in the south of Poland. He had liked to draw ever since he was a child. His sketches depicted a world of non-existent images and remote lands which he continues to map out to this today. Having finished school, and following his parents' suggestions, he applied to study medicine, but he failed the first stage of recruitment as he insulted the examiners by calling them "materialists". He studied physics for six months at the Jagiellonian University in Krakow, but studying exact sciences guaranteeing a stable profession was not fulfilling. Having dropped out of physics Lupa next entered the Academy of Fine Arts in Krakow, Faculty of Painting. He lists Vermeer, da Vinci, Caravaggio, Friedrich, Ernst, Klee, Delvaux and Magritte as some of his favourite artists (whose influence can also be observed in the stage designs he creates). His poetic, and very "literary", paintings are characterised by the distinct influences of surrealism and symbolism. In his drawings, Lupa becomes an illustrator of his own fantasies. Such artistic predilections were behind his move from the Faculty of Painting to Graphics at the same Academy.

During his studies at the Academy, Lupa became enchanted with the French New Wave, and the cinema of Jean-Luc Godard in particular. When he graduated from the Academy in 1969 Lupa therefore applied to the Directing Department of the School of Film and Theatre in Lodz. He was fascinated by the cinema of Ingmar Bergman, Luchino Visconti and Andrei Tarkovsky. However, he got lost in his own immature attitude and pretentious pose of "extreme avant-garde".[1] Today, Lupa likes to refer to himself from that period as "Narcissus fascinated by his own pranks".[2] He enjoys telling the story of how after the second year of studies he got

---

[1] Beata Matkowska-Święs, „Wciąż noszę te siedem dachówek – rozmowa z Krystianem Lupą," *Magazyn Gazeta*, June 1, 2000, 12.
[2] Matkowska-Święs, „Wciąż noszę…," 12.

expelled from the famous film school for eccentric and provocative behaviour. However, many of his lecturers and co-students agree that the films he presented at exams were simply poor.

Expulsion from studies brought about his two-year crisis. He was unable to decide upon the direction to follow. He tried to get to the Directing Department at the Warsaw Theatre Academy (1972). Unfortunately, he could not faint in a way that satisfied the commission auditioning candidates. Instead, he passed the exams for the newly-created Directing Department at the Ludwik Solski Academy for the Dramatic Arts in Krakow. Educators at the Academy soon recognised his talent. At the time, directors such as Jerzy Jarocki and Konrad Swinarski staged their best productions at the Krakow Stary Theatre; young Lupa was particularly drawn to Swinarski's productions. He became his assistant, working on rehearsals for *Hamlet*, however, in his own productions he was far from copying his teacher. He was not interested in Brecht, Shakespeare, or the Romantics. In his own words, Swinarski merely taught him "great distrust for all initial ideas, for general and immediate classifications. He developed a habit of penetrating the structure of each scene, its atoms".[3]

Besides Konrad Swinarski, Tadeusz Kantor had a great influence on Lupa's work. Their first encounter was when Lupa was still studying at the Academy of Fine Arts and attended his lectures on modern art.[4] (This was where he first heard of Andy Warhol and pop-art.) The first performance directed by Kantor which Lupa saw was *Dainty Shapes and Hairy Apes, or The Green Pill: A Comedy with Corpses* by Witkacy. The performance enchanted him. As a student of directing he participated in rehearsals for *The Dead Class*:

> Soon after that I went to the performance and cried my eyes out. Such great fulfilment of artistic dreams always touches me in an almost archaic fashion. I remembered Kantor's fraudulently yelling that it would be the greatest production of European theatre, and suddenly I said: yes, it is the greatest production of European theatre. After *The Dead Class* I was obsessed with Kantor. Kantor was something holy. I remember that also because of him I engaged in a fight with someone and showered them with sugar. (…) Later there was *Wielopole, Wielopole* — all right, everything was the way it should be. And later Kantor began to die inside me, but I also claim that Kantor suffocated in his own greatness and fulfilment. He

---

[3] Joanna Boniecka, „Ja służę demonowi – rozmowa z Krystianem Lupą," *Odra*, no. 4 (1992): 30.

[4] Kantor had been a lecturer at the Academy of Fine Arts since 1967.

grew old and became like a childish king, ruffling and experiencing his grandeur or godliness in a… naïve… or sclerotic way.[5]

Of the revolutionary works by Jerzy Grotowski, Lupa saw only *Apocalypsis Cum Figuris* (staged in 1969). He did not join the crowd of his followers and admirers:

> I was put off by the solemnity with which the performance tried to enforce a message and offer "soul food" to me as its viewer in some almost Eucharistic pretension. What is behind this gesture? Is this sacrifice real? Can it be real each time? In comparison, I absorbed productions by Tadeusz Kantor with fascination. He did not pretend to offer me something, as some angel of wisdom. On the contrary, he appeared with the rough energy of his nature, he revealed his buffoonery! (…) My reservation towards Grotowski began, as we can see, with superficial motifs. I did not appreciate the great effort he made creating his image.[6] (…) Everyone has different access to the instrument of their own body and their own soul. Therefore, I do not believe that the so-called collaborative training, as was the case with Grotowski, is the right way of working with actors. Such a method unifies, and as a result changes these people into a… flock of sheep… brainwashed by the faith. And even if the charisma of a breath of faith can work this miracle and allow actors to reach beyond, I still am sickened by such a brainwashed actor.[7]

(Krystian Lupa was to have participated in the ceremony to award Jerzy Grotowski with an Honorary Doctorate at the University of Wroclaw (1991). However, Grotowski, who always carefully followed what people said about him, did not allow it. Lupa, on the other hand, continues to call him a "false prophet".)

In 1976 Lupa made his professional theatre debut. He staged Sławomir Mrożek's *The Butchery*[8] at the Juliusz Słowacki Theatre in Krakow. In the performance, Beethoven's String Quartet in A minor was drowned out by the shrieks of slaughtered animals to symbolise murder of culture. Next

---

[5] Grzegorz Niziołek, „Aktor w obnażających sytuacjach – rozmowa z Krystianem Lupą," *Didaskalia*, no. 10 (1995): 11.

[6] Łukasz Drewniak, „Fałszywy mag świątyni teatru – rozmowa z Krystianem Lupą," *Dziennik*, April 4-5, 2009, 11-12.

[7] Beata Matkowska-Święs, *Podróż do Nieuchwytnego. Rozmowy z Krystianem Lupą* (Krakow: Wydawnictwo Literackie, 2003), 70.

[8] Original title of the production: *Rzeźnia*
Date and place of premiere: May 8, 1976, Juliusz Słowacki Theatre, Krakow
Direction: Krystian Lupa
Set design: Krystian Lupa

year Lupa staged his graduation performance at the Academy for the Dramatic Arts: Witkacy's *Dainty Shapes and Hairy Apes* was produced in the spirit of Kantor's work. At the production, Lupa met Alicja Bienicewicz and Andrzej Hudziak for the first time. Together, they created his breakthrough productions: *The Dreamers*, *The Sleepwalkers* and *Kalkwerk.*

After graduating from the Krakow Academy, he was employed by the Cyprian Kamil Norwid Theatre in Jelenia Góra. That was also to where he transferred his graduation production.[9] Initially, his works were received by reviewers with reservation, generally in a negative way, but the artistic director of the Jelenia Góra theatre at the time saw a mature artist in him. A distinct feature of Alina Obidniak's management was her talent for attracting young directors ready for bold artistic experiments at the theatre. It was in Jelenia Góra, a small, provincial theatre that Lupa managed to create his first theatre laboratory. He had perfect conditions for working and finding his own form of artistic expression. He created an atmosphere of constant experiment, and attracted a group of devoted actors and achieved "community" in created works. His actors were referred to as "a group of fanatics". They spent all their days together, reading, deliberating and listening to music. A "gang" was founded in Jelenia Góra, headed by Lupa, who was characterised by constant intellectual exploration. Merely a dozen or so enthusiasts came to see his productions, and usually the audience shrank by half after the first interval.

Witold Gombrowicz, Frank Wedekind, Stanisław Przybyszewski, Stanisław Wyspiański, Stanisław Ignacy Witkiewicz, Sławomir Mrożek and Alfred Kubin: looking for texts for his productions Lupa trawled through modernist and contemporary dramatic works. He tried to include them in discussions about changes in contemporary culture and spirituality. He staged texts which were difficult, grotesque, and required in-depth reading. He also staged his own literary works, including *The Transparent Room*[10] and *The Supper*.[11] He worked in Jelenia Góra for nine theatrical

---

[9] Original title of the production: *Nadobnisie i koczkodany, czyli Zielona pigułka*
Date and place of premiere: February 19, 1978, Cyprian Kamil Norwid Theatre, Jelenia Góra
Direction: Krystian Lupa
Set design: Krystian Lupa
Music: Krzysztof Lipka (consult).

[10] Original title of the production: *Przeźroczysty pokój*
Date and place of premiere: February 17, 1979, Cyprian Kamil Norwid Theatre, Jelenia Góra
Direction: Krystian Lupa

seasons. Unfazed by the approaching deadlines of premieres, he prepared nine productions. While working on them, Lupa developed his own method of working with actors. *Maciej Korbowa and Bellatrix*, based on a play by Witkiewicz, was his last production prepared in Jelenia Góra.[12] When Lupa moved to Krakow, the group of artists focused around him disintegrated.

In Krakow he signed a contract with the Helena Modrzejewska National Stary Theatre, which became a twentieth-century cultural phenomenon. The theatre was particularly fortunate in managers, directors producing, actors performing and, finally, the repertoire. The phenomenon of the Stary Theatre artistic ensemble is quite problematic to many researchers of contemporary Polish theatre. It is a phenomenon that totally warps the semantic spaces of adjectives and which is, in a way, created at the time of a performance, and constructed out of the superb coordination of great artistic individuals and a disciplined ensemble. The Stary Theatre has always attracted the greatest names in Polish theatre: Swinarski, Wajda, Jarocki, Grzegorzewski, and eventually Lupa. In 1988 he produced *The Dreamers*, based on a play by Robert Musil.[13] Initially, the production did not attract much interest: it was often performed to an almost empty auditorium. But those who did attend could sense something new in this content, a vague announcement of something great that would cause revolution in the way of thinking about the art of theatre. Despite the initial conservative reception, the production brought Lupa national acclaim (including the Konrad Swinarski Prize awarded by the monthly *Teatr*). It was recorded and broadcast by Polish Television. However,

---

Set design: Krystian Lupa.

[11] Original title of the production: *Kolacja*
Date and place of premiere: April 27, 1980, Cyprian Kamil Norwid Theatre, Jelenia Góra
Direction: Krystian Lupa
Set design: Krystian Lupa.

[12] Original title of the production: *Maciej Korbowa i Bellatrix*
Date and place of premiere: April 6, 1986, Cyprian Kamil Norwid Theatre, Jelenia Góra
Direction: Krystian Lupa
Set design: Krystian Lupa.

[13] Original title of the production: *Marzyciele*
Date and place of premiere: February 28, 1988, The Helena Modrzejewska Stary Theatre, Krakow
Direction: Krystian Lupa
Set design: Krystian Lupa
Music: Marcin Krzyżanowski.

many still perceived Lupa as a curiosity which would burn out after two seasons…

2. Insanity measured out with steps Krystian Lupa and the writings of Thomas Bernhard

One of the most controversial figures in European literature, and one of greatest visionaries of European theatre: One cannot help feeling that the two of them simply had to meet. Reading each of Thomas Bernhard's work we are struck by a maniacal, very repetitive narrative, as if addressed solely to the persona of the protagonist. It is very persistent and intrusive, a delirious repetition of thoughts circulating rhythmically around the entire text. It is frequently off-putting to readers new to his writings. Too heavy, too infantile because of visible conscious stylistic procedures by the author, who wanted to make a very specific impression on his readers. However, if we immerse ourselves in this manner of imaging and expression of thoughts, with time we will notice that it becomes so infectious that we are no longer able to think independently and begin to filter the world in a brand new fashion. Reading it, we sense that this fierceness and intensity of Bernhard's prose is untranslatable. Austrians refer to its musicality; literary theorists find it to be babbling and barbaric. We could quite justifiably raise doubts as to whether these texts can be used in theatre at all.

Krystian Lupa staged *Kalkwerk* in November 1992,[14] two years after the death of Tadeusz Kantor. Looking back, the two events have much in common: the death of the creator of *The Dead Class* closed a certain era in Polish theatre, whereas the premiere of *Kalkwerk* is the symbolic beginning of another. To this day, *Kalkwerk* remains one of the most important productions staged in Poland after 1989. It was Lupa's first encounter with Bernhard's prose. It was the first of the author texts he read, and which he immediately decided to stage. He faced the challenge of translating the extremely complicated system by which Bernhard's characters expressed themselves into the language of theatre, but succeeded in

[14] Original title of the production: *Kalkwerk*, (adaptation based on the short story: *The Lime Works*).
Date and place of premiere: November 7, 1992, The Helena Modrzejewska Stary Theatre, Krakow
Direction: Krystian Lupa
Adaptation: Krystian Lupa
Set design: Krystian Lupa
Music: Jacek Ostaszewski

creating his own adaptation.[15] After the premiere, reviewers were convinced that it was Lupa's greatest achievement, his crowning work so far (the director was almost fifty at the time), but it soon became apparent that *Kalkwerk* was merely to be the first of his greatest theatrical achievements.

Scenes from *Kalkwerk* are nocturnal. The ascetic composition of the stage space immediately brought to mind the productions by Tadeusz Kantor: old, rusty equipment with paint peeling off; a cold, metal bed; brown police uniforms; cold, blue and grey light streaming through the window. Lupa himself comments on the window reappearing in his theatre sets:

> A window is a kind of valve or opening to all kinds of possibilities, to the outside world. (…) The mere fact of there being a window and its opening is a symbolic act aimed at changing the space and filling it with new meaning and new power. The spaces are staged; they grow and at some point develop roots in the audience, stem from acting and reach outside with their branches where they create a metaphysical model. The character's universe infiltrates the universe of reality which penetrates the character.[16]

Kalkwerk, appearing in the Polish title, is the name of an old lime works. Its interior, filling the entire stage space, resembled an abandoned factory hall with cast iron ornaments in the windows, which Konrad (Andrzej Hudziak) had removed as soon as he bought the house. It seems that Kalkwerk was an eerie place from the very beginning, not unlike its inhabitants. Had they been that way before they moved in here? We cannot tell. Konrad bought the house to finish his monograph on the sense of hearing to which he had devoted the past twenty years of his life. Each day, for hours on end, he tortured his disabled wife by testing the so-called *Urbantschitsch's Method* on her. Tension growing between the two eventually results in crime.

The entire production was presented in reverse order. Policemen enter the stage. They finally find Konrad, who had been hiding in a cesspit for three days. Screaming at each other and at Konrad, the policemen try to conduct an initial interrogation. In the middle of the stage is a wheelchair covered with an old sheet over a woman's body. Konrad cowers from the cold and is clearly scared of the increasingly aggressive policeman who

---

[15] Lupa added two scenes in his adaptation: the initial scene with police officers and the scene of Konrad's dream.

[16] Aleksandra Szydłowska, „To nie znaczy, że jestem fryzjerem - rozmowa z Krystianem Lupą," *Notatnik Teatralny*, no. 11 (1996): 93-96.

repeats the accusatory word “murderer!” He changes into dry clothes. He is slow and clumsy. His fingers are numb from the cold and seem to be holding on to the buttons of his trousers as though to prevent himself from falling to the ground.

This opening scene is followed by a sequence of events leading to the murder. Morning at the Konrads. Warm morning light streams through the window. Konrad’s wife is lying on a bed. She is trying to summon her husband with a bell but he does not arrive. She rings the bell once again. There is growing impatience, even in the movement of the wrist. There is growing impatience in the movement, in the sound of the bell which keeps ringing in vain. The bedroom door remains closed. She has to manage on her own. She removes an overly heavy, mouldy, down duvet. She makes the effort to sit up by holding on to the bed rail and slowly moving her paralysed body. She lowers her numb legs to the floor carefully and slowly. Everything happens in real time, every moment is needed to draw a breath of air and gather new strength. (During her meetings with members of the audience, Małgorzata Hajewska-Krzysztofik often said that as early as in the morning on the day of a *Kalkwerk* performance, her body as if subconsciously, begins to feel ill, and adopts poses typical of Konrad’s wife.) Struggling with the dead weight of her crippled body she moves into the wheelchair only succeeding after several attempts.

Lupa is exceptionally sensitive to unplanned coincidences happening during rehearsals. On one occasion, the moment that Konrad’s wife was already sitting in her wheelchair, exhausted by the effort, coincided with the sound of an aeroplane flying over the theatre. The airplane became part of the production. Having heard the sound, the woman follows the plane with her eyes as if it might become entangled in the fly-tower mechanism above her.

Konrad appears in the door of the room. He puts a tray with breakfast on the table, as he does every day, and does not even notice the extreme effort she must have made a moment before, without his help. Konrad opens a wardrobe and takes out one of the dresses; his wife sits with her back to him. She cannot see him, yet she shakes her head — not that one. Lupa’s actors are masters of comedy in such situations. They use a slightly extended pause, or catch the partner’s eye. Konrad dresses her like a rag doll. He pulls the clothes over her head and keeps tugging at her. He is unceremonious and indifferent. His thoughts are constantly immersed in his study. His duty towards his wife only gets on his nerves — every morning, the same questions are asked:

Konrad's wife:
Did you sleep well?

Konrad:
I obviously did not.
(*after a while*)
Did you sleep well?

Konrad's wife:
Obviously, I did not.[17]

Konrad pours tea and sets up plates, impatient that all these activities interrupt his work. They eat without saying a word. Konrad finishes breakfast abruptly, and without a word of warning takes away his wife's plate, and grabs a tea cup from her hand before she has finished drinking it: "The creative process hates prolonged breakfasts!"[18] He is a domineering tyrant whose entire life is subordinated to his work on hearing. There is no way for his wife to protect herself or refuse him. She has to surrender to the brutal discipline imposed by her husband who is ruthless towards her. Konrad begins his tirade (iconic for theatre researchers) on the sense of hearing:

> There is a distinct difference between listening and hearing. Listening and hearing. On the one hand listening, and on the other hand hearing… LISTENING?... LIS?
>
> (*he says it softly, gently, carefully*)
>
> … and… HEARING!!! HEARING!!! He goes on: catching, listening in… can you hear and distinguish it?… Pricking up one's ears and eavesdropping. PRICKING UP ONE'S EARS AND EAVES-DROPPING (*higher regions of longing and lower regions, sneaky and clandestine*)
>
> …and on: being hard of hearing, mishearing and so on… Lending an ear, overhearing, hearing through the grapevine…TRYING NOT TO HEAR!!! TRYING NOT TO HEAR!!! TRYING NOT TO HEAR!!! Can you hear? TRYING NOT TO HEAR!!![19]

Konrad's body follows every syllable, as if becoming an apparatus for emitting and receiving stimuli. His body shrinks compulsively, as if the sounds he makes are provoking his muscles to physical response, not unlike the rapid repetition, in ever-changing ways, during therapeutic, schizophrenic exercises, of the short "i" in "Im Innviertel habe ich nichts".

---

[17] *Kalkwerk*, stage script, (Krystian Lupa's private archive), 13.
[18] *Kalkwerk*, 13.
[19] *Kalkwerk*, 13.

Quickly, in a high pitch, as if surprised. He is joined by the off-stage voice of Lupa, sitting, as always, in the back row of the auditorium, and chanting individual sounds into a microphone. Eerie and ominous. Konrad's wife falls into a trance and begins to speak about laughing mice and pins.

Their entire married life has been subjected to Konrad's study on the sense of hearing. They sacrificed everything to the study — has it been in vain? Is Konrad merely a psychopath sadistically tormenting his wife? Or is he a genius? Could he hear more than others? Were the voices he heard merely spectres of a sick mind? Or was he a jester, as his wife often thought? Did she believe in her husband? In his study? Or perhaps she gave up because she had no other choice, anyway? "I would rather not see what is in your head..."[20] We do not know whether her words express dread of some terrible brain dysfunction, or fear that all that joint effort will prove futile. Lupa himself made things even more complicated in one of his texts:

> It is not an accident that it is a study of the sense of hearing. The ear is, so to speak, a prophets' choice of a sense organ. God comes through the sense of hearing, nature whispers its mysteries through the sense of hearing in such a way that it almost becomes speech. (...) It is through the sense of hearing that world comes to man and becomes word. Particularly in special, critical moments...[21]

Konrad kept pacing up and down the stage, as if his growing insanity could be measured out with steps. Trying to protect herself from his despotism, the wife becomes intoxicated by memories, reading old letters, looking at photographs taken when she was young, at a time when their life was completely different. It was filled with travel, receptions and new dresses. When she reads them it seems the letters had just been delivered, envelopes had just been torn open, and not picked up, for the hundredth time. It seems that the people who posted them still care about how she is.

Everything had been subordinated to his work. It seems that everything had already been gathered, thought through, but at the climactic point, when he should simply sit down and put the study to paper, everything falls apart. Every day there comes the ideal moment to write the study but there is always an interruption. A postman, a baker, the wife demanding her pillow be straightened. Everyone thoughtlessly ruins Konrad's work with their petty needs, and he always has to treat these people politely

---

[20] *Kalkwerk*, 25.

[21] Krystian Lupa, „Kalkwerk Thomasa Bernharda," *Notatnik Teatralny*, no. 7 (1993/94): 61.

because he cannot write anything today, anyway. The whole day is wasted. "Our reality is shaped by what we neglect to do, not by what we actually do…"[22] *Kalkwerk* is a production about great inaptness, great unfulfilment. About an idea which explodes in the brain. Which cannot be resolved as easily as Konrad would wish:

> One should empty one's brain from time to time, drain off the surplus brain, as we do taking a leak, nothing more (…), empty the brain like the bladder, answer the call of nature, take a brain break like you take a bathroom break.[23]

The study is put on paper only once. In Konrad's dream about a vision come true.[24] In that dream, Konrad wrote his work down. From the beginning to the end. All the words have finally been arranged in the right order. All it took was to sit at a desk. To quietly take out the paper, carefully, so as not to scare away the words which came to him that night. His wife also appears in this dream. Healthy, beautiful in a blood-red dress. She burns the study.

We will never know why Konrad actually killed his wife. The final scene is another return to the memories of a past life. Trying on long-unworn dresses and the sudden, categorical demand of powder; Konrad's wife will apply layers of cloud-creating powder. After a while the powder will settle on everything, her face, her shoulders, and the table. Its particles in the air will carry the final words of the performance: "Scandal has hit our house."[25] But even after they could no longer be heard the audience would remain silent in their seats. In dead silence, as if any sound penetrating this space would be a *faux pas* in the face of the immense drama which had just unfolded on stage.

Lupa and his actors managed to create a production with unusual intensity. The air on stage seemed to thicken around Konrad and his wife from the very beginning, when we started observing their psychomachia. They both implemented a scorched-earth policy. The participants in this marriage had nothing more to say to each other. Not one scene made the cold emotionality of the performance brighter. The only ray of happiness was going back to the memories of the time from before the illness... of both of them. Andrzej Hudziak, who played Konrad, was slim, petite, "the

---

[22] *Kalkwerk*, 37.
[23] *Kalkwerk*, 21.
[24] Scene added by Lupa in his adaptation.
[25] *Kalkwerk*, 44.

embodiment of mediocrity".[26] Nevertheless, he created a legendary performance which landed him in a psychiatric hospital. Cast alongside him was Małgorzata Hajewska-Krzysztofik, not quite thirty at the time, who was given the task of playing a mature woman, wheelchair-bound for years, mentally drained by her domineering husband. Looking back, it seems inconceivable that such a difficult production was created by such young people. The production was difficult both for the artists and the audience who often found it hard to bear. People were leaving, running away during performances. There were also those who came to see the production several dozen times. Each time they allowed this peculiar story about the demon of the brain to drain them inside.

Another text by Bernhard directed by Krystian Lupa was *Immanuel Kant*.[27] It is widely considered to be the funniest and the most absurd of all texts by the Austrian author. Once again, it would seem that it is completely unstageable, but to Lupa it was ideal. The plot is historically impossible: Immanuel Kant (Wojciech Ziemiański) is on board a transatlantic liner, going to America for cataract surgery. In fact, the philosopher never left Königsberg. Even Lupa realized his struggle with the text he was staging:

> Are we going to demonstrate that Kant used to be Kant, or is it completely unnecessary? Or do we simply answer the question: "how did it actually happen?" with: "Whatever…" The myth of a truly GREAT MAN became (gave rise to) a kind of FREAK… A whim of imagination. Undermining historical truth. Everything is a contradiction of itself. Where did this creative gesture stem from? This question should somehow be answered… We are cast-off pupal skins. What remains is piteous… It is an excuse! The meaning of this caprice seems deeper… As if an inexplicable cataclysm of perspective… A sudden emetic reflex in response to once-worshipped (also personally) figures of authority. What remains from past admiration is a silly and embarrassed distaste… It all does not make sense![28]

---

[26] Marek Mikos, „Konrad. Bernharda, Lupy i Hudziaka," *Notatnik Teatralny*, no. 7 (1993/94): 77.

[27] Original title of the production: *Immanuel Kant*
Date and place of premiere: January 13, 1996, The Polski Theatre, Wrocław
Direction: Krystian Lupa
Adaptation: Krystian Lupa
Set design: Krystian Lupa
Music: Jacek Ostaszewski.

[28] Excerpt from Krystian Lupa's journal published in the brochure. *Immanuel Kant* (Wrocław: The Polski Theatre, 1996), 10.

In his writings Kant compared the human struggle with the metaphysical element to a voyage across a dark ocean. In his text, Bernhard propelled Kant two centuries forward to throw down an intellectual gauntlet to the New World as a representative of the Old one. Europe, proudly boasting its history and culture, failed to notice that its position based on Reason had been shaken by American culture, which had just came to life. Europeans travelling across the ocean still believe that they are carrying the torch of knowledge. At a reception, representatives of the European intellectual elite celebrate, but fail to observe, that islands with unconquered civilisations pass them by along old railroads behind their backs.[29] Kant is presented in that contemporaneity and carelessness of a civilisation developing in affluence, wearing a frock coat and a wig from his time, and, with a whim typical of great minds, insoles anachronistically made of asbestos fibre (the philosopher was worried he might burn when giving his lecture) — a VIP of European humanistic thought. In the performance, however, he is merely a mumbling, capricious old man bullying other passengers with fits of bad moods. He is only interested in his own contempt for people and the surrounding world. Like a person who in old age mistakes real memories for creations of his imagination, Kant keeps referring to events which did not occur until after his death. From time to time, he blurts out comments: “Socialism is lethal”, “Communism is a faddish delusion”, “Marx is a ne’er-do-well”, “that poor feebleminded sap, Lenin”. Time is on a loop and, as we can deduce from the ending of the performance suggested by Lupa, the voyage will probably never end.

Kant is in fact racing against time, and saving his eyesight is at stake. In America he is to receive an Honorary Doctorate from Columbia University and have the cataract surgery. He will bring reason to America — America will give him his eyesight. Bernhard ridicules the figure of Kant throughout the text. However, the philosopher’s progressive blindness could be an allusion to Schopenhauer, who compared the influence of Kant’s thought to “an operation for a cataract on a blind man”. Bernhard loved to hide subliminal messages for “insiders” in his texts. Nietzsche’s name is not mentioned even once, although the sentence “a married philosopher belongs in comedy”[30] is attributed to him. Bernhard therefore came up with a completely banal reason for the great thinker’s voyage. It is Kant’s wife (Krzesisława Dubiel), obviously. A typical, not particularly intelligent, snob who has always dreamt of a

---

[29] Lupa used the potential of the stage located in the old railway station very well. Mobile change of theatrical scenery was possible using an old railway.

[30] Jerzy Łukosz, “Kant tańczy,” *Teatr*, no. 4, (1996): 10.

voyage to America. Therefore, when Columbia sent the letter informing about the honorary degree, Kant no longer had a reasonable excuse. The voyage was also scheduled sooner because of a sex scandal which broke in Königsberg at the time. Kant's wife's affair with Friedrich (a great performance by Krzysztof Dracz) came to light.

The ultimatum with which the philosopher presented his wife, "either him or me," is probably even more absurd than the entire idea of Kant's voyage across the ocean. Friedrich is a parrot: in Bernhard's play, merely a prop, whereas in Lupa's it is a living man squeezed into a cage. We do not know whether historically Kant had a pet. Bernhard chose a parrot as "the most philosophical animal" for a reason. After all, everything is repeated in European civilisation. Kant can only repeat clichés at this point. Friedrich loves to repeat his master's words. He shouts them out, as if enjoying just playing with their sound. For some reason the favourite word he shouts time after time is: "imperative"… Kant always delivered his most important lectures in front of Friedrich first. He always took him to university. He claimed that no living creature, no professor could concentrate the way Friedrich could. In fact, Friedrich could have travelled to America on his own, and have faultlessly presented his master's every thought. Bernhard's Europe is therefore a place where even a parrot is more intelligent than scholars. Even Leibniz does not dare give a lecture in Friedrich's presence: he chooses to cancel his speech.

Kant and Friedrich's coexistence has a peculiar character. They had lived together for twenty-five years, and we can observe how Friedrich sympathises with his master, as if he had adopted some of his emotions in order to filter and express them. When Kant begins to get angry, or lose patience, it seems that Friedrich is about to destroy his cage. When Kant falls asleep the bird sinks into lethargy. Kant tastes his pet's seeds: like a real "whole meal sommelier", he rants about the superiority of Guatemalan over Brazilian seeds.

It is certainly one of Lupa's most static productions. On a stage created in the building of an old railway station time drags. Passengers surrender to inertia and pointlessly walk up and down the deck. In the background is the quiet hum of the ship's engines. The content is fixed in the characters' dialogues held while sitting in deckchairs arranged on the deck. In his text, Bernhard presented a cruise which was to become part of the history of philosophy. Kant is travelling with his great lecture to America, but he is not going to give it. Just as Konrad in *Kalkwerk* did not write his study, when he stands in front of other passengers in an attempt to rehearse his great speech, he falls apart. It is possible that at the end of his life he lost faith in his own words. He is unable to gather his thoughts: "It is impossible... to speak of reason… on the high seas." Kant's voice cracks. He collects sheets of paper from the lectern and throws them behind him.

The liner in Lupa's production becomes a contemporary representation of the mediæval motif of the ship of fools. Bernhard ended his play with the ship reaching New York and the passengers being greeted by orderlies from a psychiatric hospital. Lupa's ship does not reach port. The audience is left with the image of Kant dancing.

In 1984 Thomas Bernhard wrote the play: *Ritter, Dene, Voss*. When writing it, he had in mind specific Viennese actors: Ilse Ritter, Kirsten Dene and Gert Voss. Initially they thought of staging the Krakow production under the title *Hajewska, Mandat, Skiba*; eventually, however, they decided on *The Siblings*.[31] Analysing the story of the three egoists raises the question as to whether this would have been the fate of the Professor's family if the main character in Luchino Visconti's *Conversation Piece* had had children. The children are what remain of a family representing a Krakow-Vienna type of bourgeoisie, the bourgeoisie of the nineteenth century which cannot truly be themselves in the twenty-first century. It is a bourgeoisie on the verge of a nervous breakdown.

Lupa had previously preferred minimalist and very symbolic settings, whereas here his realism is so increased that when dinner is served in one of the scenes, the audience could smell the roast. The set design was utterly middle-class. Heavy chairs, tables, buffet — "an altar of a bourgeois sanctuary",[32] with plates, sauce boats, cups, saucers, platters, carafes, jugs — everything which had certainly been in the family for generations. And the ghastly presence of ancestral portraits: "We always suffered in front of these awful paintings"[33] says one of the characters at one point, although it is their dead parents' fortune that allows them to live so comfortably; a life which has not changed for the past thirty years. For

[31] Original title of the production: *Rodzeństwo*
Date and place of premiere: October 19, 1996, The Helena Modrzejewska Stary Theatre, Krakow
Direction: Krystian Lupa
Adaptation: Krystian Lupa
Set design: Krystian Lupa
Music: Jacek Ostaszewski.

[32] Krystian Lupa, *Utopia 2. Penetracje* (Krakow: Wydawnictwo Literackie, 2003), 126.

[33] *The Siblings*, stage script, (Krystian Lupa's private archive), 66.

thirty years they have been spreading the same butter on the same bread. "Isn't it reason enough to kill oneself?"[34]

> Ritter:
> A matinee
> which was always our salvation as children
> is now out of the question
> afternoon tea at Aunt Margaret's
> how easy it was then
> to escape from despair
> cup of cocoa
> and the map on the floor
> that's no longer enough
> Soon it won't even be enough
> to take a biography to bed with you.[35]

Even the sound of broken plates seems hysterical in this house.

Lupa's production is a fragment of the family's day. It is a holiday — Ludwig (Piotr Skiba) returns from a psychiatric hospital in Steinhof.[36] So far, every attempt at bringing the brother home has ended in catastrophe. Doctors kept warning the sisters that their lives were under very great threat. However, Dene (Agnieszka Mandat) insists on bringing their brother home, safely. The servants have been given the day off. She has arranged for them to be alone when Ludwig comes home from hospital: "Just us — siblings."[37]

For the first hour the sisters are alone. They wait for their brother to finish washing off the remains of his stay at the psychiatric hospital. Ritter (Małgorzata Hajewska-Krzysztofik) is smoking a cigarette, turning the pages of a newspaper, slowly getting drunk — as she does every day. She allows herself to relax. She stretches like a cat on a hot windowsill. There is a certain eccentricity of irreverence about her. She openly manifests her disregard for bourgeois conventions and family fortune. She carries herself like an artist, but is aware of the mediocrity of her talent. She gets cast owing solely to the shares her parents bought in the theatre. They allow her and her sister to play two-minute episodes in productions of their choice. Lupa lets off steam when writing about them in his journals:

---

[34] *The Siblings*, 14.

[35] *The Siblings*, 44.

[36] The character was modelled on Paul Wittgenstein, a nephew of the famous philosopher, whom Bernhard met during his stay at the hospital in Steinhof.

[37] *The Siblings*, 6.

> The house becomes a place of unresolved childhood. Theatre is an imitation of mature life for the sisters. They go to rehearsals and pretend to perform real (mature) problems in humility (although, it seems, quite unconscious and automatical — unprofessional). Although indeed — taking theatre seriously is far from being mature. The fifty-one per cent of the shares appear to be ambiguous as well. Seemingly, the sisters have freedom of choice, at the same time we are forced to perceive their acting through the prism of financial machinations. Shakespeare! They come to rehearsals and remain alienated. They do not belong to the ensemble — real actresses sit at the bar at a different, separate table, only exchanging polite bows with the sisters. The director, also, addresses them as rich amateurs, who play only to satisfy a whim. Working has always been something alien to them. It has always been something done by the servants. Adult life, however, brings about an authoritative demand: one must work! They agree to it without resistance, but there is something not right about it. They simply do not know how to hold their tools. Even in acting. A heated up dinner is a shamefully exposing piece of evidence. "Hand-made" cream puffs are "mentally indigestible" because they had been created in a grotesque act of intense heroism. Why does Dene so badly want to present herself as a "housewife"? She obviously senses that Ludwig does not believe in the maturity of their theatrical profession. The house should immediately become "trustworthy". It should not be "helplessly neglected" but "kept". The sisters make a fetish of housework: "What can one do on a rainy afternoon?" Read a biography, do the dishes, receive some guests…??? The list is short, which surprises everyone. It is embarrassing indeed.[38]

In fact, the dinner has been prepared earlier by the servants who now have the day off. "Heat it up yourself, at any rate."[39] Dene, as opposed to her sister, is a typical middle-class woman. Officially she does not allow herself to do anything wild. Ritter is always threatening to leave: Paris, Rome, Amsterdam… but it is obvious she will be back home in a week's time, on the same sofa, with a pack of the same cigarettes and a new edition of the newspaper. There are some constellations in life which are impossible to escape. Hence Ritter's cynicism towards her sister who tries to rebuild her family's closeness at all costs. She ridicules her efforts because the success of the entire undertaking really does not depend on cutlery neatly arranged on the dinner table. Dene obsessively checks everything, everything has to be perfect when their brother arrives. She perceives Ritter's distance as an attempt at destroying the home she fought for, and for which she was ready to give up everything. For the family, for

[38] Lupa, *Utopia 2*, 113-114.
[39] *The Siblings*, 14.

appearances. She is pathetically naive in her simple perception of the world. She tries her best, but Ludwig loves the reserved Ritter more. His sensitivity requires that a person's presence cannot be more intense than he expects. He distributes his acceptance neurotically, and those ignored face a death sentence. He reacts nervously to affection. His relationship with Ritter is incomprehensible and unacceptable to Dene. She insists on enforcing her affection. She goes to Steinhof every day, buys expensive shirts, talks to doctors, and manifests her devotion so that there are no grounds to reject her love. That love is suffocating. The relationship between these siblings is a complicated, unequal, triangle. In Dene's eyes, Ludwig is fragile, weak, and helpless, whereas Ritter can very well recognise the tyrant in him who hides behind the philosopher's mask. Dene and Ludwig also represent the convention of incestuous love: alone in the bathroom, they touch each other with their looks. It is not clear who provokes whom more. Unspoken words hide forsaken thoughts whirling and desperate for attention… Only after Dene reluctantly leaves them alone will Ritter reveal to her brother that their sister secretly changes into his clothes. Some nights she sits naked in a window, eating yoghurt and listening to Schumann.

When, after an hour, Ludwig finally stands in the middle of the living room it turns out that the three of them have nothing to say to each other. The return home is only illusory:

> Ludwig:
> lack of comprehension is the one bond
> between myself and my sisters
> that's what I thought.[40]

The situation is not even saved by cream puffs, Ludwig's favourite dish, served to humour the moody brother who terrorises the sisters with his whims. Perhaps the cream puffs can bring back the old world when cocoa and the map on the floor were enough? The most ordinary middle class scene, but which ends in disaster:

> Ludwig:
> Cream puffs
> that I am so fond of
> Ludwig
> who's fond of cream puffs
> who's fonder of cream puffs than of anything else

---

[40] *The Siblings*, 44.

The whole time I was in Steinhof
I thought of nothing but those cream puffs
(*looking round*)
It's like the inside of a tomb here
we're really already buried
a delicious tomb
in which cream puffs are served
(*sniffing at his cream puffs*)
the typical cream puff aroma
(*to his younger sister*)
that's right
isn't it
they are freshly made for us
so that finish them up
(*exclaiming*)
The highest art is the art of baking cream puffs![41]

The tablecloth embroidered by their grandmother, pulled sharply, propels plates and cups into the air. Dene runs out of the room — this afternoon's critique (as it were) of cream puffs was a deliberate insult. Only Ritter is amused by the performance. Only with Ritter does Ludwig have a warm, open conversation. He is always reproachful when talking about his sister:

Ludwig:
despises my inmost being
but insists
that I eat her cream puffs (…)
Here, you see
where I burned myself
a burn scar
intentionally
I held the candle
under my hand until it was half burnt through
and here on my neck
(*showing it*)
I still have the marks
of my strangulation attempt
What have we here
asked the resident
in his sly manner
A strangulation attempt
last night

[41] *The Siblings*, 58.

I replied
at which he laughed out loud
Then why on earth didn't you hang yourself p r o p e r l y
said the resident
Do you think I'm crazy
I replied.[42]

The Siblings ran for twenty years, until January 2017. It was another great production by Lupa, an intimate performance by three actors, constructed around their powerful presence. Around the tenderness of looking at one's burnt hand. Around the clinical observation of partners pacing up and down the living room like predators guarding their territory. A mundane dinner in this production was able to focus the audience's attention to the maximum. Each uttered word contained a challenge where everything was at stake. An accidentally broken plate which slipped off unintentionally was an ominous announcement of the end of the world. Words woven in statements seemed to belong to another register, their meaning not matching the on-stage reality. They blew up before becoming meaningful, and sometimes their meaning was piercing. Every scene showing normal attempts at being cordial towards another person became absurd. *The Siblings* was also a remarkably funny performance. Intelligently directed by Lupa and his actors who managed to perform through all the cream puffs and clumsy words which were to save the situation, the remains of a relationship… Audiences regularly burst in laughter seeing how inaccurately the words were used, how they constantly missed their destination. This show contained three great performances. Throughout the production Lupa directed his actors so that they engaged in polemics with the text they were performing. There is no doubt that Agnieszka Mandat was aware of the fact that she had to perform the part of a particularly rough character. At times she acted as if standing next to her character. Małgorzata Hajewska-Krzysztofik was fierce, and coexisted perfectly with Piotr Skiba, always provocative and ruthless towards his partners.

After each premiere, critics unanimously announce: behold, Krystian Lupa has reached the peak of his artistic ability. With every new show Lupa proves that he has outdone himself once again. *Extinction*,[43] in which

---

[42] *The Siblings*, 79-80.

[43] Original title of the production: *Auslöschung/Extinction*
Date and place of premiere: March 10, 2001, The Dramatic Theatre, Warsaw
Direction: Krystian Lupa
Adaptation: Krystian Lupa

Piotr Skiba created his greatest part, has been unanimously proclaimed "a manifestation of the potential of Polish theatre".[44]

Like *Kalkwerk*, it seems that *Extinction*, a novel of six hundred pages, is completely unsuitable for staging. There is no action, plot or situation, and the German original is not even divided into paragraphs. The novel was written in a style which was to create an impression that everything was written down in one go. Someone sat down and committed everything that hurt from their soul to paper, erasing their memory. Like a snapshot reminiscence which is suddenly overexposed in memory and sinks back in the darkness. Everything is written in prose typical of Bernhard, with a hermetic construction of thoughts and statements. The main character's monologue, reminiscences, associations, stream of consciousness — sometimes completely alogical, and therefore real, believable…

> I could not have been indifferent to *Auslöschung*, a provocatively helpless book. Showing a broken man and a broken writer… with scattered literature. As if Bernhard had fallen into a puddle, dropped his schoolbag, and his pencils and notebooks fell out. This is what the novel is like. And I lean over these muddy things and suddenly see… some mysterious writing. I take one notebook and carry it home under my arm. I try to decipher what is written in it. I do not understand it entirely… I don't understand… Yet, I carry on through this incomprehension. And I produce *Auslöschung* not understanding this book entirely.[45]

The performance does not have a linear plot. Franz (Piotr Skiba) shows us scenes from his life to make it easier for us to understand a child from the first flash of the play. It is not a scene. The entire event lasts no longer than a minute. "I hate them!!! I HATE THEM!!! I WANT THEM DEAD!!!" The boy is crying, screaming the words out, running up and down the stage. We can hear plates being broken, the spotlight illuminating the stage for split seconds. The cook is running after the crying boy trying to control him. The light goes off. We can only hear crying.

When the light goes on again we can see Franz's Rome apartment. A telegram has just arrived: "Mother, father, brother, dead." Years later, the boy's wish has come true, but Franz is already far from home and from those things. He has been living in Rome for years, leading the life of an

---

Set design: Krystian Lupa
Music: Jacek Ostaszewski.

[44] Beata Guczalska, *Aktorstwo polskie. Generacje* (Krakow: The Ludwik Solski Academy for the Dramatic Arts, 2014), 342.

[45] Matkowska-Święs, *Podróż do Nieuchwytnego…*, 30.

intellectual, surrounded by books which do not hurt. He is far from his family home, but you can be far away and certain things remain so deeply rooted that no amount of time can heal the wounds. There are things we cannot forget and certainly cannot forgive. And the demons, once in one's soul, have a natural tendency to always reappear: if someone claims otherwise, they are lying.

The demons always return out of the blue and stand in one's way. Franz has just returned from Wolfsegg; he needed the visit to confirm that there was nothing to return to. The suitcase is still not unpacked and he needs to return again. There has to be a squire at the estate. The matter is all the more surprising as Franz has always been an "extra" child, not really wanted. The estate was to be inherited by his elder brother Johannes. Johannes was perfect for the job, he loved the countryside and hunting. Johannes was the embodiment of the world of landowners, and Franz is not. When the family were culling deer on their estate, Franz preferred to sit in the house library with the windows closed and read Dostoyevsky. He escaped from Wolfsegg, from the bosom of his family. He wanted to let the world into his mind, because "in Wolfsegg they never had fresh air in their minds."[46] He hated his country, in which he saw only falsehood. And so he escaped all the way to Rome. And once again it turned out he has to return to Wolfsegg. To face the inevitable, that which cannot be deferred for the undefined, never-to-come future. It can be put off until tomorrow at the latest: tomorrow is when any possibility of delay ends.

Wolfsegg used to be wonderful, but his relatives turned it into a hell, into the ordeal of family lunches, a huge oak table at which several dozen people could sit, but only five do. "At this family table, from the father's place only death sentences were passed. I do not recall them ever praising me, I cannot have missed it…"[47] says Franz when he finds himself once again in his family dining room. He escaped from people,

> people to whom, the words such as shame, sensitivity, and consideration meant virtually nothing. And who never felt the slightest need to improve themselves, having stopped in their tracks decades ago and been content to stay put ever since. (…) All of my closest people, how silly the word closest sounds, finished their education early, remained on their pitiful level in full self-admiration, full self-satisfaction… (…) Looking at these photographs, I am inclined to think that they could have made something of themselves — and perhaps even achieved something great — yet they made nothing of themselves... Because they settled for indolence like

[46] *Extinction*, stage script, (Krystian Lupa's private archive), 5.
[47] *Extinction*, 36.

> everyone else, for that matter... They risked nothing, and chose to take it easy as soon as they could… Lie back and relax…
> My sisters stopped in their tracks as soon as they had graduated from high school, which they left with their heads held high... oh... and clutching their graduation diplomas, which they regarded as guarantees of something absolutely extraordinary.
> High school, high school — my sisters took every opportunity to repeat these words.
> This happened before high school, that happened after high school…
> Now, at thirty, they still remain at the level of seventeen — year-olds…
> My father ended his education having graduated from the technical high school, and my brother, Johannes, ceased to develop after graduating from the forestry school at Gmunden…
> Like ninety per cent of humanity...
> They leave their schools and stop and stop in that pitiful position.
> Human beings exert themselves only for as long as they can look forward to obtaining diplomas… having gained enough of these idiotic diplomas, as soon as they feel them in their hands, they no longer develop.
> For the most part, their sole aim in life is to obtain diplomas and... titles.
> They do not strive for the natural development of their spirit, but for diplomas and titles.
> They value themselves and their lives so little that they see only these diplomas and titles. They proceed to hang the diplomas on their walls and spend their lives staring at them from their sofas. We may say that most associations take place not between human beings, but between titles, not between Mr. Kurt and Mr. Meier but a doctor and an engineer…
> Whenever I go on a train I have the impression that the compartment is occupied solely by professors…[48]

These remarks are not addressed to the audience. Most of the time, Franz is sitting on the desk of his student, Gambetti (Andrzej Szeremeta). To Franz, Gambetti is a perfect listener. He is still sensitive to falsehood typical to the world of grown-ups. He can sense when his teacher speaks to him because he feels the sincere need to talk to someone close. He can also pick up moments when Franz shifts from sincerity to creation, like Bernhard, who also liked to delight in indignation and spread out his negativity. Gambetti is still unspoilt, has a nose for false dissonances typical of a young man. He laughs at the exaggeration that his teacher falls victim to when he chokes on his own hatred. He is amused when Franz cannot see how grotesque he becomes when he demonstrates his righteous indignation over the hypocrisy of this world.

---

[48] *Extinction*, 10-11.

Franz's best friend is also perfectly identified by Gambetti as a show-off. However, it is rarely that Bernhard presents a female character sympathetically — Maria (Maja Komorowska) is an exception. She is supposedly modelled on Ingeborg Bachmann, with whom Bernhard became friends in Rome. Maria, a poet and best friend, whom he met when she "did not have thousands of books yet at home… hundreds at most…"[49] Franz revealed his idea for *Extinction* to Maria. How much time will he need to write it? A year? Two years?

> Franz:
> By writing… I annihilate what has been creating me so far… me and everyone else in here… what has been deforming me, what has distorted… Because it has never been pronounced… Now an enormous rubbish dump will be created where everything will burn through, everything will be annihilated…
> (…)
>
> Maria:
> You cannot write solely from pain, it would only be revenge…[50]

Franz tells Gambetti his dream about Maria. A "high-mountain" dream. Maria runs into a guesthouse located high in the mountains. She is wearing a red party dress and heavy men's shoes. Alexander (Waldemar Barwiński) runs in right behind her. He's a friend. "We swapped shoes!" Alexander is trying to stand straight in high heels. They are surrounded by a cold wave coming through an open door and by snowflakes falling outside the window. Maria and Alexander, two bright rays of light in this world. Happiness, so simple to handle, and occurring so seldom in Franz's life. There are books lying on the table, with Maria's poems among them. The best ones, the unwritten ones. How much tenderness there can be in holding pages with someone else's, treasured poems…

> The table with blessed books… They are works by Schopenhauer and Maria's poems, perhaps also by someone else, a beloved philosopher, a beloved poet. But quite truthfully they were not works from this world — where everything is born poor and mediocre. They were probably works which these authors could have written, had they removed their coat of indolence and helplessness. They are promised works, secret works… These books secretly fell to our lot — we reached these books… Who reached them? Alexander or Maria… Yet these books are a surprise and

[49] *Extinction*, 41.
[50] *Extinction*, 85.

astonishment to me, I do not know too much about these books myself… But Maria as well is not fully knowledgeable. Upon hearing that we have her poems she screams "thieves", yet later comes over attracted – curious. (…) I remember dreams in which suddenly in my apartment or my study I discovered my paintings which had somehow escaped my memory, paintings created in another region (…) Such works have to be paid for with something…[51]

At this moment of tenderness, the owner of the guesthouse appears at the door, he has Franz's father's face. A stranger who can knock all the books off the table with one steady pull. Maria becomes a bird, throws her arms in the air. She screams as if she is trying to scare a predator away from her nest.

Maria is an antithesis of the character of the mother (Jadwiga Jankowska-Cieślak), who is stupid, greedy and cruel. Her face is always implacable: not once do we see her smile. The only moments that Franz could have been close to her were when they were filing letters together, once a week. Once Franz was absent-minded and read for too long in the library and missed this moment…

Franz:
It was nine when I awoke from a peculiar dream terrified, put the book away and ran out of the library,
which I was not allowed to be in anyway, and showed up downstairs where the family had finished dinner a
long while before...
They were all sitting in the so-called green drawing room, waiting only for me...
I was perhaps nine or ten at the time.
I'm not sure exactly, Gambetti.
I was trembling all over.
My sisters, though still only very small girls, were already familiar with malevolent excitement, longing to
see some sensational punishment, ruthless and merciless...
My mother asked me after a long speech filled with the most extreme accusations;
Now, what were you doing in the library?
I said, I was reading Siebenkäs...
(*with a sudden frenzy of a charging memory*)
What?
I was reading Siebenkäs...
Whereupon she jumped up from her chair and slapped me in the face...

[51] Lupa, *Utopia 2*, 369.

Go to bed! — she yelled — Get out of here at once! To bed!
And when I was already at the door:
You are not to leave your room for three days...[52]

And yet, for him, it was punishment enough that he missed the one moment in the week when he was alone with his mother and when his mother seemed like a woman who could be kind and nice to him. They get closer years later when his mother visits him in Rome. When they walk together in the city streets, and windows of shops are rolled in front of the actors:

Mother:
What is that Siebenkäs actually? Can you tell me now?

Franz:
Siebenkäs? It's an invention of Jean Paul... A book...

Mother:
Jean Paul? Who's that?

Franz:
Jean Paul is a writer, and Siebenkäs is one of his books...

Mother:
Oh, if only I'd known... I thought Siebenkäs was your invention... Your invention to spite me... A common
excuse...

Franz:
(*laughs long, loudly and continuously*)

Mother:
Is this correct? Is Jean Paul really a writer, and is Siebenkäs one of his books?

Franz:
Yes, correct.

Mother:
Are you sure? Are you not lying even now?

Franz:
No, I'm not lying...

[52] *Extinction*, 14.

Mother:
So Jean Paul is a writer, and Siebenkäs is one of his books...
So Siebenkäs is one of his books, and Jean Paul is a writer...

Franz:
Yes...
(*after a long while in silence, when we walked down the street...*)

Mother:
And is Kafka a writer too?

Franz:
Yes, Kafka's a writer.

Mother:
What a pity. I thought you'd invented them all. What a pity... And he wrote... *The Trial*?[53]

They agreed that, after all those years, Franz could only accuse his mother. She had frightened off his father's best traits. Always the best, after the wedding he became mediocre. She cheated on him with Cardinal Spadolini (Marek Walczewski/Władysław Kowalski), whom she regularly visited in Rome using a visit to her wayward son as an excuse. And over and above all that, she is "a hysterical Nazi", involved in the movement with all her heart. On Hitler's birthday she always raises a swastika in front of the house. She hosted Nazi officials at receptions. Later on, she was in hiding from the Allies.

When Franz is walking down the estate which has now suddenly become his property, he goes to Kindervilla. It is missing the colourful rocking horse; there is a huge, cold, empty space. The world of childhood desecrated by his parents hiding Nazis in this place. War criminals. All these murderers, his father's friends, will come to the funeral — how can he shake their hands? Suddenly, during the funeral, all official titles granted back in *those* days will become present. Austria is full of silent murderers — this is another accusation thrown by Bernhard at his homeland.

The parents' spirits appear in Kindervilla. "They do not know what had happened to them. They think they are coming back, that it is only some indisposition… they are too narrow-minded to recognise death…"[54] The father gives him commands, instructions. Now Franz will be able to settle

[53] *Extinction*, 20.
[54] *Extinction*, 77.

down comfortably in Wolfsegg. He will be able to open all libraries, he will not find a better one in all of Italy. The son listens to him carefully but in response asks him only why he did not try to save the Jews he knew from concentration camps. Why did he consciously betray them, knowing very well the fate he was condemning them to?

In the final scene Franz goes towards the audience for the first time. He stops at the very edge of the stage. Standing behind him, at the back, are mourners; sounds of a funeral piece composed by Jacek Ostaszewski become louder. At Franz's signal — "Out!" — the lights go out, the music dies. A will is read out by an off-stage voice:

> I hereby decide to bequest the entire Wolfsegg estate and all property belonging to it as an unconditioned
> gift to the Department of Culture of the Jewish Community in Vienna…
> Signed:
> Franz Josef Murau
> born in 1934, died in 1983…[55]

The lights go out. No one in the stunned audience feels like applauding. A seven-hour story created from a monologue. From a war declared on everything that is uncomfortable in an unaccepted reality. The construction of this performance is broken. It follows the narrative of Bernhard's novel, breaks off, like a stream of thought and associations of the main character, which are incoherent and achronological. They disperse in the huge spaces of the setting: Franz's Rome apartment, the drawing room in Wolfsegg and the orangery where the coffins with bodies are carried. Dynamic changes of scenery whirl in our heads. The acting is intimate, personal, directed towards one's own thoughts and the text ground in our minds. Krystian Lupa, who strove to adapt the work for the stage made it possible for characters and parts to emerge from the main character's monologue, thus creating one of his greatest artistic achievements:

> In *Auslöschung* — his last novel which, if only because of the scope of problems it discusses and limitless intransigence becomes a type of will — Thomas Bernhard does not sum up his personal and artistic experiences, but subjects them to radical revision. Sudden death of the main character's parents (he is in fact the author of this fictitious autobiography), death in a car crash, is the starting point. The time between receiving the news and the funeral is the time of "Auslöschung", a monologue at times gigantic, full of contradictions, and suspended between the temptation to make a

[55] *Extinction*, 87.

> general change of life so far, in which everything negative, everything that tampers with and deforms a human being and their perception of the world will be annihilated, and the pressure of returning onto the bosom of the family and accepting the responsibilities and privileges of an heir... It becomes an opportunity to settle the score with contemporary (general and local — Austrian) philosophy of life, its system of principles and values, as well as a settling of accounts with the traditions of literary creativity. All of it, according to Bernhard, is false and leads to further irreversible falsehood. *Auslöschung* is a total resignation from external assets that literature boasted so far — what remains is a bare, dismayingly real and helpless human voice. *Auslöschung* is a suggestion of expurgation, saving human dignity and truth by "erasing" — an uncompromising and unconditioned reduction, the most radical amputation of the diseased spiritual tissue... For the creators of theatre adaptation it is a great challenge to have the deepest reflection about the truth and lies of theatre...[56]

Five years later, on the boards of the same theatre, Lupa staged "another Bernhard".[57] Everyone already knew how precisely the Lupaesque synapses are tuned to the wretched derisiveness and genius of Bernhard's observations. Therefore, everyone expected a... masterpiece.

The stage was lit by the screening of the sky moving over actors. The action takes place in the house of a writer, Moritz Meister (Władysław Kowalski), a beautiful villa at the foot of the Alps. The performance opens with tea being taken on the terrace. Moritz's wife (Maja Komorowska) hosts Fräulein Werdenfels (Agnieszka Śnieżyńska), who is writing a doctoral thesis about her husband. Cups of freshly brewed tea overflow with the wife's awe of her husband. Even a rhyme about a lark, an example of the worst kind of graphomania, is recited by her with the reverence worthy of the deepest analyses of human existence. Anna is a guardian of the house and of her husband's genius. She remembers perfectly when and in what circumstances each of his works was written. The PhD student, probably happy to find a better source of information than any state archives could offer, makes a note of every word. Eventually Anna begins to dictate her thoughts about wealth and life, all

---

[56] Krystian Lupa, "Wokół *Auslöschung* Thomasa Bernharda," in *Extinction* (Warszawa: The Dramatic Theatre of the Capital City of Warsaw, 2001), 5.

[57] Original title of the production: *Na szczytach panuje cisza*
Date and place of premiere: September 23, 2006, The Dramatic Theatre, Warsaw
Direction: Krystian Lupa
Adaptation: Krystian Lupa
Set design: Krystian Lupa
Music: Paweł Szymański.

the time looking over her shoulder to see if Fräulein Werdenfels is writing everything down. She suggests ideas for the thesis: "my husband adores vowels."[58]. She is married to a great writer, she is the guardian of his genius, to which she owes the fact that today she lives in a luxurious villa. She is the co-author of her husband's greatness. After all, this was not the first PhD student: so many had taken the trouble to analyse the master's work before her. Anna already knows perfectly well what to tell them. And how to engage their enthusiasm. She talks about the trip to Knossos ahead of them. She calls it "an educational trip in the footsteps of King Midas". Knossos, Phaistos, Evans, pseudo-intellectual speech about the origins of European culture, but she also did some research in Knossos… And the stupid, naive PhD student eagerly writes down every word. She does not know the answer to questions asked by Anna. She has never been to Knossos, she has not seen the Regensburg Cathedral. She has experienced too little to know what is there to be discovered in the world. Such kind of curiosity does not get you good grades in your diploma. She comes from an academic family, is ambitious, but has little more to show for herself than as a well-mannered student. She is the type who always does everything properly, perhaps even very well, but not extraordinarily well.

If she really *listened* to Frau Meister's words she would notice that a much more interesting project for a doctoral thesis was taking place right in front of her. If she had raised her eyes from her notes written down in a neat school-girl hand only for a moment… Callas, *La Traviata*, Moritz Meister knows all of Beethoven's symphonies. When they are sitting together in the library he begins to talk about a friend he used to have who introduced him to music. How much he owed to her… but the Master says she died… but it cannot be, she is sitting next to him. Anna gave up a promising career as a pianist for the sake of her husband's creative work: "Only one of us can be devoted to great art, we said to each other when we got married. The choice was that it would be me."[59] When Moritz says this, there is no hint of reflection that for his sake she had given up travels, concerts and audiences. They joined the intellectual elite, but at the cost of one of them giving up her dreams. An unattempted future, this intrusive conditional mood, condensing all thoughts so thickly that all you can do now is let them sink to the bottom of the tea-cup while Moritz rants and raves about Mendelssohn, and about Professor Stieglitz, the central character of his recently finished tetralogy. The rhyme about a lark, a cycle about the Morello cherry… Lupa's perfectly tuned actors play out all

[58] *Over All the Mountain Tops*, stage script, (Krystian Lupa's private archive), 16

[59] *Over All the Mountain Tops*, 11.

meanings on all levels with great precision. With a slight raising of the eyes from the tea cup they signal to us… there is something here to think about. And yet Moritz would be completely helpless without his wife. When he enters into an empty room convinced he was going to find her there he does not know what to do. The ominously immobilised revolving stage which normally speeds up the changing of a scene can be pulled from under him any second.

Is Moritz just a self-obsessed buffoon? He had just finished his tetralogy. He removed the weight of creative effort from his shoulders and is now savouring another literary victory. The final i had been dotted. Muses predict poetic glory to people like him. What is the first sentence the master says when he appears on stage?

> Goethe did not understand bees.[60]

Bees and literature, the master's two passions. He had even written a study… about the secret of bees. Thomas Bernhard hides behind the character of Moritz Meister. Just like the character in the play he escaped from Viennese middle-class life to the Tyrolean village of Obernathal. Meister, on the other hand, created his literary *alter ego* in the character of Professor Stieglitz, the main character of his tetralogy. Following this trail of thought we can say that Krystian Lupa is self-mockingly hidden behind Władysław Kowalski playing Moritz Meister.

Everyone in this play keeps referring to Professor Stieglitz. He, too, loves Beethoven, he, too, loves Knossos, and he obviously knows a great deal about it. Anna has to read chapters of his work to Moritz every day, especially fragments referring to Professor Stieglitz. Moritz keeps emphasising the similarities between them, but this Stieglitz has to be an incredible embodiment of perfection: well read, well listened, knows the answer to every question. This is also how the PhD student treats Moritz. How greedy he is for her flattery, how his face radiates when she compliments him on his genius…

Based on what we hear from the characters in the play we can deduce that the recently finished tetralogy is some long-winded, two-thousand page monstrosity of erudition. Utterly incomprehensible unless we have the complete Encyclopædia Britannica to hand. If no one can understand it, if no one has the willpower to plough through the only correct interpretation of inscriptions from Knossos, such a work is easy to promote as a masterpiece. The author's final task is to believe his own (so tediously earned) genius and protect it persistently later on. In his

---

[60] *Over All the Mountain Tops*, 8.

production, Lupa shows the psychological process of becoming a creator. From lonely self-denial to believing in oneself, which over time can develop into indiscriminate megalomania. Meister has been elevated to the role of national genius. He has to face it somehow. It is easier for a human being to cope with a problem they believe in, but his belief has developed into *hybris*.

However, we can clearly see that there is something wrong with this masterpiece. When we listen carefully to the questions asked by the PhD student it is momentarily unbelievable. Is she really that stupid?

> When did the first thought of writing a tetralogy come to your mind?[61]
>
> Did you have an idea for the tetralogy?[62]
>
> Such a vast work… such a two thousand pages long work in which the entire history of culture is processed… How is it possible?[63]
>
> Why is the chapter devoted to Robert shorter than the one about Edgar?[64]
>
> Doesn't Robert represent a kind of villain in your tetralogy?[65]
>
> Did you experience stylistic problems writing the chapter on Edgar?[66]

The stupidity of these questions clearly shocks the author, but he decides to treat them seriously. The Master can speak about himself under any circumstances, and keeps talking into the microphone, undiscouraged (however, shocked considerably). Eventually, he begins to manifest irritation with the fact that a PhD student writing a dissertation about his book can be such an idiot. They are sitting in the library, surrounded by heavy volumes, but when Meister reaches for one of them it turns out to be a designer-box for pills. Taking into account the level of questions asked by the PhD student, they are either tranquilisers or heart pills. A PhD student… a mediocre mind, who by asking banal questions tries to fill them with the appearance of sublimation. However, it is not the student's mind that can be the problem. Is it the student who is that stupid? Or is it the work she is writing about. Her questions are endlessly stupid. No

---

[61] *Over All the Mountain Tops*, 20.
[62] *Over All the Mountain Tops*, 21.
[63] *Over All the Mountain Tops*, 21.
[64] *Over All the Mountain Tops*, 26.
[65] *Over All the Mountain Tops*, 23.
[66] *Over All the Mountain Tops*, 23.

literary scholar would ask such questions. However, judging by excerpts from the tetralogy quoted in the performance, there are no smarter questions to be asked. She simply tries her best to dissect anything suitable for an academic dissertation.

After Konrad, after Kant... unfulfilled artists who never managed to put their life's work on paper — fear me, those who succeeded. Perhaps it is not worth climbing the intellectual peaks because there is nothing there. Just the clouds flowing picturesquely over the brightly lit stage. Meister lives like Professor Stieglitz, in a villa granted to him by the state, in an area "almost untouched by the terrible present".[67] With the daily ritual of picking up the mail and responding to letters from admirers. There is also a letter posted in Stockholm… but it is only a travel agency brochure. Journalists and editors come to visit (of course, only those who publish the greatest). They have created a shrine of talent in the house. A villa from the state, but this house must have had previous owners. One of the maids still remembers them. When asked, she is unwilling to talk about them. They emigrated to America, driven out by the Nazis. Professor Stieglitz is also an avid anti-Semite, delighting in fancy quotations from the ancient Greeks. "We deceive the apocalypse," says Meister, "we do not question it — we deceive it — and this is the tragedy of the Germans."[68] Says Meister, says Bernhard.

In the final scene, during a dinner with friends, the Master reads out the final chapter of his tetralogy:

> Meister:
> now I will read out a piece of the chapter on Edgar.
> Conclusion.
> Robert arrived from Trieste The city fraught with history an empty port in the dark
> Marlene knows nothing about his tragedy with Edmund
> Who stayed in London
> The scandal with Cyrus is forgotten
> The papers decided not to publish anymore about Cyrus
> The article Edgar discussed with Robert
> did not come out as *Times* does not publish such articles
> There is a strong wind blowing in Germany at the moment
> Robert simply cannot accept
> Edgar's decision
> (…)
> We presume the disaster must have struck

---

67 *Over All the Mountain Tops*, 3.

68 *Over All the Mountain Tops*, 51.

much sooner namely at the moment
when Edgar gave up his estate
and returned to Switzerland to meet his mother
That lonely woman suffering from pneumonia
Awaited Edgar at the hotel in Lausanne
at the hotel which
what a strange coincidence
belonged to Professor Stieglitz
Thus the circle of siblings finally closed

Publisher:
Well...
This is a master…
… piece.[69]

But who says it, and in what context? The finished tetralogy is "a work masterfully nonsensical, whose absurdity is shocking".[70] It is a very fragile talent and greatness, just built on a base of words. The acting by Maja Komorowska and Władysław Kowalski creates a great composition with the ending. They mock themselves, their words and gestures are always in inverted commas: "You see? How we turn on the charm in all this fame and wealth?" Komorowska has her pseudo-academic tirades but peeps at the audience all the time — You see who I have to play now?

What is such a person really thinking? There is, however, no impudence in this effect, no indiscreet agreement with the audience. There is, rather, the awareness of the fact that one can do more in front of audiences who come to see a production by Krystian Lupa. These audiences will detect humour even in the most serious dialogues.

The peak: what are the impressions of those who conquered Everest? Allegedly, an ecstatic sensation… but there is no one around. Just the cold, fatigue and the sun hurting the eyes.

Lupa proved that he has a unique sense for staging Bernhard's plays. He understands his way of constructing thoughts, his sense of humour. He can translate his intensity into the language of theatre. However, if we really let ourselves be carried away by this fascination, greedily reaching for new publications we will realise that in fact Bernhard strikes the same chords in every work. In every work there is the same aggressiveness, fierceness, obsessive dripping of poison. Productions directed according to paths marked out by these texts have to share the same pitch. At some point, therefore, subsequent masterpieces produced by Lupa with well-

[69] *Over All the Mountain Tops*, 61.

[70] Jerzy Koenig, „Jeden dzień z życia pisarza," *Teatr*, no. 12 (2006): 22.

tried methods became less attractive to audiences. It is already certain that every new premiere will be *Bernhard bien faite*. A revelation to those who are only beginning their literary adventure with this author, but quite predictable to those who have been following Krystian Lupa's work a little longer.

In *Woodcutters*,[71] Bernhard once again attacked Vienna's intellectual elite. By producing this work Lupa wanted to provoke a discussion on the condition of the Polish "aristocracy of the spirit" on the cusp of the twenty-first century. With Bernhard's mockery, he wanted to create ferment over the commercialisation of the Polish theatre which, in the artist's opinion, had become a form of undemanding entertainment for the masses. He wanted Polish artists and people active in culture to break away from their comfortable satisfaction with the status quo. In interviews he complained that there were not many creators left who would venture to take a real, artistic risk which would not be measured by commercial success. Some critics obviously joined him in his conviction, others approached the problem from a distance, observing a certain manifestation of hysteria in the artist's attitude, to which I will refer at the end of this book.

Going to see the play, we join Thomas (obvious *alter ego* of Bernhard, played by Piotr Skiba) and accept an invitation to an artistic dinner, hosted by the Auersbergers after Joana's funeral (Marta Zięba). Together with the invited guests we will be sitting in their dining room until late at night (the play is almost five hours long). Unfortunately, during the course of the evening, it will become apparent that remembering the late Joana was not the main reason for this meeting.

The performance begins with a video. Thomas, who has just returned from London after twenty years' absence (Bernhard's favourite motif of "impossible escape") is walking in the streets of Vienna. There is something obvious about his going to the Graben on arrival and meeting the Auersbergers there. He had broken off contact with his best friends twenty years before, with the intention of never restoring the relationship. The camera catches them at a bookshop window. Thomas is looking at the copies of *Woodcutters* on display, and hears a familiar, female voice

[71] Original title of the production: *Wycinka*
Date and place of premiere: October 23, 2014, Polski Theatre, Wrocław
Direction: Krystian Lupa
Adaptation: Krystian Lupa
Set design: Krystian Lupa
Music: Bogumił Misala.

calling him. Maja Auersberger (Maja Lampersberg, a Viennese singer) and Gerhard Auersberger (Gerhard Lampersberg, composer and art patron who, among others, promoted Peter Handke), had just purchased the complete works of Wittgenstein. It is always good to complete one's education thematically…

"You know? — I know…" — He had unwittingly gone to the Graben on the day of Joana's (Elfriede Slukal – dancer, associated with the Wiener Gruppe) death, and hastily accepted the dinner invitation, hosted by the Auersbergers after the funeral. Friends only, as usual. An exceptionally artistic dinner, meaning, accompanied by a discussion at the highest intellectual level. Artistic dinners with a theme, be it Wittgenstein, or a friend's death. On evenings like this all of the old friends, once so close, are gathered together. And now, the only feeling Thomas might have for them is hatred and distaste. At moments like this, people suddenly see things clearly and reject everything with uncompromised criticism. But indeed, Bernhard could not have it any other way.

Before Thomas's escape to London they used to meet to create things together. Now, all they can do together is destroy. They come flying from afar like vultures. Celebrating the fact that it is not them… Elfriede Jelinek had already called to say she was not coming. She used "the malady of literary crisis"[72] as her excuse. Jeannie Billroth, "who fancies herself as Virginia Woolf,"[73] is coming (this character is based on writer Jeannie Ebner). Also appearing are Anne Schreker — the local Gertrude Stein who "followed the path from a young talent to a repulsive state artist,"[74] (Friederike Mayrocker — poet and writer) and Albert Rehmden (Anton Lehmden — painter and founder of the Vienna School of Fantastic Realism).[75]

Dinner is in progress. It is already very late but their discussions are about nothing. They are all waiting to discuss "real issues" until a "phenomenal actor" (Jan Frycz) playing in an "enchanting" performance of *The Wild Duck* at the Burgtheater arrives, but he is running late. On the day of the funeral everything is subjected to the phenomenal actor who reached the peak of his artistic abilities playing the part of Ekdal. Still, as

---

[72] Thomas Bernhard, *Woodcutters* (Wrocław: Polski Theatre, 2014), 44.

[73] Bernhard, *Woodcutters*, 45.

[74] Bernhard, *Woodcutters*, 117.

[75] The double identity of the characters in *Woodcutters* ended in court. Gerhard Lampersberg recognised himself in the figure of Gerhard Auersberger and filed a lawsuit for defamation. The court ordered all copies of the book to be confiscated.

the host was not embarrassed to admit: "The Burgtheater is a pigsty."[76] The entire performance takes place in the dining room, at a table where everyone is gathered to remember Joana, or perhaps to celebrate the great actor of the Burgtheater? The actor, who probably does not even realise that his co-diners have just returned from a cemetery. Throughout the evening Thomas is sitting to the side, in an armchair. He is observing everything with the typical distance of a person who can see through them all. He wonders what had happened to all these artistic souls that his friends used to carry at the bottom of their hearts. Thirty years before, every one of them dreamt about something great. Today, all they do is collect government awards: "This city is a monstrous machine annihilating geniuses, a monstrous machine destroying talents."[77] They began a dangerous affair of servility towards the Government. Suddenly, somewhere on the red carpet, they lost their ability to criticise. Suddenly, the system became bearable, it became "their own". They started joining commissioners and ministers for tea. They renounced the ideals which created them. "The Burgtheater has always been attacked, especially by those who have been eager to join and been rejected. This has always been the case."[78] They do not even realise how far they are from the ideas they gestated at their youth. They are too busy with national events.

Finally, definitely too late, after midnight, the actor of the Burgtheater arrives. A megalomaniac, another Moritz Meister, who turned *The Wild Duck* into the event of the season in Vienna. He complains about the condition of contemporary theatre. If only he had better partners on stage… Because, apart from him, the choice of actors for all the other parts was accidental. He was the only one who left for three weeks to the Tyrolean Alps to work on his part. A few minutes after 2am, when everyone is barely alive after a hard, mentally draining day, a discussion begins on which character is harder to portray: Strindberg's Edgar, or Ibsen's Ekdal… And about Joana falling into poverty before her death, about her taking her own life, forgotten… Her friends do not feel like reflecting on whether or not she should have been helped. John (Marcin Pempuś), Joana's partner, had striven to save her. He is the only mourner who cried real tears at the cemetery, and is now becoming more and more vividly aware that his presence at this dinner is a great misunderstanding. Their Joana, their memories have nothing in common with the Joana he knew. He leaves angry and alienated.

---

[76] Bernhard, *Woodcutters*, 66.
[77] Bernhard, *Woodcutters*, 82.
[78] Bernhard, *Woodcutters*, 112.

The lights are dimmed. The artistic dinner is coming to an end. The exhausting day affects the audience. At this point, only the best friends remain. The other guests had left a long time ago. Half-asleep audiences delay collecting their coats and walking out into the cold night. The air is heavy. Those present sink into their seats. Only those for whom it was fitting to be the last to leave remained. They formulate sentences from behind half-closed eyes and discuss topics to which they will not return next time they meet, the ones that grind to a halt inside ashtrays overflowing with cigarette butts and scraps of food. Conversations take place outside the censorship of regular meetings. Hushed voices, final remarks. Perhaps Joana had to kill herself to make this meeting possible? As Thomas is leaving, the hostess still manages to call him on the stairs:

Maja Auersberger:
Thomas!

Thomas Bernhard:
Yes?

Maja Auersberger:
Don't write about this!

Thomas Bernhard:
...I ran through the streets as though I were running away from a nightmare... and as I ran I reflected that the city through which I was running, dreadful though I had always felt it to be and still felt it to be, was the best city there was, which I found detestable and had always found detestable, was suddenly once again the best CITY in the world, my own CITY, and that these people, whom I had always hated and would go on hating, were still the best people in the world: I hated them, yet found them somehow touching — I hated the CITY, yet found it somehow touching — I cursed these people, yet I have to love them and I hate the CITY, and have to love, I ran and ran and thought I had run away from this monstrous so-called artistic dinner in the Gentzgasse, as I had run away from all monstrosities, and I thought I'll write something about this artistic dinner in the Gentzgasse, not knowing what, I'll simply write something about it, and I ran, ran and thought that I'll write something about this artistic dinner in the Gentzgasse at once, at once, I thought, right away, I kept thinking, running through the inner city, right away and at once, right away and at once, before it's too late...[79]

[79] Bernhard, *Woodcutters*, 149.

3. *Рукописи не горят*[80]
Krystian Lupa and Russian literature

> Newsweek: You were born in 1943, during World War II. Was the topic of Russia discussed at your home?
> Krystian Lupa: I love Russia, despite the family experience. My father was a linguist, a Russian teacher; he read Dostoyevsky, Tolstoy, Chekhov in the original. At the same time he had no problem obsessively hating Soviet power and Communism. He was a Russophobe who, obviously, was also a member of the Polish-Soviet Friendship Society. He would come home from meetings full of hatred and poisoned us with it. He preferred German culture.
> Newsweek: Did you become a Russophile to spite your father?
> Krystian Lupa: Yes, and Fyodor Dostoyevsky became the most important author, he was God. I was also greatly fascinated by Moscow, especially old, Orthodox Moscow from the period of the Napoleonic Wars, which I caught from Tolstoy' *War and Peace*. This strange demonic myth of the city in which strange, ghastly things take place. I had a recurring dream in which I am on a train to Moscow, get off at the railway station and run to the centre down a wide street, I look at my watch to see I have to go back and I don't get to the Kremlin, those Orthodox churches. Russia's religious nature has a great impact on me. All that you can see in the monasteries of Zagorsk or Moscow. The zeal of old people is unbelievable, ecstatic. You cannot see that here.[81]

From time to time, to expand the imagination, Lupa succumbs to his idealistic Russophilia and reaches out towards Russian culture. As early as the nineteen-eighties he gradually began to retreat from staging drama and move on to the great works of literature. He explained that it was more and more difficult to express aspects of the contemporary world through dialogue. With the development of psychoanalysis, humans stopped believing their own words and the words of their interlocutors. The truth, the essence of what one intends to express — hid behind words. "Dialogue ceased to be the basic carrier of the human mystery".[82] To him, the novel was an interesting performance matter exactly because it does not impose theatricality. It is in itself a suggestion of a certain, very specific, reality. It does not create its world merely through dialogue. It does not distribute it

---

[80] Ru. "Manuscripts don't burn.", Mikhail Bulgakov, *The Master and Margarita* (Moscow: AST Moscow, 2006), 320.
[81] Jacek Tomczuk, „Przyzwyczailiśmy się już do pokoju. I tu nagle Ukraina – rozmowa z Krystianem Lupą," *Newsweek*, March 22, (2014): 41-43.
[82] Matkowska-Święs, „Wciąż noszę te siedem dachówek…," 12.

among characters. In his adaptations of novels, Lupa always looks for a palimpsest, a second level of meanings, which can be fully realised only on stage. Rehearsals frequently begin without a script. He selects characters and situations from a novel and tries to illuminate them at rehearsals from different angles to provide different motivation for actions. He observes the results of how this approach works on stage. He often develops events and problems barely mentioned in a novel. Sometimes, he also prepares two versions of a performance, directing them according to different interpretive keys.

Lupa first worked on the text of *The Brothers Karamazov* when preparing a graduation performance with students of the Krakow Academy for the Dramatic Arts (1988). He then suggested that the Dostoyevsky novel be read through the texts of Mikhail Bakhtin, and his theories tested in specific scenes. The essence of the performance was based on the characters of Alyosha and Ivan. "I compared the performance to circling around a well — the death of old Karamazov was only a dark hole, barely sketched with dialogue; it was not talked about or shown. This principle was maintained in the later performance at the Stary Theatre."[83]

A "full length", eight-hour performance staged two years later at the National Stary Theatre in Krakow did not provide the answer to who killed old Karamazov.[84] Everyone was a father-killer in the performance. In 1891, Nikolai Ge, a Russian artist belonging to the Peredvizhniki group, painted *Conscience: Judas*. It depicts Judas with his back to the viewers, watched by guards leading Jesus. It is a dark night. The light is falling on the road from behind his back. The reality presented in the painting is the pitch of Lupa's setting. The entire performance is immersed in darkness, underexposure. It is a theatrical tenebrism. Monochromatic costumes in dimmed colours often make the figures invisible on the dark stage. The represented world of this production brings to mind mouldy bed linen or an old sticky banister we subconsciously avoid touching. Spectators are surrounded by invisible, yet noticeable filth. All objects on stage are covered with a layer of dirt, grease and passing time. Relationships

---

[83] Fyodor Dostoyevsky, *The Brothers Karamazov* (Krakow: Stary Theatre, 1999), 8.

[84] Original title of the production: *Bracia Karamazow*
Date and place of premiere: April 10, 1990, Helena Modrzejewska Stary Theatre, Krakow
Direction: Krystian Lupa
Adaptation: Krystian Lupa
Set design: Krystian Lupa
Music: Stanisław Radwan.

between characters are the same. A window is the only source of light here, as if a ray of hope suggesting that there is a God, and that there is immortality. And this ray falls on the living room of old Karamazov (Jan Peszek)… Lupa has always been ironic.

The darkness of this world will not be brightened up, even by the character of Alyosha (Paweł Miśkiewicz), whose faith in God and immortality accepts no half-measure compromise. Neither will it be brightened up by the character of Lise (Beata Fudalej). In Lupa's production she is a grown woman. Possibly, her love for Alyosha makes her the only clearly pure character in the story. The whiteness of monastic habits is greyish. Lise's dress is also grey, not white, as if the costumes of these bright characters unwittingly reflected the darkness in which they were immersed. Lupa's production raised questions about the existence of God and the nature of evil dormant in human nature. Situations between characters did not summarise the book, but attempted to raise topics described in it. They discussed the questions all characters asked themselves. All the brothers, so different from one another, are tormented by the same question: "Does God exist or not?"[85] The entire production is focused around this problem. The performance began with an off-stage question: "Who are you?" and Alyosha appearing in a single spotlight. Another blackout, and spectators were transported to Father Zosima's hermitage (Andrzej Hudziak) where pilgrims have gathered. An elaborate scene in the novel was reduced to the character of Lise and her mother. People came to Zosima for advice, comfort and support in moments of weakness of faith. They expected a miracle but instead the devil appeared.

In the darkness we can hear a jester, old Karamazov. Jan Peszek, cast for this part, is perfectly equipped to play the character. A glorious rogue, disgusting, obnoxious, wonderfully sarcastic. Jan Peszek's performance was a symphony. He will be asked to leave this holy place of seclusion any minute. However, we know from the novel that it is not going to happen. Four hours into the performance (to the bewilderment of audiences who know the plot of Dostoyevsky's novel), Fyodor Karamazov is still alive and well. The death of this character is going to be a representation from an Old Rusyn icon. An illuminated cloud will flow from his mouth to the sky. In Lupa's production, everyone is a father-killer; the audiences also become accomplices to the death. Ivan (Jan Frycz) wanted his father dead, but did not have the courage to carry the burden. He did not even have the courage to find out who did what he wanted done so much; he was not strong enough. In his adaptation, Lupa

---

[85] *The Brothers Karamazov*, stage script, (Krystian Lupa's private archive), 20.

does not determine who killed old Karamazov. The thread of investigation was completely omitted.

All the brothers have a guilty conscience. They all, each in his own way, have doubts. There is no immortality? Not even a little bit? Ivan's conversation with Alyosha, when Ivan confides in the younger brother about his loss of faith, takes almost thirty minutes of dialogue over a plate of soup, and the audience's minds do not drift off from the meaning of their words even momentarily. Ivan and Alyosha are two completely contradictory characters, with two different world views. Together, they are two parts completing one figure. Ivan believed he was not rebelling against God but against the world he created. He instils his doubts in Alyosha. In the novel, as well as in the production, a human being is a testing ground on which God fights with Satan. Never before could it have been said that Krystian Lupa is interested in religious topics, and in this production he completely followed Dostoyevsky who put forward arguments to test them on humans. His characters keep mulling over whether there is despair great enough to kill one's thirst for life: how much can we expect from a human soul? Was God so indispensable to the world that he had to be imagined? "And the strange thing, the wonder would not be that God really exists, the wonder is that such a notion, so holy, so moving, so wise a notion which does man such great honour, could creep into the head of such a wild and wicked animal as man."[86] Mysticism will not be beaten out of simple folk with a stick. But the simple folk usually optimistically stop at the notion that man created God in his own image. They forget that Satan was created the same way. No other species can be as cruel, with such artistic sophistication, as man.

In Dostoyevsky's novel, the eponymous brothers are in their twenties. In this production they are several years older, more mature, their characters heavier. Lupa directed his characters by slowly illuminating them. Their contradictions came to light slowly, as action on stage developed. Growing doubts, questions arising were asked incidentally, as natural consequences of events. Importantly, in most dramatic scenes, such as Dmitri's (Zbigniew Ruciński) leaving for Moscow, Lupa often brings to the surface the comedy of his characters' situation, the naïveté of their convictions. In his adaptation, Lupa put together dialogues at a different angle than Dostoyevsky did. Where a reader sees another wrongly interpreted plan, a person hearing the same dialogue on stage would burst out laughing.

[86] *The Brothers Karamazov*, 34.

The performance ends with *Et Resurrexit* from Bach's *Mass in B Minor*. Everything is effectuated: a grand finale, a perfect place to end the production on a high note, but it is something Lupa never does. After the highest note there is always blackout, dimness, muffling of emotions. The entire performance, the eight hours spent with the Karamazovs is like a dream, a hallucination in a weak light of the lamp hanging over the stage. Lupa's adaptation does not have a continuous plot consistent with the novel. The performance breaks off with the conversation between Ivan and the devil (Piotr Skiba). This final scene is when the production is finally real. Satan comes to Ivan half-naked, dragging a dirty quilt behind him, insolent, malicious, ruthless towards Ivan on the edge. How could such a banal devil come to such a great man? But even such a Satan is mighty, and shows Ivan his power although Ivan keeps trying to deny his existence. Talking to the devil is when Ivan realises that it was not a dream and that everything really happened. The real ending of the performance is the moment when Ivan comes up to the window and opens it. The light falls in. A promise of redemption? Expurgation? After eight hours in the darkest areas of the human soul viewers would welcome at least a semblance of a promise that, despite everything, there was a chance of salvation: "The world stands on absurdities, and without them, perhaps nothing at all would happen."[87] — Lupa has the ability to find the perfect punch-line for his productions.

The so-called "literary tourist" in London avoids the National Gallery or Westminster Abbey, and heads straight to 221B Baker Street. The Moscow equivalent would be Patriarshiye Ponds, where Mikhail Berlioz (Zbigniew Kosowski) and the young poet Ivan Homeless (Bogdan Brzyski) wander one day. Not far from the pond is the *Memorialnaja kvartira* — a museum-apartment dedicated to Mikhail Bulgakov. However, much more important than the museum is the staircase of the house in Sadovaya guarded by an entry phone and residents reluctant to listen to strange steps on the staircase. Bulgakov's apartment is located on the fourth floor. The walls of the staircase are covered with drawings and quotes from the ground floor all the way to the top. There are scenes from *The Master and Magarita*, portraits of characters, magic spells, and prayers to Woland. Fantastically colourful, carefully thought out, polished up: they are not careless graffiti, hurriedly scrawled. Lupa made such a "humanist pilgrimage" following Bulgakov's footsteps before he began

[87] *The Brothers Karamazov*, 36.

rehearsals for his adaptation of *The Master and Margarita*[88] (a reference to this magical staircase was made in the production design in the drawings by patients of the asylum to which Ivan Homeless was admitted).

Berlioz and Ivan Homeless appear at Patriarshiye Ponds. Talking about the existence of God they are joined by a mysterious foreigner. He is enchanted by their conversation. What an amazing country in which atheism is nothing special and proofs of God's existence are of no value. In *The Brothers Karamazov*, the question of God's existence dominated. The first scene in *The Master and Margarita* is a conversation between Berlioz, Ivan Homeless and Woland (Roman Gancarczyk) precisely about proofs of His existence (obviously refuted by Communist science.) Berlioz to some extent replies to Ivan Karamazov's question: yes, it is man, granted free will, who decides his own fate. However, in the production Woland and his entourage will prove to him how illusory faith is and that we can plan our future ourselves: "Yes, man is mortal, but that is not the worst of it. What is bad is that he sometimes dies suddenly." Because, as Woland argues, Jesus really existed, and there is nothing to argue about. And does the devil exist? With his production, Lupa speaks about the insanity of unbelief. The worst thing man can do is to adopt omniscience, and even Woland does not know where his own fate would send him next. Woland's entourage, "the devil's quartet", are eternal wanderers whose job is to disrupt people's destiny. They resemble a circus troupe with a cat, always on the road. Moscow is just one of their stops. At the beginning of the performance, one of Woland's companions moans: "To Moscow, to Moscow. Why to Moscow, I didn't want to go to Moscow". It sounds a little like a variation on Chekhov's: "To Moscow!" But why indeed *did* Woland especially choose Stalinist Moscow as the next destination? And was it, in fact, *his* choice?

> Jacek Romanowski (Asasello): At the beginning of the scene at the "ill-fated apartment" we are arguing that we don't like Moscow and we don't know why we got here. It was Woland's decision — let him answer.
> Roman Gancarczyk (Woland): Why to Moscow? It simply had to happen this way. It is difficult to say who gave the first impulse. Clearly, we can speculate about it but in my opinion Woland didn't know he would appear

[88] Original title of the production: *Mistrz i Małgorzata*
Date and place of premiere: May 9, 2002, Helena Modrzejewska Stary Theatre, Krakow
Direction: Krystian Lupa
Adaptation: Krystian Lupa
Set design: Krystian Lupa
Music: Jacek Ostaszewski, Jakub Ostaszewski.

> in Moscow. It was a so-called "controlled accident". Evidently, this was an arrangement of the cosmic force which caused them to get there. (…)
> Piotr Skiba (Koroviev): Two perspectives can be adopted. The first one suggests that Woland is an autonomous character who consciously sets out for specific destinations. The other — which seems to us more interesting and which we approached in this production — assumes that the devil appears from a specific kind of space and place; certain energy, weakness and disorder in man cause the devil to emerge. A potential of anarchy, lurking in the space, brought about the devils who find it to be great substance and sponge on these events.[89]

Lupa's adaptation was directed in such a way that with the help of apocriphal additions the characters engage in polemics with Bulgakov's original. The director broke the illusion of the novel, when Woland's entourage wangle their way in the apartment in Sadovaya. Koroviev nervously looks for something to read in the owner's library: "No one, no one reads anything in here." He moves on to another room, and after a while returns with a copy of *The Master and Margarita* under his arm. He opens it at random, and begins reading the description of the apartment in Sadovaya. His companions listen carefully, indeed, it is them "happening" at that moment in the action of the book. When Koroviev grows bored with reading, he puts the book on the table: "I don't feel like getting into this". Further disassembling of the novel will take place at a Moscow literary café. Koroviev and Behemoth (Adam Nawojczyk) try to get in, but Sofya Pavlovna (Alicja Bienicewicz), who worked at the reception, does not want to let them in without a membership card of the Writers' Association. She remains unaffected by arguments that Dostoyevsky did not have a membership card either. Walking past the audience, Krystian Lupa enters the stage. Sofya Pavlovna lets him in without blinking an eye. There is always a place for someone like him… He sits at one of the tables and with an extended arm commands her to let the strangers in. He finishes a drink served by a waiter and disappears from the stage to sit in the back row again and navigate the performance from there.

Koroviev and Behemoth, finally allowed inside the café, sit at one of the tables. They finish reading excerpts from *The Master and Margarita*, trying to understand their situation better. They take the fate of the characters in their own hands in order to turn the story of the Master (Zbigniew Kaleta), Margarita (Sandra Korzeniak), Berlioz and Pontius Pilate (Jan Frycz) into a meaningful, cohesive whole. They read

---

[89] Agnieszka Fryz-Więcek, „Okazja czyni diabła – rozmowa z Romanem Gancarczykiem, Jackiem Romanowskim i Piotrem Skibą," *Didaskalia*, no. 49/50 (2002): 15.

subsequent fragments of the novel, and ridicule incompetent images created by Bulgakov: a naked Margarita, flying high above the earth on a pig, and the troubles with gravity resulting from it. Izabela Połabińska, in her notes taken at a rehearsal, captured the unbelievable circumstances in which most brilliant scenes like that are created:

> 26 April
> Writers' café. Koroviev and Behemoth leave the audience. And we're in a pickle. The situation repeats itself, like in a bad dream. Koroviev barely finishes the first sentence: But this is the writers' house. Stop. But it is from some operetta — Krystian says — you are not entering a new reality. From the top. After a few sentences by the infelicitous diablitos another Stop. You don't bring anything, you don't react, you don't see. Once again. They get to Sofya Pavlovna as a "bouncer". Stop. There must be some misunderstanding — the director is already irritated. I can't hear any adventure, Sofya Pavlovna isn't stopping anyone. There is no event whatsoever. You are slipping on tiny tones! From the top. What of it, if they keep lying. Stop. What's going on? — Krystian is angry. You already had it! And from the top. Worse and worse. Krystian has had enough; he decides to have a reading rehearsal. He does not interrupt. He walks in circles, growing more and more sullen. End of text. I understand it is just a reading — the director concludes — but there isn't anything left of this scene, is there? Everything is pretence. There are no characters in danger, exposed. If you show a character's weakness — it is a vaudeville or a cabaret. We are to protect these people, their dignity, and their sense of self-worth. End of rehearsal.
> Actors are slow to leave, with their convictions shaken. Eventually, the three satanic outcasts remain. Koroviev begins a conciliatory conversation with Krystian about how they had just got the book and cannot find their lines, that a manuscript might help… What manuscript? Krystian explodes. A manuscript is good for a literary scholar, not a common passer-by — and you could have prepared the book! You take a book out of your pocket and put it on the table like a cigarette case. The viewers don't care that you can't understand the book. What I hear are some pre-recorded tunes, like Frico and Coco, the clowns!… But — Koroviev is not giving up — aren't they written exactly like Frico and Coco? Krystian gets involved: Yes, it is Frico and Coco who have a problem! They are like two tramps at a sophisticated writers' house. These scoundrels don't have such things in their capitalist country, and here, look, such marvels in the Soviet Union… Authors of *Don Quixote* and *Faust* mature in such orangereys, but you have to be careful, because they might rot, and bad fruit occasionally does happen. It is, as if two graffiti daubers had entered the Sistine Chapel and fussed about what that Michelangelo doodled, while theirs was real Art!!

> Aha! — Koroviev is enlightened — we have to put forward hypotheses and not perform commentaries! Eureka.[90]

Woland's thugs are incredibly bored. They are like naughty children who begin rocking their chairs. They don't have anything to do, so they come up with entertainment at the expense of the inhabitants of Moscow. They take control of reality. They bend it to such an extent that everyone begins to go mad. The heroes are bursting with supernatural powers and things such as riding on hogs begin to happen… The turning point marking this collective madness is a masterly performed evening at the Variété Theatre. The audience of the production becomes the audience of a black magic séance. Actors are sitting mixed together with the spectators. Woland's troupe are carefully watching the hysteria of women with their dreams of new dresses exposed. They carefully watch Bulgakov ridiculing Soviet dreams of the West and its dollars. They turn the intensity of emotions up.

Far away from these events is Ivan Homeless, locked up in a Mental House, who after Berlioz's tragic death started talking about a mysterious foreigner sitting on a terrace of Pontius Pilate's palace. The paint peeling from the wall covered with patients' drawings has probably seen tsardom. We can guess we are in poor suburbs of Moscow, in areas where respectable citizens do not venture. No one can be sane in such a grim place.

> 9:03 p.m. April 1, 2012
> The biggest uncertainty… what about Ivan Homeless, having read aloud both scenes at the mental hospital I became completely discouraged. J. Ś. took the floor. Wonderful, funny and scary… Why do they only see the political content? If something presents something horrible, it is incredible in itself, regardless of the price of truth.… I listened completely discouraged. I looked at our table… I could feel them… Bogdan with his head down, Ula, distrustful Piotr… They are really looking for something else… That… the tastes of truth — how I would like it. Others — would like it to match convictions, to confirm convictions and to have something to perform… Why do people need to be constantly reassured in their convictions, why are they afraid to let their convictions out, put them at risk, in jeopardy?… Perhaps they are afraid of such a situation, perhaps they find themselves constantly among enemies, among the enemies they find outside… I began to blabber… I thought it would all come to nothing… I was even certain it would all come to nothing, embarrassment crept in. This embarrassment often appears, like a pupil who came to a class unprepared… What will I do with these two scenes I had my assistant rewrite?… Why have I summoned them here for a rehearsal? They must

---

[90] Izabela Połabińska, „Notatki z prób," *Didaskalia*, no. 49/50 (2002): 19-25.

> have thought about something like this. They need to be tricked into some method, they need to be shown — persuaded that there is a strategic objective… Then I will be able to start working. So I have summoned them today only to force myself to think… They looked at me in disbelief — it is either going to be complete disgrace, or I am up to something… There is no other choice… Sandra is looking at me with an apprehensive smile and tears seem to fill up her eyes… I think I am imagining the tears… (…) Perhaps this is the right track? Perhaps Homeless (hence the pen name) was born in a far away Russian village, surrounded by a thousand-year-old magical mentality; perhaps his father was a clairvoyant and a primitive adept of ecstatism — rushing his revelations with alcohol, perhaps his mother lost her mind crying about not being able to understand her husband, with candles in front of icons and there was consistent crying in the room, and swearing and pleading to God… The child was discovered by a mad teacher at school who sent it to town for a crash course and ideological training at the Komsomol. A poet was discovered in the young man… his world view was changed in two years, objects of faith and fetishes replaced… everything he had from the tradition which was poor but reached to the bottom of his soul was simply snatched away from him. This change obviously must have been superficial. They tried to compensate this superficiality with fanaticism and pressure… the pressure of new ethics… Ivan became a totally incoherent creation — one thing was quietly smouldering inside him, and quite another thing was pressing him on the surface… Such a man cannot develop — such a man can remain compulsively consistent or become sick.[91]

One could run away from such a place, but to where? This is when, in the middle of the night, through an open window, the Master comes to see Ivan Homeless. He is visiting his trusted next-door neighbour. He tells the story of his madness. The madness so deep, one could forget one's own wife's name. He is proud to be the gravest case in the entire institution. He talks about Margarita. About nights when things are so dramatically bad that we keep thinking and pleading for that someone to guess that we need help, we need to be dragged back to the surface, we need them to come, but there is no one coming… it was on such a night that the Master burnt his work. And now he has nowhere to go. He is afraid of dogs and trams. The ball at Woland's is possibly a chip of his broken perception of the world. The ball at Woland's. Surrounding the stage, in ominous silence are the deceased. There is no shouting, no greetings, and no music. Pontius Pilate meets the resurrected Yeshua (Andrzej Hudziak). This is the scene when Woland concludes, "A fact is the most stubborn thing in the world."

---

[91] Lupa, *Utopia 2*, 416-417.

Although Margarita was wasting the wishes granted to her by Woland on other people, she will have the privilege of meeting the Master. They will make one more attempt at returning to reality, but there is a predominant coldness and sadness on the stage. It is not the idyllic vision of love that Bulgakov imagined. The Master is completely absent. He is smoking a cigarette, virtually not noticing Margarita. Does the danger of her leaving him for Woland make any impression on him? Eventually, both of them leave Woland. Asasello brings the poison to them. They embark on another journey with confidence, with a naive conviction that everything will turn out right — the world is built on that.

The final scene is a conversation between Woland and the Master. All the characters are squatting on the stairs at the back of the stage. They are following the final dialogue. The novel is completed. The Master can finally see his protagonist. Pontius Pilate, suffering from a headache for two thousand years, is sitting at the top of the mountain alone. Lupa's low voice can be heard off-stage reading out a description of Woland's entourage transforming into knights of darkness.

Izabela Połabińska, notes from rehearsals:

> May 1
> In the morning, Krystian appealed to the group not to get involved in psychological reasoning of everyday life — in some washed-out Stanislavskian method — and welcome the principles and requirements of the absurd, yield to irrational reactions in confrontation with irrational reality.
> After twenty hours of rehearsal my head is full of chaos. I can no longer see things from a perspective. The premiere is tomorrow![92]

Lupa had selected spectacular comical tricks from the novel which, performed intelligently, created brilliant stage wholes. He presented characters to whom magic was a habitual procedure. From sophistication he was able to move on to cheap effects such as a housemaid flying on a pig. There was no trace of Stalinist Moscow in the show. Lupa removed the filter of Communist Russia present in the novel and referred only to the absurd. He allowed the devils to figure out the ending. However, not all critics were impressed with the production:

> Blue light of a bare bulb. An old, cast iron bed, a dead grandmother's ancient duvet, crumpled pillows and yellow sweaty mould on a sheet now

[92] Połabińska, „Notatki z prób," 19-25.

> serving as a duster. There's as much life around as in a fly's buzz when it feels like moving its wing. The depth, let me tell you, the depth of dreamy endurance... Yet, something starts to move in the sheets, there is something wheezing under the lumpy feather stuffing, the bed is wailing underneath the heavy load of somebody's awakening body, something is clearly about to happen... But it is calm again. It was just someone's dream, it was just someone rolling over. The hole is calm again. All we can hear is water dripping from a rusty tap. And suddenly — wham, bam!!! I hear a rumble behind my back, a thunder out of this world. I check to see what is happening, after all I am at the theatre, not in the Wild West. I look, and it is all clear. It is Krystian Lupa. He is pounding on a drum with a huge club, from time to time shouting out old shaman's spells into a slightly slobbery, clip-on microphone, to intensify the atmosphere, kicking at the doors of the auditorium. Admittedly, he is not jumping up and down, but that is only because he is attached to a web of cables connected to a keyboard on which he is playing a classically hazy rhythm of intimate metaphysics. Yes, my world suddenly collapses on me, as I see a grey-haired, cultural older gentleman and a great artist playing Indians once again. Stretch this duvet-Indian image over two nights, blow it up to eight full hours and you will come up with the principle of *The Master and Margarita* according to Lupa, you will get alpha and omega, the metaphor, the principle, the taste, the smell and rhythm of the whole, in short — blow up an image and you will receive Bulgakov as an old woman who spends an eternity lying in old rags and is unable to do anything else.[93]

To speak about acting, art and theatre truth Lupa combined two texts in one evening: *The Seagull* by Anton Chekhov and *A Spanish Play* by Jasmina Reza.[94] He wanted Reza's text to be a commentary on Chekhov's, and for the two works combined to form a complete diptych. *The Seagull*, with which the performance begins, starts with an image of the historic world premiere at the Moscow Art Theatre: a row of chairs is set, backs to the audience on the edge of the stage. In the background — a huge swimming pool filled with twelve tonnes of water. Lhasa De Sela in the speakers. Her voice is muffled, liquefied, and dangerously hazy. Actors enter the stage through the audience. They are getting ready to see

---

[93] Paweł Głowacki, „Bzyk martwej muchy," *Dziennik Polski*, May 14, (2002): 11.

[94] Original title of the production: *Niedokończony utwór na aktora/Sztuka hiszpańska*
Date and place of premiere: October 1, 2004, Dramatic Theatre, Warsaw
Direction: Krystian Lupa
Adaptation: Krystian Lupa
Set design: Krystian Lupa
Music: Mieczysław Miejza.

Konstantine's (Andrzej Szeremeta) play. Lupa's *The Seagull* is a moving story about finished artists. About creative torment. About talent which can kill. But how can we talk about acting without talking about human nature?

Nina Zariechnaya (Marta Król) and Konstantine are at the beginning of their artistic path. Digging their way with bare hands towards life's experiences is still ahead. Lupa intensified the problem of actor's/artistic presence even more. Marta Król playing the part of Zariechnaya was a actress at the start of her career, her steps on the stage still very insecure. Zariechnaya was ashamed to perform in front of Arkadina, a great actress, played by Maja Komorowska — a great actress. We can assume that Marta Król experienced the same actor's anxiety in the presence of Maja Komorowska. It was a perfect shift of an off-stage situation into the reality of the play. Intimidated? Perhaps so, but Zariechnaya had to find the courage to close her eyes and face the doom awaiting her on stage. If she really cared, if her true goal in fact was to escape the provincial backwater and conquer the world; if she was ready to do anything to achieve this goal, the first step she had to take was to forget that Arkadina was watching. Whether she liked it or not no longer mattered. Krystian Lupa best summarised the opposition between the young and the old during one of the rehearsals: "We've made a nice production, and now we'll destroy every fucking thing because we want to incite something in you." Lupa's Zariechnaya is like a dream of a career from a glossy magazine. Her monologue in the performance is brutally interrupted by Arkadina's guests. Konstantine finds himself in an even worse predicament: after all, Arkadina is his mother. He has to look for a compromise, between a rebellious search for his own path and a natural need for acceptance. His words are very ambiguous: "Mother hasn't seen my play, but she hates it." Is this just a rejection of rejection, or is the smouldering sorrow there because he was still hoping his mother would truly understand him? During rehearsals, Lupa asked Konstantine and Zariechnaya to do some homework and prepare a real production which would be presented to the guests. They worked on monologues and spent hours arranging consecutive scenes. They came up with a text on the verge of madness which they recorded and showed to Lupa. This was what brought them back from the chaos in which they had immersed themselves.

Maja Komorowska's acting was the highlight of both parts. Her Arkadina is an emotionally drained woman, a has-been celebrity who can no longer show her feelings other than by acting them out as characters. We could spend a long time debating whether she truly loved her only child, whether she was trying to follow his choices, or whether it was just another part which she performed in the presence of an audience. There is too much unnatural weight in her attempts. It seems that honesty should not be strenuous. In *A Spanish Play* she plays a matronly woman whose existence should only be limited to living her daughters' lives. However, when Maja Komorowska starts dancing flamenco at the end of the show, the entire reality begins to twirl. The fabric of her dress seems to capture everyone all the way to the back of the theatre. Lupa always creates spectacular, emotionally-loaded scenes which would be perfect for a performance finale. He builds them up, and sets them in motion only to silence them again. He always paces the rhythm of the performance from the peak of emotions to calm silence, for both cast and audience. The scene of Maja Komorowska dancing flamenco, happy and in love, is seemingly a perfect moment to close the show with a storm of applause from the excited audience but at this point Lupa always adds an extra fifteen minutes of dialogue to ease the tension in the actors' muscles.

All the characters in *The Seagull* are transformed into the characters of *A Spanish Play*. Reza's text was to shed light on the text by Chekhov. There was, however, a technical problem of how deeply one can play an actress playing an actress. Are there a limited number of inverted commas for such a situation? Jadwiga Jankowska-Cieślak (Aurelia) moves towards the audience:

> I am rehearsing a Spanish play
> in which I play an actress
> who's rehearsing a Bulgarian play.
> I teach piano to a married man
> whom I fall in love with.[95]

Stage situations keep throwing the actors off their characters. Something always discloses their careful attempts at building stage illusion. Again and again, the actors are ready to get off the starting block; they get on stage from the foyer, through the audience. Soon after, they themselves have to transform into spectators, because Konstantine is going to show his play. Lupa disembowels all theatrical constructions. He drops a wall with a door for an actor to walk through and lifts it up again. He lets technicians be seen on the stage, almost pulling out the sofas from under the actors. Once, he makes an interruption himself by yelling at the crew from the back row. So we have actors playing actors who are celebrities,

---

[95] *An Unfinished Play for an Actor/A Spanish Play*, stage script, (Krystian Lupa's private archive), 33.

their photographs are published by tabloids, and their mobile phones keep ringing. The gala dress outrage:

> some ragged costume, in which, with the eyes
> of entire Spain on me, I will feel
> ragged, which means, that this way or another
> my night will be ruined, because a woman, Fernan, who exposes
> herself to entire Spain, cannot fall below
> people's expectations of her![96]

is a substitute outrage. The main problem is not that the protagonist cannot find the right dress to wear, she simply does not accept her mother's new partner. She does not accept the fact that there is a real estate manager (Władysław Kowalski) sitting at their family table (although they gather at it only twice a year). She does not accept that they can only talk to such a man about boundary walls, property law and the need to trim ivy. But the issue of "the common ownership status of the shared border", which keeps reappearing in conversations, is what binds the entire performance into a cohesive whole. This is the key problem, because "the common ownership status of the shared border" between the actor and the character he plays is what is most interesting to Lupa. While watching his actors in action, he is trying to catch exactly where the dividing line is drawn.

Acting as the main notion of theatre production; about its consequences when a certain framework of action is imposed by success. Do such high priests of art still have the right to show how real people eat? The problems they discuss are quite trivial, unwanted pregnancies, and old unfulfilled passions. They have normal conversations about children fighting for a scoop in a sandbox, and Lupa is able to create a little wonder from this scene for his actors. From minor topics — should a child who is happy to get a vacuum cleaner as a birthday gift see a specialist? — we slip into topics on the verge of insanity. We hear about people who having drunk one litre of vodka go out into the street and on their knees beg the cars passing by to run over them. About crazy people speeding on motorways at 290 miles per hour suddenly overtaken by a rabbit running along the road. In this performance "the common ownership status of the shared border" serves as a litmus test to determine nervous breakdown.

---

[96] *An Unfinished Play for an Actor*, 47.

4. Towards the precursor

There came a moment when Krystian Lupa grew bored with the theatre made by Krystian Lupa. Tadeusz Nyczek pinpoints it being after the premiere of *The Master and Margarita*:

> He is on the top, an unquestionable guru, after Kantor's death, successor to the throne of the Main Visionary and Leading Artist. He has enchanted disciples, enchanted critics, enchanted audience — and no longer only in Poland. He does not have to prove anything, he knows everything about theatre and has perfected his decadent-psychological style. This is when he starts playing with it. He throws it in the air and watches it fall. He spreads it over the stage, over the background and the audience.[97]

His Bernhardian interest in creative individuals developed into creating productions-biographies. He flew to Athens to meet organisers of the Hellenic Festival, who offered him production of a project. He promised to reveal his ideas when they but was in fact flying with an empty head, devoid of ideas: "There was a basketball team on the plane to Athens — athletes with an average height of two meters twenty. They were all a head taller than me. The tallest and the most beautiful one was sitting next to me. I was fascinated by this incredible Homo sapiens individual… and when we were beginning to land over Athens, the idea for *Zarathustra*[98] appeared," the idea of staging the philosophical epic poem by Nietzsche, which resulted in "the greatest dream about man theatre could offer".[99] By combining the text of *Thus Spoke Zarathustra* with *Nietzsche, Trilogie* by Einar Schleef and his own apocrypha, Lupa created a production about the search of the Übermensch.[100] He offered his spectators a psychological-philosophical vivisection of the meaning of human existence.

---

[97] Tadeusz Nyczek, „Andy II," *Teatr*, no. 4 (2008): 15.

[98] Krzysztof Mieszkowski, „Człowiek nie jest finałem - rozmowa z Krystianem Lupą," *Notatnik Teatralny*, no. 34 (2004): 32.

[99] Piotr Gruszczyński, „Krystian Lupa: wieczne dążenie," in *Strategie publiczne, strategie prywatne. Teatr polski 1990-2005*, edited by Tomasz Plata, 41. Izabelin: Świat literacki, 2006.

[100] Original title of the production: *Zaratustra*
Date and place of premiere: May 7, 2005, The Helena Modrzejewska National Stary Theatre, Krakow
Direction: Krystian Lupa
Adaptation: Krystian Lupa
Set design: Krystian Lupa
Music: Paweł Szymański.

The first notion which is always brought up when discussing the text of *Thus Spake Zarathustra* is the death of God. Questions about God and the meaning of religiousness were already present in *The Brothers Karamazov* and *The Master and Margarita*. Lupa himself, when asked about his religious worldview, refers to the words of Rainer Maria Rilke:

> There will be God. God is born in people. I think it is totally absurd that a perfect and omnipowerful being would create an imperfect world. Why the hell would he? I believe that matter, with its unbelievable struggle, is aspiring after something. And that man, as Nietzsche says, is a bridge. I keep building this bridge.[101] Security lies in God, faith and religion. God can be referred to as the core of everything, including human seriousness and dignity. In God lies the comfort of Christians, criticised by Nietzsche, as it is a morality of the weak, of those who consider not committing a sin to be the greatest virtue. They build their lives according to a negative criterion — "NOT to do something". Nietzsche put it differently: "Not freedom *from* something, but freedom *to* something". Man lives in order to do something, and not — not to do something. To live so as not to do harm is the greatest harm. (…) Zarathustra does not come with some transcendental message, but a strangely intimate one, which we all carry inside. If we are to venture anything and judge the man opposite us, there is a misunderstanding. We suddenly feel attacked by the words: "Man is something that must be overcome. I come to proclaim the Overman to you, and you can transform yourselves into the Overman." This is when anxiety begins. Having swallowed the hook of God's death, man feels under attack and trapped, hearing: And now you are faced with a task. You must make the transformation. You must transform yourself.[102]

Actors playing in the performance gather on the stage near the audience, hover in the foyer before the beginning, talk to people, and greet those they know. They are dressed as if they had just walked into the theatre straight off the street: one might wonder whether they are here to perform tonight or to socialise. They walk onto the stage as if trying to define the situation they are in. They are waiting for the performance of a tightrope walker, who is about to walk over their heads. Among them is the young Zarathustra (Michał Czernecki). He is easily discernible, wearing red trousers, a white shirt and barefoot. He is trying to catch their attention: "I will teach you the Overman! Man is something to be surpassed! What have you done to surpass him?! All beings thus far have created something beyond themselves, and you want to be the ebb of this

---

[101] Ewa Likowska, „Ekstrawagant - rozmowa z Krystianem Lupą," *Polityka*, no. 37, (2006): 76.

[102] Mieszkowski, „Człowiek nie jest finałem…," 34.

great tide, and even return to the beast rather than surpass man?!"[103] But they are not listening to him. They are not listening to what he is trying to say to them. They are deaf.

> Zarathustra does not perceive the world by reflection, but by intuition, association — implementing the previously gathered knowledge, activating contexts and experiences. But he knows the bitter taste of defeat, his own inappropriateness. This made an overwhelming impression at the Odeon of Herodes Atticus on the slope of Acropolis. Imagine a tall weakling such as myself walking in, standing in front of three thousand spectators to announce that he had learnt the truth, to share this great revelation. I shout to them but no one is looking at me. Three thousand people are looking at the subtitles over my head. I look them in the eyes, but see no reaction, just the heads held up high, out of sight. At that moment I felt what Zarathustra might have felt: People, I am speaking to you — to you only, with my whole body, not with words, but you do not look at me.[104]

The tightrope walker, who "turned danger into his profession",[105] is falling from high above. He failed to rise above people. Zarathustra draws an outline of his body, as if in a scene of an accident. He buries him with his own hands. This is when Johannes (Bogdan Brzyski) arrives. He wants to accompany Zarathustra to ease his own pain after the death of a friend. Because suddenly there is no more that person to whom one could tell anything, whom one loved… His despair will become the Eagle — Zarathustra's companion. Mateusz, who left his woman, also appears. Mateusz will become the Snake. Together they will embark on a journey to overthrow all boundary stones. They will be guarding Zarathustra's sleep when he goes through consequent transformations, like a dog nudging its master with its nose to encourage him and rush him to go on. They meet the Jester and the Prophet of Great Fatigue. Zarathustra will also be greeted by kings wishing to escape the falsehood of the world. They come to Zarathustra, listen to him, but still do not understand anything. They arrive earlier than anyone else and they do not understand anything… The last pope (Zygmunt Józefczak) also appears on his way. There is a non-accidental resemblance to Pope John Paul II in his final years. He is stooping and falling apart. Tubes and cables of the devices to which he is connected disappear behind the papal throne; there is the frame a hospital bed connected to a fish tank behind his back. In an

[103] *Zaratustra*, stage script, (Krystian Lupa's private archive), 1.
[104] Łukasz Maciejewski, „Chcę - rozmowa z Michałem Czerneckim," *Notatnik Teatralny*, no. 34 (2004): 82.
[105] *Zaratustra*, 4.

unpleasantly brown liquid there is a naked human body vegetating, feeding leaches. From his blood, the pope gets the energy to travel. Zarathustra faces a difficult conversation with the Church Father, about the death of God:

> They say that sympathy choked him, when he saw how man hung on the cross. (…) There was something of the priest-type in him. He was equivocal. He was also indistinct. How he raged at us because we understood him badly. But why did he not speak more clearly? And if the fault lay in our ears, why did he give us ears that heard him badly? If there was dirt in our ears, who put it in them? Too much miscarried with him, this potter who had not learned thoroughly. That he took revenge on his pots and creations because they turned out badly… that was a sin against good taste… (…) He was a hidden God, full of secrecy. Truly, he did not come by his son otherwise than by secret ways. Whoever extols him as a God of love, does not think highly enough of love itself.[106]

In the play we could see Zaratusthra's three "personas": Young, Mature, and Nietzsche. Nietzsche's character (Krzysztof Globisz) was the last personification of Zaratusthra. His body is unable to carry his whirling mind. From the wilderness through which Zarathustra wanders we move to a middle-class interior. Fritz (ie Nietzsche) is already very ill. There is virtually no contact with him, his words are mainly monologues. He is unable to get dressed on his own, he cannot even hold a book in his hand. It is an illness his close ones turn away from and which his Mother (Iwona Bielska) and Sister (Małgorzata Hajewska-Krzysztofik) decide to manage. The illness has alienated him. Helplessness becomes anger at the son's physical detachment, at the fact that he had never married, at him turning his back on the world and wasting everything. His mother is helplessly trying to penetrate the darkness of his mind where "shadows are groping one another". She is trying to force him to speak. Let him speak, even if she cannot understand him. Just let him speak. And Fritz speaks only when Snake and Eagle come to see him, the animals accompanying Zarathustra in his quest. However, the ignorant mother is trying to chase them away.

Getting ready to wash. The painstaking responsibilities of caring for the sick Fritz. They have to lift a cast iron tub and bring the hot water. Both women, however, are already used to everyday struggles. They undress him, help him get into the tub. There's no pretence in Lupa's performances, spectators will see the whole bath. Washing a clumsy body

---

[106] *Zaratustra*, 24.

which had lost all control. They will see the calm of hot water, relaxing and dilating the blood vessels. There is no Übermensch. Fritz turns to look helplessly towards the audience, as if to apologise for the state of affairs. "Zarathustra has crashed, but not into someone greater."[107]

The Mother is turning for help to memories, when Fritz was still well, when he used to play the piano to them in the evenings. She is trying to force him to play again. They need a holiday to awaken the life that has passed and is never to return. She is trying to force them to play and to dance: "Go on, children!" She begins to hit the piano keys, playing the ghastly *Moonlight Sonata*, while Lupa is wailing to the microphone from the back row. Fritz takes his mother's place at the keyboard, banging on the keys with his fists and caterwauling *Silent Night*. Nothing heals tattered nerves as well as music…

The mother cannot accept her inability to understand her own child. Only the sister can make contact with him. However, their conversations have different meanings. Their dialogues pass each other by. She is telling him about their father, he is telling her about ripening figs and this is how they communicate. They go for a long walk all the way to "the Streets of Babylon". They watch the homeless queuing humbly for soup. They are the characters Zarathustra had met on his way. Now, gathered over a plastic plate of soup, they do not notice the strangers watching them. A bleeding and beaten-up prostitute appears among the people: "Males think they are Übermenschen, and they think we are whores. But who turns us into whores?!"[108] Fritz is trying to save her but it is already too late. He is standing at the epicentre of despair and misery. Wilted sorrow pervades the stage. There is no chance of escaping the reality. The appearance and emotional strain of this scene are unbearable. The music itself, composed by Paweł Szymański for this fragment, is heartbreaking.[109] "The higher man is an eternal mistake…"[110]

Krystian Lupa most probably first heard of Andy Warhol at Tadeusz Kantor's classes when he was studying at the Krakow Academy of Fine Arts. *Factory 2*, produced in 2008, was a collective fantasy inspired by the artist's work.[111] When rehearsals began, the news of Lupa completely

---

[107] Gruszczyński, „Krystian Lupa: wieczne dążenie," 42.

[108] *Zaratustra*, 55.

[109] The music for the performance was voted "Theatre music of the year" by *Teatr's* readers, and awarded best music for the film *Plac Zbawiciela* (*Savior Square*) at the Polish Feature Film Festival in Gdynia.

[110] *Zaratustra*, 54.

[111] Original title of the production: *Factory 2*

changing his way of working on a production quickly spread around Krakow. Like that time in Jelenia Góra, he isolated himself and his actors for over a year to devote themselves solely to this project. They were not interested in the artist's personality, nor in the origins of pop culture, but in the phenomenon of the group who gathered around Warhol in his Silver Factory. The community of the Stary Theatre actors decided to tackle the issue of the communal life of the group of artists. Together with the director and playwrights they all conducted research into the topic, reading books and watching films about Warhol. They painted their rehearsal room silver, and all the actors could go there whenever they wanted, to listen to music, read books, or try on costumes. Several hundred hours of improvisation, the so-called "screen-tests", were recorded at the time. As Katarzyna Warnke (Nico) recalled: "Krystian set up a farm of personalities (…) At the beginning, our work was to lie down on the floor and watch films or read books. It was like a strange Warhol-themed play centre."[112] Catching every gossip about the theatre, people were anxiously awaiting a great artistic event.

The stage space was to imitate the interior of the famous New York Factory. Silver walls, silver tables, silver chairs, with the exception of a red sofa in the centre. There was a huge screen over the stage displaying the actors' improvisations (screen tests) during the performance and screening *Blow Job*, the film directed by Andy Warhol, at the beginning. For twenty minutes, Warhol filmed the face of a man as he receives oral sex. The real action takes place fifty centimetres below the frame — and these words will become the catch phrase of the show.

The production is not organised by a script. Two days before the premiere actors were still learning new texts provided by the director. The whole thing was designed as a fantasy on what a typical day at Andy Warhol's Factory might have looked like. Conversations and actions are to a large extent improvised. Things the characters might say or do and what resulted from their personalities. They are variations on real and possible events which might have taken place. The audience were therefore in for a seven-hours session on the meaningfulness of using a vacuum cleaner,

---

Date and place of premiere: February 16, 2008, Helena Modrzejewska National Stary Theatre , Krakow
Direction: Krystian Lupa
Adaptation: Krystian Lupa
Set design: Krystian Lupa
Music: Mieczysław Mejza.

[112] Julia Kluzowicz, „Faktoryjka – rozmowa z aktorami," *Didaskalia*, no. 84 (2008): 17.

capital punishment and taxes. Unfortunately, numerous improvisations, constituting the majority of the performance, ended up being quite pretentious études about sex and the meaning of life. The strategies behind this forced eccentricity were quite easily recognisable, and impatience with the actors' inability to manage the characters they played was noticeable. The conversations were incredibly long. The boredom applied to this production is premeditated. These people represent nothing on their own, they have nothing to say. They are kids, harmed by life and gathered around Warhol who promised them five minutes of fame. They are all driven by an overpowering need to be "somebody", to draw Warhol's attention, as he turned people into celebrities, sent them into another orbit and, when bored, left them on their own.

During rehearsals, unsupported by an otherwise obligatory script, they improvised, inspired by biographies of the Factory members. They took events from their lives, combined them with films produced by Warhol, recorded improvisations and added them to the production. For a long time, none of the actors knew which character they would play and which character would be included in the production.[113] They read, researched, and when they got to know the characters well enough, members of the cast were selected. Each actor was to write down his preferences on a piece of paper and indicate which part/character was closest to them, and which one they would definitely rather not play. Lupa made the final selection. He wanted his actors to reach towards the historic precursors rather than impersonate them. He wanted them to stop halfway between their characters and their own personality. While working on the production, actors even changed the way they dressed privately. Lupa ostentatiously started drinking Coca-Cola. They were looking for appropriate props. But the props were more for the actors than the audience. In the final scene, the actress playing Ultra Violet (Urszula Kiebzak) enters the stage with a beetroot: how great an expert on the Factory do you have to be to know and recognise that Ultra Violet used beet juice to stain her lips?

The "screen tests" proved to be crucial in preparing the production. Actors locked themselves alone in a room with a camera, and improvised for half an hour on a topic assigned by Lupa including "My fucking me". The greatest burden, however, was not direct confrontation with the

[113] Eventually, the following characters/prototypes for the production were agreed on: Andy Warhol, Paul Morrissey, Brigid Berlin, Gerard Malanga, Ondine, Edie Sedgwick, Viva, Ultra, Eric Emerson, Nico, Freddie Herko, Holly Woodlawn, Jackie Curtis, Candy Darling, Mary Woronov, International Velvet, Andrea Feldman, Valerie Solanas.

camera, the necessity to expose oneself or to strip away any intimacy. What actors found most stressful was the awareness that the recordings would be included in the show what if it turned out that they had no personality? For half an hour they had to "be on their own and face the stress of the fact that there is no text or acting task and you have to be interesting, and at the same time refrain from the temptation to perform, because that would be false".[114] Katarzyna Warnke (playing Nico in the production), when asked about the screen tests in one of interviews, confessed:

> - Were they your real tears or actor's tears?
> - I cannot answer this question with complete honesty because what was happening in my mind at the time applies to me personally. At the time, I could not hide behind Nico, I still did not have my character. I selected a song from an iPod, a song which makes me emotional and which I identify with a personal memory — it is associated with longing and impermanence of happiness. I don't know if it's noticeable but these tears were unexpected for me. It's really cool that there is an honest smile, and a moment later there are tears and emotion.
> - Is the screen test we saw in *Factory 2* your personal statement?
> - It is. We were all trying to be as close to ourselves and our real feelings as possible. Krystian instructed us to be natural. The question was to what extent, even a non-actor, would be able to remove the everyday masks. I've noticed that we make faces when we are alone, walking towards a mirror. Practically everyone does it — we flex the muscles in a specific way. We lie, even to ourselves: I don't know if it is at all possible to stand this way "naked" on our own. Perhaps only in an intimate situation with another person? I mean safe situations, when we feel loved or in a relationship of friendship. The cold eye of the camera was so cruel, so intimidating, because there was no way of establishing contact with it, and yet you knew it was recording. There is nothing else, just you alone, the greatest prosecutor and the greatest judge.
> - In one of the texts in the *Factory 2* brochure Krystian Lupa writes that actors were protesting against the screen tests. Didn't you want it?
> - They were not real protests. That was more our way of expressing fear of seeing something we didn't want to know about ourselves. Because, as actors, when we stand in front of a camera or on stage, we usually have a lot of things protecting us. And Krystian wanted us to get closer to the boundary and to share something intimate. And he triggered our suspiciousness — what would you like us to interest you with, Krystian? Who are we to be? And he repeated that we do not have to be anybody, that we are simply to show what we are like. But what does it mean — what I am like? Actors are used to putting on a mask. And here they have

[114] Kluzowicz, „Faktoryjka…," 17.

> to turn the mask around — show what has collected behind it. The challenge to "be interesting" was horrible.[115]

Actors who had been working with Lupa for years (including Piotr Skiba, Małgorzata Hajewska-Krzysztofik) were joined in *Factory 2* with the "theatrical youth" who chose drama school because of their early fascination with *Kalkwerk* or *The Brothers Karamazov* and later took Lupa's classes during their studies. Generations, sensitivities, fascinations and influences were integrated. In this context, the improvisation by Zbigniew Kaleta and Sandra Korzeniak, the former Master and Margarita, seems even more interesting. They are in bed, alone: "This improvisation was exceptional, indeed. It felt as if the Master and Margarita were meeting years later in another place. Things went wrong in their lives and now they meet to go to bed together. For the first or the last time — we don't know. And there was magic there, this scene is completely upside down."[116]

Actors in this production were constantly doubled: by the screened images and their own presence on stage. Therefore, their performance was directed at themselves, to the audience, to the director sitting in the last row and to the screening over their heads. Every evening their improvisations had to fight for a new life on stage. Actors had to perform against each other with their senses constantly tuned to the audience to see whether the energy was flowing beyond the footlights or whether there was a need for a change of direction.

> - Did you understand the reasons behind creating this production?
> - Krystian often repeated that babbling is what is most valuable. There were times when we had reservations and said: "But it is uninteresting," and all these months Krystian kept saying: "But it's exactly boredom that interests me. I'm now interested in boredom. Boredom is a great force."[117]

When after seven hours the artists face the audience to pose for a group photo, instead of a shutter we can hear a gun shot. Blood appears on Warhol's T-shirt. Fans consider this production to be the boldest of Lupa's works… Everyone agrees on one thing — something has come to an end.

Factory 2 was designed as part one of a trilogy of biographies devoted to Andy Warhol, Marilyn Monroe and Simone Weil. To briefly summarise the production: in *Persona* Sandra Korzeniak played the part of Norma

---

[115] Kluzowicz, „Faktoryjka…," 18.
[116] Kluzowicz, „Faktoryjka…," 23.
[117] Kluzowicz, „Faktoryjka…," 22.

Jeane Mortenson who “played” Marilyn Monroe preparing to play the part of Grushyenka.[118] *Persona* is a three-hour performance about Marilyn Monroe’s struggle with her own personality, about Sandra Korzeniak’s struggle with a dreamed ideal. It is about a battle for oneself when one’s psyche falls apart and every piece has to be picked up again without destroying oneself. The production depicts a single day, the last day of Marilyn Monroe’s life, when she ran away from the set of *Something's Got to Give.* The whole thing takes place in a deserted film studio where she is hiding. We wander this solitude to reach the real Monroe, considering what this word actually means. Tired, intoxicated with sedatives, she is lying on the table among dirty pillows, cigarette butts and empty bottles. She is half naked, wearing an old, stretched out sweater. She is hiding in a deserted, studio afraid to go home — this is where it starts. The studio has not been used for years but there is a still working landline which Marilyn uses to communicate with the world. She summons a friend, a photographer and a psychoanalyst. This is where Monroe records a screen test of Grushyenka from *The Brothers Karamazov* — her dream part — on her own.

Paula Strasberg (Katarzyna Figura) walks in — she is the wife and collaborator of Lee Strasberg, the founder of the Actors Studio in New York.[119] She is an acting coach detested by directors, so Marilyn only listened to her advice on issues relating to the characters she played. She begins to rehearse the part of Grushyenka, Monroe’s greatest obsession, to chase her depression away. This is her greatest, unfulfilled dream. They work on the part even though there is no chance of Monroe playing it. The two of them rehearse the scene of a meeting in Mokre. It is a scene of a dance which should represent total captivation. The captivation of a person who has lost all her strength and is no longer able to get up, but despite this collapse makes a final effort, hoping that, with the force of earlier momentum, something might click and work. Awareness and potential might blend together to trigger the mechanism of Great Art. However, everything they do is clumsy and heavy. You cannot expect someone who's down on her knees to jump higher than she used to.

---

118 Original title of the production: *Persona. Tryptyk/Marilyn*
Date and place of premiere: April 18, 2009, Gustaw Holoubek Dramatic Theatre, Warsaw
Direction: Krystian Lupa
Adaptation: Krystian Lupa
Set design: Krystian Lupa
Music: Paweł Szymański.
119 Monroe studied with Lee Strasberg at the Actors Studio.

Andre de Dienes (Piotr Skiba) walks in. He is an American photographer who worked with Monroe. They have a photo shoot in this mess, among all the alcohol and mouldy linen. Photographs of Marilyn appear on a big screen over the stage. It is Marilyn-the-dream, in far better physical and psychological condition than the Marilyn on stage. Dr Ralph Greenson (Władysław Kowalski) also walks in — he is a psychiatrist and psychoanalyst. Some believe that he was responsible for Monroe's nervous breakdown because he encouraged her dependence on him. Apparently, his ill-conducted therapy, based on sedatives, accidentally led to her death. He conducts a psychoanalytic séance in which the strategies he adopted to subjugate her are revealed. He is eager to have the star in control. He persuades her that further therapy is necessary. He breaks her childhood into pieces. He deceives her with psychoanalytic clichés. When Marilyn begins talking excitedly about the future, he quickly changes the subject.

The basic problem is that everyone who comes to visit has a different vision of Marilyn. Her acting coach, her photographer, and her psychoanalyst. And she has to implement each of the visions. Paula Strasberg infected her with absurdities about creating her own image: "You are the greatest symbol in the history of humanity, everyone knows it and recognises it and you must recognise it, too!"[120] This is when Lupa presented a documentary recording of a rehearsal. Korzeniak is completely broken, crying on the stage: "How am I to present an idea, I am far from ideal…"

We do not know where she finds the strength, but in the end Marilyn washes herself, does her hair, and gets dressed and leaves for a rehearsal. She has not had enough time to rest, and is still feeling depressed and ill, but they have to start working. Assistants undress Marilyn, and get her ready for a take. She lies down naked on a platform. The cinematographer gives final directions. Lights go on in the audience. The camera catches Marilyn from above and slowly turns towards the audience. After one full turn it returns to Marilyn's body, which begins to be consumed by fire in the dim light of the stage. Flashiness blends with the overpowering seriousness of her sacrifice, but perhaps this is how the great of this world should end? Krystian Lupa wanted the production to be

> about telling a tale which cannot come true — a non-existent absolute film starring Marilyn Monroe — which would in fact be the most real, the essence of her life — because her real life was always unreal and temporary — she was a vampire, a non-existent being, a being likely to (potentially) exist. (…) So maybe this motif. Not to talk about the illness,

[120] *Persona*, stage script, (Krystian Lupa's private archive), 12.

the falling, the getting closer and closer to the edge — balancing between a psychoanalyst and being unable to exist on its own — or rather to talk not only about that. A vivisection of the fall is too popular a topic. But the connection between the falling and a more and more persistent and fantastical creative idea which is a spiritist séance between a few artists who are creating, hypnotised, and paralysed — or unwittingly dragged into the trap of ineptitude — thus animating a miraculous homunculus that is Marilyn Monroe… Creating in another person — because that is what she wanted… Dreamers of the impossible. All of them — our characters — were dreamers of the impossible…[121]

5. Centaur

I carry suitcases with the characters' souls behind my actors.[122]

Krystian Lupa draws, paints, and takes photographs. He writes a journal with notes about everyday matters, meetings, conversations, films he watched, texts he read, his battles and struggles with actors. Fragments of the journals are often printed in production brochures or as separate publications. Throughout all these years, he has managed to create his own, hermetic language to talk about theatre. If we go through post-premiere interviews with his actors we will soon notice that after months of rehearsals they are permeated with Lupa's own imagery. They subconsciously adopt his way of speaking and formulating thoughts.

Rehearsals often begin without a ready script. There is a book/topic and a sketched-out direction which it would be interesting to follow. When rewriting an adapted text, Lupa often reduces it to its essence, a report. He turns it inside out and throws light on it to see if there is something underneath. He radically tears the seams of a text in order to sew it back together, adding some outside elements. He constructs a performance based on emotional states and situations they evoke. He involves his actors in the creative process. They collaborate, co-create, searching for new contexts for their characters' actions. They bring their characters to life by equipping them with their personal experiences, their bodies and their sensitivity. In Russian culture, icons are "written" not painted. I think that in the case of Krystian Lupa's theatre we can speak of the "writing of characters in actors".

---

[121] Krystian Lupa, *Persona* (Warszawa: Dramatic Theatre of the Capital City of Warsaw, 2010), 36-37.

[122] Magdalena Rigamonti, „Artysta żyje krócej niż człowiek – rozmowa z Krystianem Lupą," *Newsweek*, July 24, 2010, 78.

A characteristic image for the process of rehearsals is Lupa engaged in hours-long monologues about his vision for a production, circling the stage barefoot hundreds of times, like an animal locked in a cage. His words cannot be taken down in notes which, after the discussion, would ideally have formed a historically valuable record of a creative process: "Say the word and fall apart…" Still, when we watch him at a rehearsal and follow the cascade of his thoughts, associations, adjectives and childhood stories — everything is absolutely clear and wonderful. The point is not to remember Lupa's words, but to remember one's emotions at the moment of hearing them, and use the emotions for the character. Working with his actors, Lupa creates a strong and very hermetic world. Rehearsals mainly involve exploration of the topics which are to be performed. Conversations, improvisations, following intuitive reflexes. Sometimes subconscious and inexplicable. Actors draw from their inner realms, they have to retrieve a character from their own intimate world.

"A memorised part is something dead — it needs to be enraged by something."[123] To be Lupa's actor means to continuously cross one's own boundaries. To do the impossible as if it was the easiest step to take on the floor. Each time his actors enter the stage they have to create their character anew, opening new emotional baggage for it. Each time there is the need of freshness to avoid a mechanised presentation of the character. Actors must not settle into a routine "Actors should go to another rehearsal like someone driven by a sexual yearning goes out on the town, and not like someone going to a dentist's to have an aching tooth pulled out."[124]

> Actor as a centaur. I once wrote down a kind of fantasy on the phenomenon of being an actor. I used the following model to help me illustrate the relationship between an actor and a character: initially the relationship resembles a horse and a rider, the actor being the horse, and the character being the rider. The character gradually begins to control the horse. The rider-character makes the actor serve someone else's brain and someone else's will… (…) This original "horse-rider" relationship (which is not too flattering to the horse) gradually transforms into a particular mythological creature: the centaur! This usually takes place during dress rehearsals, with the premiere inevitably approaching. It is impossible to sleep at the time. It would be difficult to blame one's nerves, it is the awareness of initiating a process one cannot fully control that is to blame. (…) Actors cast in smaller parts become very nervous — these parts are unable to possess a person. Whereas, if an actor portrays a broader, more complex character — he is forced to "carry it to term" before the premiere

[123] Rigamonti, „Artysta żyje krócej niż człowiek…," 78.
[124] Matkowska-Święs, *Podróż do Nieuchwytnego*…, 97.

like a foetus. And then comes the performance, which is like a dream, and the mechanism of connecting different details begins to work. An actor does not control his character, the character controls him. We are afraid to trust such situations but when darkness falls in the theatre, operators inevitably begin doing their job and the curtain goes up, an actor often feels that — like in a dream — everything starts following its path, and he serves some purpose. And occasionally a character appears and is fulfilled… It isn't everyday that an actor becomes a centaur…[125]

Lupa is himself a great actor, and can show perfectly well what result he expects to achieve in a given scene. However, he never demands to be directly imitated, copied. He always leaves his actors space to gather thoughts and plan the remaining part. It is necessary for an actor to become a character, rather than to perform it. Sometimes this can be seen in the way the text is presented, as when an actor seems to be creating a character during a performance. Such a character is always fresh and has an air of truth about it. Without pretence. Actors make mistakes, add things on their own, react to the audience and to Lupa's signalling. His actors have to be tuned to play in two directions at the same time: towards the presence of the director sitting in the back row and towards the impulses reaching them from within. As Lupa claims, an artist must feel like a genius, otherwise he will not find the energy to act or the courage to take a step. An artist should always aim beyond his abilities. Which is not to say that the director's high expectations are always fulfilled:

4:24 p.m. January 11, 1997
Oh my God, I don't know if this profession has given me more happiness or unhappiness… certainly more unhappiness than happiness…
The constant falling!
The constant losing of what one would like to have forever…
An actor is a leaky bucket… what's best in him constantly leaks out, only mud remains… something completely worthless. I don't know if it is his (their) fault. They are doomed to yearn for success so much. They cannot hide it… (…) As artists do, by creating outside their own bodies — without transferring the pride from their souls onto their work, besides they can create at the opportune moment, and wait for the opportune moment. An actor has to create at a set moment, "after the third bell", inevitably "after the third bell"… and he has to drag it all out on the stage, he cannot leave anything in the dressing room… and the intensity of the yearning for success is at its peak and he has to bring it with him, because it refuses to

[125] Krystian Lupa, „Aktor jako centaur," in *Świadomość teatru. Polska myśl teatralna drugiej połowy XX wieku*, edited by Wojciech Dudzik, 234-235. Warszawa: Wydawnictwo Naukowe PWN, 2007.

remain and wait in the wings. And this yearning is often like a hunch. Especially when the body is exhausted, and the soul is filled with anxiety — this is when the success-hungry monster enters the stage in full light — naked — like a tramp flasher — eager to cause a scandal which he needs in order to live. (…) This does not refer only to the generation of mastodons at all. This is the way of protecting their dignity — their "creative dignity". I can feel that besides laziness, besides sluggishness, besides the inability to construct a character as a chain of inspiration for the inner dialogue — there is also the basic, subconscious, deep unwillingness to lose oneself in a character, to burn through one's own style. Even if they agree to accept a suggestion of mine, they execute it only half-way — not to lose their cultivated figure, the majesty, the seriousness of an actor of the Stary Theatre. I have an impression that they sense — it's still the case, although in a way they surrender to me like you surrender to an authority — they give in superficially, cowardly, without greater consequence, I can feel that in reality we grow further and further apart — they do not share my effort — they do not share my effort of reaching for the requirements of new mentality, for the impressions resulting from reality, they can't understand it… why the hell would they change anything in something so well done. This certainly refers to the "old" partners of mine, the young are humble, but somehow pressured and fearful, as if I was asking them to wander about in the middle of the night, while they are cold and sleep-deprived. "This is extremely difficult, the things you expect from us" — they say. I don't understand it — to me it would be difficult to repeat the routine in such a dull and hopeless manner. To me it would be difficult to do something without the joy of discovery. Whenever I appeal to their imagination, whenever I suggest that they do something using a vision, they perform some peculiar dance — and I can see clearly that they do not employ anything, merely pretend to employ something. Yet, I see them later on in various private situations — impassioned and mobile — when they are directed by their private, inner monologue — when they are fighting in the dressing room about money or politics… Suddenly they are real, equipped with bodies, legs, torsos… even their arms don't move in such a hopelessly dumb way as on the stage. I don't understand — how can an actor not observe himself and draw conclusions — how can he not examine, not experience his own mechanism (organism)… For example, why does an actor have to be told: You mustn't be easy here, resistance cannot be absent from your intonation because (for instance) you (your character) has just been humiliated. It is simply a very straightforward consequence of an inner monologue — and an inner monologue is a spotlight (a beacon) of inner energy; it is only under the pressure of the inner monologue that an actor SHINES. I often get the impression that most actors (artists of their own bodies and personalities) do everything in their power to escape the possibility of letting a "steam of genius" in. To a lesser degree, it is a lack of skill, a mental strategy of those who want to be geniuses so badly — they do not let this faith in — this madness — as if afraid that their "fragile genius" might break under such pressure.[126]

"It must be one scene — like one breath!"[127] Lupa often happens to produce shows which are over ten hours long. They are often performed in one day, as theatrical marathons, and sometimes they are divided into two nights. Sometimes we might get the impression that Lupa decelerates the narrative time. He lets it expand in the box of the stage and pours it onto the audience like dough. Time seems so physically material that it can be combed through with one's fingers. In the lazy, thick air, in the dimmed light, the narrative time of the performance becomes actual time infecting the audience. This applies, among other productions, to *Woodcutters*, when after a late dinner the characters start falling asleep in their armchairs. Consumed alcohol is floating in the air; the light of the chandelier is fading. Exhaustion from a night of conversation and cigarette smoke flows into the audience who become an organic part of this meeting. Ravel's *Bolero* lasts seventeen minutes, so if characters in a play are listening to it, in the production listening to it will also last a full seventeen minutes. But what is most important is that the experiments with time are not performed through music, the pace of events, dialogues, or changes of stage situation: time-lapse in Lupa's productions is directly related to the characters' inner experiences.

Legends are told about his work with actors. It is probably the dream of every Polish actor to perform in one of his shows. These experiences, however, are not easy:

> He is extremely patient, as long as the rehearsals are in progress. He trusts that actors will finally manage to achieve the intended result. Perhaps this is why rehearsals last so long. The degree of expectations from actors is immense. He runs out of patience after the premiere. When something already discovered suddenly disappears, when an actor takes a step back. Krystian becomes bitter like a child, almost sick, and then he gets ruthless. And we want to be praised. It's normal, after all. Meanwhile, a bucket of cold water is a source of stress which lasts all the way until the next performance. And that is when we can discover that the stress was constructive, creative.[128]

---

[126] Lupa, *Utopia 2*, 446-447.

[127] Lupa, *Utopia 2*, 43.

[128] Piotr Gruszczyński, „Nie wymaga wirtuozerii - rozmowa z Piotrem Skibą," *Notatnik teatralny*, no. 18-19 (1999): 90.

Lupa is very rarely satisfied with his actors. Legends are circulated about his blow-ups. He can walk on the stage during a performance and order the audience out. Sometimes, driven to the end of his tether with frustration caused by a poor performance, he will get up from his seat in the back row and leaves, ostentatiously slamming the door to the audience. He is always present at his performances. He is always sitting in the back row. He always disappears before the lights go up on the auditorium. Nobody ever knows where he goes, but as soon as the next act begins he is back in his seat. And he always disappears after the performance, when everyone wants to congratulate him, talk to him, take him out to a restaurant:

> I run away during intervals, because no one should see me then. And I cannot talk to anyone. If someone caught my arm at the time, and not everyone knows this, I would be unhappy. Because it is a bad sign for me. A bad omen. Any contact with anyone is a bloody interference, a distraction.[129]

It is also very rarely that Lupa takes a curtain call:

> I admit, with no sarcasm at all, that I admire actors who after a dose of suffering or humiliation are able to make the obligatory courtesy gesture and even smile. I cannot. I am so distraught that I'm simply not fit to make any appearance on the stage. Such radicalism and the state we drive ourselves into do not go unpunished. You cannot snap out of it in a second and perform the curtain call. I cannot. After the performance there is such strong mental and physical disintegration that certain things are simply impossible. Setting the world in motion costs me so much that if it's broken apart — I have to go to my place and switch the phones off. I lie down as if afflicted by a disease.[130]

6. The time to plant…

Many young people have experienced a period of fascination with Krystian Lupa's theatre. I think that we can even speak of a generational phenomenon among the "theatrical youth". There is a flock of his disciples spread around Polish theatres at the moment, infected with a certain way of thinking, and a certain way of researching reality. What is most important, however, is that his students (meaning, obviously, the most

---

[129] Matkowska-Święs, *Podróż do Nieuchwytnego…*, 78.

[130] Paweł Łopatka, „Przezroczysty niepokój – rozmowa z Krystianem Lupą," *Didaskalia*, no. 53 (2003): 28.

talented ones) do not copy his aesthetics. Lupa is not interested in producing directors like him. It is only at the beginning that he helps his students ask the right questions. But he never helps them find the answers. He only advises that the answers are not offered too quickly. Students value his intuition and attentiveness when talking to another person, his constant need for experiment, taking a risk. Unlike many other teachers, he can discover talent in students considered by most lecturers to be mediocre. Everyone likes to be perceived as naturally talented, however many admit today that it was Lupa who originally sparked that flame of passion in them.

In 1983 Lupa started lecturing at the Directing Department of the Ludwik Solski Academy for the Dramatic Arts. From 1990 - 1996 he served two terms as Dean of the Academy. He always supported unconventional projects, which caused reservations in more conservative teachers. He protected the students' right to make individual decisions, mistakes and failures. Reading his texts about teaching theatre artists, we are enchanted by the utopian vision he intended to implement in the Academy. He wanted it to be something more than just a place of perfecting one's skill, he wanted it to become an open space for meetings of artists, teachers and students. A place of joint experiments, discussions and unrest — like Plato's Academy. He firmly rejected the erudite model of teaching directors, as he found it obsolete. He tried to create a new canon of theoretical subjects. He wanted his students to wander freely through many fields of the humanities. The ability to establish communication between a director and an actor played a key part in their education. In order for the students to achieve a deep understanding of the process of creating a production, he demanded that they themselves perform in études, create stage and costume designs, write plays and look for music to illustrate them. He always begins his classes with conversations. What does theatre mean to you? What kind of a reality is it? Third year students, on the other hand, are asked: what was the biggest difficulty you faced at the Academy? He forces them to provide serious and personal answers, although not private. He talks about his own experiences. He can diffuse the distance between both parties very quickly. Later, he formulates the kind of topic for the classes. For instance (this is a task from a few years ago): reconstruction of subjective space, connected with an intense personal inner experience. The task was to find the experience, name it and create a spatial equivalent for it. Students described subsequent versions of their spaces, changing them according to the influences of communal readings and analyses. Later, there was an exchange of texts, and so one person's version was prepared on the stage by someone else. In the second semester, students returned to their own texts. This time, the task was to find a subjective and objective version of the space for the selected event. The term "space" was very broad, anyway: it could be created with sounds, colours, light, or merely human behaviour. Everyone aspired to discover their own inner space and translate it into the space of the stage where a personal message would have an organic sound.[131]

> From the Journal:
> 11:29 p.m. May 11, 1999
> I really don't know, I think that there is one basic flaw in my educational pygmalionism — my horrible seduction, my aiming for an educational miracle… (…) "What time is it?" I asked. Twenty-five to six. I was just about to finish, I was just about to finish, so it wouldn't go wrong again. It's a shame — I'm so old, I am an esteemed director, I am a professor students ask for, and still, at every class, there is this fear, of something going wrong, of interrupting something magical, the power over acceptance, the delight with the so-called charismata. Is everyone this afraid of the possibility of losing them? (…) So I finish, I finish… moving on, downstairs, to meet a group who feel loved less and now want to seduce me, so I don't wiggle out of making a diploma production with them… (…) They were already waiting for me downstairs. (…) Never mind, anyway, they're making mysterious faces and announce they're taking me to a certain place. Where? Ah, that's going to be a surprise. But soon they gave it away. Let's go see Oberc! It's a mountain with a castle on top, I thought. Go see Oberc? To Sebastian's! Ah, Sebastian's, and I thought it was a hill with a castle on top… and, of course, they laugh, although I'm not sure if they'd be laughing if I weren't… Once again, I'm ashamed of being spoilt, being spoilt only because of the shape of the nest the young people are building for themselves. They may not notice it, but it's exactly because of such things, not just because of the way I look, that I am old to them. We get into a taxi. Will I manage, will I be able to connect with their young theme, their rhythm, otherwise I will expose them to pampering an old professor? How on Earth can I escape it? (…) After all, I'm going with them to say no. And I'm already thinking about their disappointment, of which they know nothing yet. Krystian Lupa — you're an old megalomaniac, a cheat! Where are we going? To Karmelicka. Good, it will be close to home, and they are already quiet, already sad, as if I had just told them I wanted to go home soon. So they tell me that Sebastian had been cleaning all day, besides, he lives over a place where someone was murdered. We get off, a red brick tenement house… (…) Still, I cannot

[131] Beata Guczalska, „Krystian Lupa w krakowskiej PWST," in *Gry z chaosem. O teatrze Krystiana Lupy*, edited by Grzegorz Niziołek, 58. Kraków: Narodowy Teatr Stary im. Heleny Modrzejewskiej, 2005.

disregard such a declaration of the young — shouted out, sung… The only, monumental armchair was for me, Teresa and Ula were sitting on a couch, Magda on a chair at the table… at the table… the others found places appropriately, picturesquely, on the floor… Will I know how to talk to them… I ask about classes, what else can I ask about. (…) What about those fails directors got? They are not protesting. Apparently, they are critical towards their fellow directors… And towards their various teachers and academy authorities they are also sarcastic… I add my own sneers, they laugh humbly and cordially… After a while they are talking to each other — unpretentiously, easily… as if they were giving me an instruction… So far, they were unable to cover me with the blanket of their own, intimate conversation, and obviously they do not want to produce something extra for me, it's a matter of taste… they are counting on me getting under the blanket, where it's homely and warm, they hold a place for me, but I'm stuck on top, clumsy and grotesque. (…) Then the dancing began… they danced and were asking me to dance. As if they were refusing to notice the age difference, as if they wanted to connect with my claim to youth which they must have sensed from me. It was their favourite crazy record, they could dance to it with abandon, singing at the top of their lungs. It was definitely a magical ritual, however, they could not snap out of the current, disco pattern… But no… But they did! It was a trap that I also had to dance with them in that — well known — intention. It was, to them, a magical guarantee, a spell — a kind of pact signed with their own youth. In a moment, driven by some magical, exactly magical continuance, which I was already fully dragged into — gasping for air after the dance — I would offer them a toast to be on first-name terms. Something was still stopping me. A feeling that I cannot give them a hundred per cent guarantee of that diploma production, and it would be something vile — to promise them so much by the ritual of the toast — and not hold on to the other end — the well-known one? Could they be expecting a spectacular result more than I was? Even if they were — what of it? After all, their objective was sacred. After all, it can justify everyone. And so, I was fraternising with them in youth — grey-haired and young, gasping for air, I was remembering some dance moves from years ago. Not much has changed in dancing. As soon as I caught the old rhythm by the throat and fell into a "trance", they shouted maniacally and encouragingly. As if their dance was waiting for my ecstasy, as if it was an offering in a magical ritual…[132]

[132] Krystian Lupa, *Podglądania* (Warszawa: Wydawnictwo W.A.B., 2003), 215-221.

CHAPTER THREE

KRZYSZTOF WARLIKOWSKI

1. My life is in my productions[1]

The "difficult child of Polish theatre" was born on 26 May 1962 in Szczecin, into a working-class family. His parents wanted him to become a truck driver. Warlikowski confessed in one interview that that wish is still strongly present in him, like an unfulfilled threat which he is still subconsciously running away from.[2] He felt alienated in Szczecin. When he passed his high school finals in 1981 he escaped all the way to Krakow, at the other end of Poland. He studied Romanesque philology, history and philosophy at the Jagiellonian University:

> I dropped out of history and Romanesque philology before the Year Four examinations. I did not write an M.A. thesis in philosophy. At the same time I was learning languages: Latin, Ancient Greek, English, French, and Italian (…) I was driven by the love of antiquity. Studying Greek was a revolution in my outlook on life. I look at what is useful and what is useless differently, and I perceive words from the perspective of their etymology. The studies were at the same time a disturbance, because they forced me to speculate and use an unnatural, formula-based language. It was not until the directing studies that they wanted to hear me describe myself, my language and tradition. Future scholars, language teachers or historians are never asked such questions.[3]

During his studies at the Jagiellonian University he met Małgorzata Szczęśniak, who is today his life and artistic partner and who prepares the costumes and set designs for all his productions. They met thanks to a

[1] Mike Urbaniak, „Warszawa to nie bułka z masłem – rozmowa z Krzysztofem Warlikowskim," *Przekrój*, no. 20 (2013): 6.

[2] Katarzyna Janowska, „Inspirują mnie nie miejsca, lecz widma – rozmowa z Krzysztofem Warlikowskim," *Przekrój*, no. 28 (2010): 65.

[3] Krzysztof Mieszkowski, „Do jutra - rozmowa z Krzysztofem Warlikowskim," *Notatnik teatralny*, no. 28-29 (2003): 229.

cancelled lecture and a coffee they had during that sudden break between classes:

> I studied psychology for ten years and later we studied philosophy together (…) we were searching for a similar thing. If you are searching and at one point you meet someone searching for similar things you feel glad, empowered. It is certainly more difficult on one's own. All in all, we were people from the university. We were fascinated by knowledge and experience. We took studying very seriously, read a huge number of books, wrote papers, analysed texts, spent time in libraries – it was work, it was something that fulfilled us.[4]

However, the reality in which they developed intellectually was closely restricted by the Communist framework (since 13 December 1981 Poland had been under Martial Law). That reality was grey, uninteresting and biased, with no access to latest trends in European culture. So they decided to leave. As soon as Martial Law was lifted (22 July 1983) and crossing the border became possible again (although receiving a passport still required much effort), they both left for Paris where they lived in the Oberkampf district. They were driven away from Poland by their interest in life: they wanted to observe and get to know a different world. They were studying and working, they went to the opera and to museums. Warlikowski remembers evenings spent in the opera particularly well (particularly at the Opéra Comique and Opéra-Garnier). He watched productions by Ingmar Bergman, Giorgio Strehler and artists performing at the Theatre of Nations festival at the Odéon theatre. He attended a seminar on ancient theatre at the École Pratique des Hautes Études. He continued his studies in philosophy at the Sorbonne and became acquainted with French literature. For both of them, the time they lived in Paris was most of all the time spent working their own development, learning, and getting to know young, creative people like them. They explained their decision to return to Poland as "pragmatic".[5] They realised that too much time spent in one place, even so mind-broadening a place as Paris, would eventually cease to have any developing effect. Intellectual celebration provoking fervent brainstorm would become ordinary routine. They had to return to Poland.

They returned in 1989 and both undertook artistic studies. Warlikowski studied at the Directing Department of the Academy for the Dramatic Arts

---

[4] Agata Skwarczyńska, „Wolność wyboru - rozmowa z Małgorzatą Szczęśniak," *Notatnik teatralny*, no. 62/63 (2011): 41.

[5] Skwarczyńska, „Wolność wyboru…," 42.

in Krakow, and Szczęśniak at the Department of Stage Design at the Academy of Fine Arts in Krakow. There is a note in Krystian Lupa's journal describing Krzysztof Warlikowski's entrance examination:

> 11:09 a.m. May 3, 2003
> It was one of the most peculiar entrance examinations. Before the examination board saw this black-haired boy with provocative features, they had praised highly a stage script for Maeterlinck's *The Blind*, which was a properly refined vision, filled with curious associations and references. Well, interesting, they said, and later looked at the photo… well, well, they said, because in the photo there was a seductive face looking at them, a face that makes an impression, and not only on women… So this black-haired young man arrived in heavy boots (…), he said hello, sat down where he was asked, and for most of the first interview — the one devoted to the defence of the staging copy — he remained silent. He repeated a question asked and thought suggestively for a long time until someone on the board could not wait any longer and rushed with another question or answer. However, there were a few times when the board waited until the end of the deliberation to hear the answer, uttered in a hushed voice, words seeping slowly — an answer so odd, and in fact hermetic, that it was difficult to deem it deep or absurd. Eventually, Professor Goliński decided to get to the bottom of it. "Do you know Słowacki?" he asked. "Słowacki?" The entrant hesitated. "Yes, I do." The tone of his voice, however, did not give away a full emotional confirmation, as with his previous answers. You expect something like that from a candidate — this additional acting that they know, even if they do not. "Which dramas by Słowacki have you read" — pause —"*Balladyna*" — pause… "Well…" — said professor Goliński — "what else?"… Pause… "*Fantazy...*" — "All right" — now it was time for an about-face, one of Goliński's famous about-faces — "Do you play the piano?" — "A little." — "Well, why don't you… improvise on the piano… y'know…?" — the Professor began in his favourite manner but he quickly stopped seeing the candidate's face twitch as if questioningly, like a bird, a sudden nod of the head, a sign that someone stops understanding… "Well, what are your feelings towards that *Fantazy* and that *Balladyna*?" — "How do you mean?" — "Well, why don't you sit at the piano and first improvise about *Fantazy*, and then about *Balladyna*, or the other way around, if you wish." The piano was placed in the corner of the examination room. "Now?" — "Now, now." The entrant slowly approached the piano and sat at it. He was sitting with his back facing us. And he was sitting like that for a moment in silence. It was as quiet as a graveyard. The entrant turned his head to the board: "So now *Fantazy*" and plink, plink… plink, plink, plink… plink… unrushed gems of high notes, a bit like Debussy in his themes of water, a bit like Satie… That lasted around two minutes. Then there was a pause and the candidate continued sitting with his back to us. And once again it was completely quiet… Finally his head turned to the board once

again. “So now *Balladyna.*” and plink, plink, plink, plink… plink, plink. And again Debussy in his water areas and again there was Satie with his piano sighs. And once again it took around two minutes… “Hmm…” said professor Goliński in the end, “Thank you, sir.” After the candidate left someone voiced their doubts: “Did he really write this stage script of *The Blind* himself?” “I’m certain he did.” — I said, because I had known Krzyś for a while then… Later the candidate presented a scene from *The Blind* and any doubt was dispelled — it was certainly someone who had to be accepted….[6]

During the studies Małgorzata Szczęśniak had already became involved with Warlikowski’s works at the Drama School. In the assigned tasks, etudes, examinations. Jacek Poniedziałek, today one of the most important actors in his company, recollects the beginning of their friendship:

We met in 1990, when I was finishing the School, and Krzysztof was starting it. He was certainly the most eccentric and interesting student of the Directing Department. People were saying he was from France, not Poland, although he only spent a few years there. He was wearing different clothes, he looked and behaved differently from the others, and he aroused general curiosity. (…) Krzysiek was a student of Krystian Lupa, who was at the time working on a diploma production of *The Man Without Qualities* with students of my year. We often discussed that production, we were arguing. Krzysiek was really provoking with what he had to say about my part. In general, he was either praising or criticising the whole project. It was a strong theatre experience to him; he came to see the production several times. He adored us but also hated us, probably out of jealousy. At one point he suggested that I perform in a scene which he was preparing. Year Four actors hardly ever play for directing students because in general they are not up for it any more, they do not see anything interesting in it any more. I agreed because Krzysiek interested me as a person. I played in a scene from *Two for the Seesaw* by William Gibson, lasting around an hour, which was quite long for an examination. Quickly, I don’t know why, we felt that we could be very direct with one another, very sincere and very tough. (…) It was at the time when he wasn’t yet irritating, annoying, or provocative, at that time all he did was fascinate.[7]

In 1990 a hidden dream was fulfilled. He became Krystian Lupa’s, assistant working on the production of *Malte, or the Prodigal Son's*

---

[6] Krystian Lupa, „Krzysztof W. – notatki z dziennika,” *Notatnik teatralny*, no. 28-29 (2003): 33-35.

[7] Katarzyna Łuszczyk, „Podróż w siebie - rozmowa z Jackiem Poniedziałkiem,” *Notatnik teatralny*, no. 28-29 (2003): 41-42.

Triptych based on the prose of Rainer Maria Rilke.[8] At the same time he was fiercely fighting for the opportunity to go on international training. In Stockholm he observed Ingmar Bergman's rehearsals. Inspired by Robert Bresson's film *Four Nights of a Dreamer*, he chose Fyodor Dostoyevsky's *White Nights* for his diploma production in 1992. Peter Brook saw the production and invited Warlikowski to his directing workshop in Vienna. In time, Warlikowski became his assistant at the production of *Impressions de Pelleas* (Debussy's opera *Pelléas and Mélisande*) at the Bouffes du Nord in Paris.[9] In 1994 Warlikowski participated in a directing workshop facilitated by the Piccolo Teatro di Milano. In 1998, upon invitation from Giorgio Strehler, he directed Shakespeare's *Pericles* on the Teatro Studio stage of the Piccolo.

From the very beginning he has worked with Małgorzata Szczęśniak as stage designer and Paweł Mykietyn, who arranges the music, and this collaboration continues to this day. At the start, they were running away from existing structures. They did not want to work where they would be forced to live in the shadow of their great predecessors, where everyone knows each other very well and existing relationships decide the way a theatre operates. Warlikowski wanted all the people surrounding him to be at the outset of their theatre journey. He did not want to inherit actors from great directors, together with their working habits.

His theatre debut was on 20 February 1993, on the stage of the Helena Modrzejewska National Stary Theatre in Krakow. *The Marquise of O.*, based on a short story by Heinrich von Kleist, was received by the audience and critics as a clumsy imitation of Krystian Lupa's theatre.[10] Even so, in 1996 he returned to the Stary to prepare *Old Clown Wanted* by Matei Visniec.[11] Reviewers compared the production to *The Clowns* by

---

[8] Original title of the production: *Malte albo Tryptyk marnotrawnego syna*
Date and place of premiere: December 19, 1991, The Helena Modrzejewska Stary Theatre, Krakow
Direction: Krystian Lupa
Set design: Krystian Lupa
Music: Stanisław Radwan.

[9] Premiered on 13 November 1992.

[10] Original title of the production: *Markiza O.*
Date and place of premiere: February 20, 1993, The Helena Modrzejewska Stary Theatre, Krakow
Direction: Krzysztof Warlikowski
Set design: Małgorzata Szczęśniak
Music: Jacek Ostaszewski.

[11] Original title of the production: *Zatrudnimy starego klowna*

Federico Fellini, and it was unanimously deemed a misunderstanding. Reviews of his first productions reveal contemptuous incomprehension by critics who are today perceived as lacking the good will to tune in to the meaning of new proposals by a not-so-young, yet beginner, artist. After the flop of *Old Clown Wanted* Warlikowski permanently parted ways with the Stary Theatre:

> It became apparent that he cannot work without acceptance, in opposition to the atmosphere of the city where he is about to present a premiere performance. This is how we have to explain the cause of absolute failure of his debut activity in Krakow where he staged *The Marquise of O.* after Kleist or *Old Clown Wanted* by Visniec. He was directing under stress — sometimes in panic — texts which were not always his own choice. Ever since, he has given the place a wide berth since Krakow is conservative to the core and does not accept the quality of being distinctly different. If you want to do something in theatre here you have to talk to the spirit of Swinarski, follow Jarocki's footsteps, and dig where Wajda had been digging before. And Warlikowski did not want to do that. His priority was aesthetic, combined with an intimate vivisection of man, rather than the wretched Polish problems, the heritage of Romanticism and dialogue with society.[12]

He has always been interested in characters from "beyond", excluded, acting and living outside the traditionally accepted rules. In *Ludwig. Tod eines Königs* (based on a short story by Klaus Mann: *The Barred Window*), his first international production, at the Kammerspiele Theatre in Hamburg,[13] he focused on the fairytale figure of King Ludwig II of Bavaria. The production, inspired by Luchino Visconti's film, covers the time that Ludwig was imprisoned in the Berg castle until his suicide. Idealistically in love with the work of Richard Wagner. A lonely man. A homosexual man misunderstood by his environment, who against his will and talent had to become king and take over responsibility for his country. Warlikowski focused on the king's need to retreat. On the escapism of an

---

Date and place of premiere: June 9, 1996, The Helena Modrzejewska Stary Theatre, Krakow
Direction: Krzysztof Warlikowski
Set design: Małgorzata Szczęśniak
Music: Tomasz Stańko.

[12] Łukasz Drewniak, „Czy publiczność oszaleje?," *Przekrój*, no. 1 (2003): 72-73.

[13] Original title of the production: *Ludwig. Tod eines Königs*
Date and place of premiere: November 12, 1994, Kammerspiele, Hamburg
Direction: Krzysztof Warlikowski
Set design: Małgorzata Szczęśniak.

aesthete who withdrew into the imaginary world of *Lohengrin*. His alienation from the outside world was particularly strongly emphasised by the stage design. All constructions (including the figure of his beloved Elisabeth symbolised by a wire mannequin), were made of metal, against which the rain was constantly banging. A toy theatre with which Ludwig liked to play, trying to push aside the thought that outside the barred window there is a real, functioning world was also made of metal sheet.

One year later, at the Nowy Theatre in Poznań Warlikowski, staged a story of a murderer for whom killing became a manifestation of freedom: *Roberto Zucco* by Bernard-Marie Koltès.[14] It was his first stage success. However, the groundwork for his theatre was to be established around four subjects: Antiquity, the Bible, the Holocaust, and Shakespeare.

2. Antiquity
A quantum leap of imagination[15]

In 1997, Warlikowski made his debut at the Dramatic Theatre in Warsaw with Sophocles' *Electra*.[16] Seldom has a production divided the critics so much as that one. One of the most frequently made accusations was that the director did not utilise all opportunities offered by the ancient text (a new translation was made especially for the purpose of this production). Critics accused Warlikowski of not having an idea for the production of the entire piece, not knowing how to stage a consistent plot, and most of all: formal superficiality. Even his supporters said that the production was laid on a "borrowed foundation"[17] of Western European Postmodern theatre.

Electra (Danuta Stenka) waits in vain for someone to arrive in Argos to avenge her father's death. A false report that her only hope — Orestes

---

[14] Original title of the production: *Roberto Zucco*
Date and place of premiere: September 22, 1995, The Nowy Theatre, Poznań
Direction: Krzysztof Warlikowski
Set design: Małgorzata Szczęśniak
Music: Tomasz Stańko.

[15] Piotr Gruszczyński, *(A)pollonia – program do spektaklu* (Warsaw: The Nowy Theatre, 2009), 68.

[16] Original title of the production: *Elektra*
Date and place of premiere: January 18, 1997, The Dramatic Theatre, Warsaw
Direction: Krzysztof Warlikowski
Set design: Małgorzata Szczęśniak
Music: Paweł Mykietyn.

[17] Gruszczyński, *Ojcobójcy*, 93.

(Mariusz Bonaszewski) — has been killed in a chariot race reaches the palace of the Atreides. Warlikowski's Electra is a contemporary woman from the Balkans — a region torn by constant turmoil, wars and fratricide. Women in the chorus accompanying her wear simple, black costumes referencing the tradition of female lamentation in the Balkans. The production evoked overwhelming intellectual coldness. A spotlight falling on the empty stage brought to mind a deserted morgue. There was a simple, metal bed downstage. Electra would stand on it to give her initial monologue. Dressed in black, against a dark background, she was almost invisible. Looking at the audience she was having a waking nightmare about the tragedy of the Atreides. Warlikowski created a production about a house in which its previous order had been destroyed. The stage design symbolized the war-torn Balkans, Chechnya, Georgia, perhaps even Yugoslavia itself. In an essay published in the production brochure Warlikowski tried to comprehend the bases for conflicts in which there are arguments on both sides… This was the case with the Inquisition, the Crusades, the St. Bartholomew's Day massacre, and the conflict in Bosnia:

> Taking justice in one's own hands can be observed to this day from Albania to Northern Ireland. Acting in blind rush, driven by a moral or ethical imperative and public opinion (obtrusive observers of our privacy who are sometimes worse than the Erinyes) sets the death-bearing machine of revenge in endless motion. This is when it becomes obvious how cold and ruthless, how inhumanely cruel, the moral rights we follow when we live our lives can be.[18]

Even if one really does not want to, one often has to pick a side and admit that someone is right, and that someone else is wrong. Photographs of Russian soldiers on a military training ground and Georgian women on the Red Square in Moscow holding photographs of their fallen sons, fathers or husbands were printed as illustrations in the production brochure.

Even if it was not the best start into the Classics that Warlikowski could have made (although his intellectual background for the presentation of this text was far better than that of most contemporary directors), at least reviewers jointly praised him for not falling for a pushy socio-political commentary. He did not modernise the ancient text with clumsy buzzwords drawn from latest news reports. To be able to stage an ancient drama today one really has to be able to defend it against the contemporary

[18] Dorota Krzywicka, *Elektra – program do spektaklu* (Warsaw: The Dramatic Theatre, 1997), 6.

perception of spectators, which is entirely different from the ancient one. Basing the whole concept on a quite superficial assumption that Electra's lust for vengeance finds its voice today in the scream of thousands of Balkan women proved insufficient to construct a performance which could defend itself on its own terms. Therefore, it had to take four years, during which Warlikowski prepared over ten productions (mainly based on Shakespeare's plays: *The Winter's Tale*, *Hamlet*, *The Taming of the Shrew*, *Pericles*, *Twelfth Night, or What You Will*, and *The Tempest*), for him to reach for an ancient text once again, in 2001. He chose to produce Euripides' *The Bacchae*.[19]

> The longer I think about Krzysztof Warlikowski's *The Bacchae*, the clearer the colours I remember of the beautiful images, which — like good paintings — can be unfolded into stories told in a hushed voice. (…) However, at the same time I know that growing vividness of colours of recollected stage images give the lie to what was a real essence of a theatre experience. The experience which was connected with a different perception of time — still very corporal but registered in a different rhythm. After all we not used to identifying the Bacchanal frenzy with sudden giddiness, acceleration of time which whirls like a dancing dervish, rather than with a decelerated almost to a standstill tension of geometric figures in which Warlikowski made Euripides' characters live. But this allowed him to almost physically open another dimension. Because the Bacchaic frenzy has become a sequence of several precise motions arranged in space, of hands holding shoes and bodies burdened with a load of another world, an arrested potential of motion with intensity similar to that driving *Dance* by Matisse.[20]

The performance begins with a storm in the dark. The light slowly brings out the figure of Dionysus (Andrzej Chyra) from the storm, who had just emerged from the sea onto the dry sand spread on the stage. He is wearing wide, white trousers, a tight jumper, and trainers. He babbles out his first words, for he is only learning to speak. He prolongs syllables, chants, minces sounds with his tongue which seems too large for his mouth. It is a dangerous creature from outside the real world, still not fully identified. Words about the necessity of vengeance are formed in his

[19] Original title of the production: *Bakchantki*
Date and place of premiere: February 9, 2001, The Rozmaitości Theatre, Warsaw
Direction: Krzysztof Warlikowski
Set design: Małgorzata Szczęśniak
Music: Paweł Mykietyn.
[20] Małgorzata Sugiera, "Po premierze," *Didaskalia*, no. 42 (2015): 19.

slowly developing monologue. *The Bacchae*, in its creators' concept, was to be a production about the arrival of a new god, but seen from the perspective of contemporary Catholicism. Warlikowski wanted to expose the flashiness of religion, the height of the façade that has distanced people from the real God, the Real, i.e. the Old Testament one… the one who is strict and unpredictable, accepts no compromises, does not forgive, and ruthlessly exercises his rights.

The entire stage is clad in metal plates which cast silver reflections in the spotlights. They cast flickering reflections of water from the pool fitted in the floor. The Bacchae, ancient acolytes (Stanisława Celińska, Magdalena Kuta, and Maria Maj) emerge from the dark upstage. In a religious procession they carry a votive statue of Dionysus wrapped in white linen. With deliberation they set it in a glass showcase lit with fluorescent lamps. Just a humble altar patched together. A reference to wayside shrines which can be found today along country roads. Instead of the skins of young deer killed with their own hands, the Bacchae are wearing cheap, karakul coats. They sit on a bench in front of the statue and open up prayer books of an unknown religion. They look like old ladies participating in a Sunday service with devotion. Their faces are covered with colours typical of the ritual. When the prayer begins, we can hear trance music and the Bacchae are seized with indescribable joy and lightness. Their old age suddenly drops away. Their religious elation is interrupted by the sudden entry of Pentheus (Jacek Poniedziałek). There are, therefore, two completely different worldviews present on stage and Warlikowski skilfully depicts the dangers of absolute atheism as well as absolute, thoughtless devotion to religion. Pentheus, in this production, is a primitive, arrogant thug. He is bald-headed, wears a white wife-beater, a red down jacket (which could be the equivalent of a king's coat), as a manifestation of *hybris*. All that he is missing to complete the sociological picture is a baseball bat with which to chase Dionysus out. His masculinity is perfectly contrasted with the androgyny of the young deity acting seductively towards him. He tediously lures him into his intricate snares. He backs away from him but at the same time pulls Pentheus with him. It becomes apparent that this arrogant tough guy gives in to him completely:

> Jacek Poniedziałek: *The Bacchae*, which I love to play, I love to play Pentheus, who is nasty, unruly, firm, heated, perhaps occasionally stupid, but so right. To me, the most important adventure is the meeting of Pentheus and Dionysus. (…) This journey, bumpy — and therefore very attractive. A journey from scornful hatred to completely ecstatic love. And to speak words which are two-and-a-half thousand years old, yet thanks to our work sound so unusually contemporary! It is very seldom that actors

> take such pleasure in acting, such pleasure in performing. It is such a strong, personal, and intense journey through the human condition.[21]

The deity, played by Andrzej Chyra, according to Euripides' drama proves to be highly dangerous. In the end, it comes down to revenge. Therefore, everything must happen according to the ancient drama. Dionysus seduces Pentheus to suddenly push him into the abyss. Agave (Małgorzata Hajewska-Krzysztofik) runs onto the stage with a giant phallus between her legs. She is drunk with Bacchaic frenzy, with the blood of the young lion that she had just torn to pieces with her own hands. As if in an act of repeated delivery she takes out Pentheus' head from underneath her dress. She does not recognise it. Old Cadmus (Andrzej Bednarz) brings the remaining parts of his body in a bucket and pours them out on the table. Grotesque chorus of believers (bringing to mind contemporary religious cults), a ghastly punishment — what religion can be so perverse? Warlikowski's question could easily be asked about the Catholic religion and its followers.

However, both *Electra* and *The Bacchae* were merely an exercise before *(A)pollonia*, a production prepared in 2009 for the Avignon Festival.[22] It is surely one of Krzysztof Warlikowski's greatest theatre achievements. A monumental production based on Greek tragedies, taking up the subject of an innocent victim. Warlikowski cut up and mixed threads from literature and history using different forms of narration. The play can be interpreted following different trails; however, Warlikowski himself does not make any interpretative suggestions. His production conveys so many symbols, references and nuances that it seems most accurate to compare it to a huge pot in which countless fishing hooks are immersed and it is impossible to pull on one without moving the others. Unfortunately, as the production progresses it becomes apparent that these hooks have been attached to human flesh.

Warlikowski used the Classics to speak about World War II and the horror of the Holocaust. For this director, the Shoah, an "exported good which is very hard to sell at home"[23], is undeniably the most important

---

[21] Łuszczyk, „Podróż w siebie…," 45.
[22] Original title of the production: *(A)pollonia*
Date and place of premiere: May 16, 2009, The Nowy Theatre, Warsaw
Direction: Krzysztof Warlikowski
Set design: Małgorzata Szczęśniak
Music: Paweł Mykietyn.
[23] Paweł Dobrowolski, „Inne czasy - rozmowa z Jackiem Poniedziałkiem," *Notatnik teatralny*, no. 62/63 (2011): 63.

part of Polish history. It is often pushed away with distaste as a burdensome pattern in thinking about our past and present. The main axes of this production have been developed around Aeschylus' *The Oresteia*, Hanna Krall's reportage on Apolonia Machczyńska,[24] and a monologue from Elizabeth Costello.[25]

The stage in *(A)pollonia* is almost thirty meters long. And it is virtually empty. The opening is performed as if taking a step back before gathering momentum for the whole play. It brings to mind *The Dead Class* by Tadeusz Kantor: two puppets of children are sitting at a desk. They are children brought up at a Jewish orphanage in the Warsaw Ghetto. Actors (later playing the parts of Agamemnon (Maciej Stuhr) and Clytemnestra (Danuta Stenka)) gently carry the puppets towards the audience. They animate them to play out the whole scene. The children dream of journeys to faraway places. Of learning about what is behind the line of the horizon. They rebel against adults' reasonable prudence. They give a performance of *The Post Office* by Rabindranath Tagore[26] for the inmates of the Ghetto. An off-stage commentary informs us that four days later spectators of that performance were deported to the concentration camp in Treblinka. Two weeks later all children of the Jewish orphanage faced the same fate.

It is not shown directly, but they could be the children of Agamemnon and Clytemnestra. In the following scene we see them at a family meeting. Iphigenia (Magdalena Popławska), a young girl wearing a too-small white dress, is running nervously around them. She is a non-uniform combination of a rebellious, courageous teenager, and a warrior's daughter who is scared to death. The Atreides family are getting ready to kill her as a sacrifice, as if it were a family celebration. To complete the false pretence,

---

[24] The beginning of Warlikowski's collaboration with Hanna Krall goes back to the time of *The Bacchae*. She was accidentally assigned a seat in the audience next to Warlikowski's seat. They started talking. Krall said that she would like someone to stage her text in two thousand years' time in the way that he staged Euripides. The first production they made together was *The Dybbuk* — a clash between her reportage and the play by Shimon An-sky: a staged story of a man who carries inside his brother's Dybbuk — the child had been strangled, because his cry could give away the hiding place of Jews hiding from the Germans.

[25] The following texts were used in the production: *The Oresteia* by Aeschylus, *The Story of a Mother* by Hans Christian Andersen, *Elizabeth Costello* by John Maxwell Coetzee, *Mother, Where Are You?* by Andrzej Czajkowski, *Iphigenia in Aulis*, *Alcestis*, *Hercules Furens* by Euripides, *Pola, The Corner House with the Little Tower* by Hanna Krall, *The Kindly Ones* by Jonathan Littell, *Battlefield* by Marcin Świetlicki, *The Post Office* by Rabindranath Tagore.

[26] It is a reference to a real life situation: on July 18, 1942 *The Post Office* was staged by the children raised in the Jewish Orphanage in the Warsaw Ghetto.

Agamemnon gives her Achilles' engagement ring. However, he is not a soulless warrior, as Aeschylus would have us perceive him. Here, he is not thoughtless, and the awareness of the lie prevents him from playing out this dressed up farce to the end. With one forceful gesture he grabs Iphigenia and drags her behind him off stage, disregarding the girl's desperate screaming. We do not know the cause of this sacrifice. We do not know which war it refers to.

> Agamemnon and Clytemnestra, Iphigenia's parents, remind me of the characters in Roman Polański's *The Pianist*. They were happy, young, they had children. And then the war happened to them. Suddenly they lost everything. One day earlier, while sitting at a table, they heard on the radio that the war had just broken out. All ideas disappear, love disappears, and we are at the mercy of God. And the next day they began hating each other. If we did not have the experience of the twentieth century and history of the Holocaust I do not know if we could understand the situation in which parents have to decide which of their children is going to survive and which is not[27]. The Jews were forced to make such choices in face of the Holocaust.[28]

Clytemnestra has waited ten years for an opportunity to avenge her daughter. When Agamemnon, returning from Troy, comes on stage, they always play the anthem of the country they are performing in:

> When we performed *(A)pollonia* at the Golden Mask festival in Moscow, Russians thought that when performing all over the world we play the Russian anthem in this scene and thus present the catastrophe caused by the Russians. After all, the Russians are imperialists and criminals as well. This scene was a huge shock for them and they felt very emotional about it. They talked about it during a discussion after the show. We explained to them that we changed the anthem in the scene depending on the country hosting us. This makes the scene very personal everywhere. During the after show discussion in Taiwan (…) Krzysiek provoked them by asking about the feelings of the Taiwanese towards Communist China. He asked whether they thought that it was the same nation divided by history, just as the Germans were divided after the war. Do they have family, relatives there, do they visit each other and do they stay in touch, do they feel like one nation? One lady said: "We are the people they did not mange to

[27] This could also remind us a famous horrific scene from *Sophie's Choice* (film with Meryl Streep in the title role, directed by A. J. Pakula, 1982).
[28] Roman Pawłowski, „Rzecz, która nie lubi być zabijana – rozmowa z Hanną Krall i Krzysztofem Warlikowskim," *Gazeta Wyborcza*, May 14, 2009, 16.

murder." (...) *(A)pollonia* enjoys a very vivid reception everywhere. Besides Austria, obviously... This is very telling.[29]

When Agamemnon returns home he does not resemble the conqueror of Troy described by Aeschylus one bit. He speaks using words based on Jonathan Littell's *The Kindly Ones*. He is a man who returned from war and it is completely unimportant whether it was Troy, or Vietnam, or World War II. The devastation in his soul and mind has already taken place and nothing will reverse that. His perception will never be the same. It is never going to be pain-free. Sensitivity has been torn to bloody pieces:

Agamemnon:
The war is over. We have learnt from this lesson, this will not happen again. Are you certain that we have learnt our lesson? Are you certain that this will not happen again? And anyway, are you certain that the war is over? In a sense, the war never ends or ends when the last child, born on the last day of a battle, lives peacefully to the day of his own funeral, but even then the war will rage on — in his children's heads, and later in the heads of those children's children. At war, a male citizen loses one of his most elementary rights, which is the right to live. But the same citizen simultaneously loses another right, equally elementary: the right not to kill. No one asks your opinion. Let us play mathematics. Casualties on the Eastern Front: 21.5 million. The Final Solution: 5.1 million. All together: 26.6 million. Armed conflict between Germany and the USSR began on 2 June 1941 at three in the morning, and ended on 8 May 1945 at 00:01 a.m., representing a total of 3 years, 10 months, 16 days, 20 hours and one minute, i.e. 46.5 months, 202.42 weeks, 1417 days, 34,004 hours or 2,040,241 minutes. Assume that the programme referred to as the Final Solution was implemented in the same time frame: a total of 572,043 deaths a month, 131,410 deaths a week, 18,772 deaths a day, 782 deaths an hour and 13.04 deaths a minute. We can also calculate the intervals between each death, with approximately one fatality every 4.6 seconds. Now time it yourselves: one dead body, two dead bodies, three dead bodies... and so on, every 4.6 seconds, trying to "see" them in front of you. It is not a bad meditation exercise. I am not trying to persuade you that I am not guilty of this or that act. I am guilty, you are not, and that is great. But you have to be able to admit that you would be doing the same thing if you were in my shoes. Perhaps with less zeal, but perhaps also with less despair, anyhow, this way or another — you would be doing the same thing. If you were born in a country or era when no one is killing your wives and children, but also no one is telling you to kill the children and wives of others, praise the Lord and go in peace. But you will bear this thought in minds forever: you are perhaps more fortunate than I am, but

[29] Dobrowolski, „Inne czasy...," 58-59.

> you are no better. I have done everything with the utmost competence, convinced that it was my obligation and a necessity, however unpleasant or unfortunate. This is also what a total war involves: a civilian as such no longer exists, and the only difference between a gassed or shot Jewish child and a German child killed by a bomb is in the implemented measure; both deaths are equally unnecessary, none of them shortened the war by even one second, but in both cases the man or men who killed those children believed that it was justified and necessary. And just like most people, I never asked to become a criminal. I wanted to play the piano. Every act I committed was committed to defend a principle — whether good or bad, I do not know, but it has always been a human principle. Those who kill are human, as are those who are killed — this is the worst thing about it. You are never going to be able to say: I will not kill; the only thing you can say is: I hope not to kill. It used to be my hope as well. Alas, my gullibility was used to create something else, something which proved wrong and evil, I have crossed the line into evil — all the evil has become part of my life and nothing can ever be fixed, ever. Words are also no longer of any use, they disappear, vanish like water in the sand, and the sand fills my mouth. I live, I do what I can, just like everyone, I am human like everyone, and I am human like you. So let us begin, since I'm telling you I am like you! Now I shall enter the house and praise the god protecting my forefathers' hearth and home. God has sent me overseas — and now has brought me home.[30]

This trick is very typical of Warlikowski, who likes to put his spectators in an uncomfortable position. He introduces a criminal such as Agamemnon, who says unimaginable things about human cruelty, who stands opposite the audience and who, after admitting his crimes, does not apologise — he concludes: "I am exactly the same as you." The director always sits in the audience. When a moment like this monologue comes he instructs technicians to turn on all the lights. All the time he sits with at a right-angle to the stage and observes, carefully monitors, people's reactions. How they struggle with the words thrown at them from the stage. Only after he reaches a satisfying level of destruction can the lights go down again.

Clytemnestra has been waiting for ten years for Agamemnon's return. She is putting on her bloody makeup. Their conversation over a crimson carpet is erratic. It is what occurs a fraction of a second before the ultimate nervous breakdown. With Aeschylus' words, Clytemnestra is trying to subdue Agamemnon, to finally humiliate him before he dies. When she takes his life her microphone begins to beep desperately, painfully penetrating the spectators' nervous systems. This death, too, must be

---

[30] Gruszczyński, *(A)pollonia*, 14-16.

avenged. In the following scene Orestes (Maciej Stuhr) comes to Clytemnestra dressed as a female employee of a mental health institution. She came to inform the mother of her son's death. A long, blond wig, a pink purse — we can see right away that it is the most unsuitable person for performing such a delicate job. She tries to talk to Clytemnestra about a potential "later on". A relative should be informed about a close one's death in such a way as to minimise the shock. A copy of Andersen's *Fairy Tales* borrowed from the library has been found next to Orestes' body. With this book the woman begins the conversation with Clytemnestra who carelessly opens it on a page with *The Story of a Mother*. This is when Orestes takes his wig off and kills the mother, fully bringing to life the practical theory of B movies: "Am I allowed not to kill?!"[31]

Athena's trial is organised as a Skype conference call. Skype, Facebook, Second Life and many other social networks allow people to adopt new identities and pretend to be someone else. It is possible that Aeschylus' "@pollo", who under a god's nickname tricked a completely oblivious Orestes into killing his mother, was a similar, deceitful product of human imagination.

The second part of the production is the story of Alcestis (Magdalena Cielecka) and Admetus (Jacek Poniedziałek). We are in Warsaw, it is a night in May, sixty-four years after the end of the War. They are both overly nice and cute. In a screen we can see a recorded interview with them, directed like material for some popular television show:

Voice: Tell us who you are.
Alcestis: Alcestis.
Admetus: Admetus.
Voice: What great thing is going to happen in May this year?
Alcestis: A big boom.
Admetus: I will be born again.
Voice: Are you loved?
Alcestis: Madly.
Admetus: I hope so.
Voice: Are you in love?
Admetus: Very much.
Alcestis: Yes.
Voice: Your dream holiday.
Admetus: On a desert island, with her.
Alcestis: In the garden, in a hammock, with him.
Voice: What do you like about him the most?
Alcestis: His shyness.

---

[31] Gruszczyński, *(A)pollonia*, 30.

Admetus: Wisdom.
Voice: Do you believe in God?
Admetus: No.
Alcestis: No.
Voice: Civil partnerships?
Alcestis and Admetus: Yes
Voice: On a scale from 1 to 10, how much does Love mean to you?
Alcestis and Admetus: 10.
Voice: Partnership?
Alcestis and Admetus: 9/7.
Voice: Sex?
Alcestis and Admetus: 15/10
Voice: Bank account?
Alcestis and Admetus: 7/9
Voice: Sense of humour?
Alcestis and Admetus: 15/10
Voice: Principles?
Alcestis and Admetus: 10
Voice: What does marriage mean to you?
Alcestis: A beautiful responsibility.
Admetus: The state's interference in a relationship between two people.
(…)
Voice: Would you die for each other?[32]

They are both clearly surprised by this question. Amused by previous ones, they suddenly look down. They are filled with consternation. Heavy silence falls, and the camera doesn't stop its invasion. It remains on for a while longer. It records their desperate need to escape the heavy look of real honesty and unambiguous responsibility.

The second part of the production is the story of Alcestis (Magdalena Cielecka) and Admetus (Jacek Poniedziałek). We are in Warsaw, it is a night in May; when the light once again draws our attention to the level of the stage we see Apollo (Andrzej Chyra), who is ironically posing as "theApolloFuckingBelvedere". The ancient statue daubed with graffiti — someone has painted a peace sign, someone else the Star of David hanging from a gallows. As a punishment for killing the son of Zeus, Apollo is staying at the house of Admetus. He walks the stage with a vacuum cleaner, dusts, feeds the hens, but also protects his mortal lover. He has even arranged for his death to be annulled, provided someone agrees to die for him. All of his close relatives have already said no, only his wife was ready to make the commitment. When the day comes, she gets ready for death. Technicians bring an elegant, cream-coloured coffin onto the stage.

[32] Gruszczyński, *(A)pollonia*, 20-28.

Alcestis prepares a farewell dinner for the family. It seems to be nice, but Thanatos (Wojciech Kalarus), the one always "terribly conscientious", refuses to eat, as if the *ananke*[33] of fulfilling his responsibilities has taken away his appetite. He ostentatiously puts his doctor's bag containing a lethal injection on the table, as if to separate himself from the family. Alcestis is still trying to entertain her guests with trivial stories. She talks about a man who fell in love with a female dolphin. True love, not like Admetus'. Admetus himself seems distanced from the whole situation. It is only when Alcestis leaves to go to the restroom that the reality hits him, as if he had only just realised all the consequences of what was about to happen. He jumps up to stop her — but the door is already locked. At the funeral he tries to explain that he betrayed his beloved wife with his own life:

> You look at me with disgust? You'd refuse such a sacrifice, would you? Perhaps someone in the audience would prefer to die? After all it is sinful to love one's own life... but... it is normal to love one's own life more than anything...[34]

The funeral ceremony is interrupted by Heracles' intrusion (Andrzej Chyra), in a cowboy costume, drunk, vulgar and loud. After the mourners inform him about what happened at the house of Admetus, he leads Alcestis from the dark realm of Hades, just as Euripides wrote originally. The whole scene is observed by a Nazi officer (Wojciech Kalarus) who only a moment earlier was playing the part of Thanatos. He interrupts the scene of a joyful welcome with a question: "Who was hiding your Jews?" The question is directed to Alcestis, restored to the world of the living, who becomes Apolonia Machczyńska (the main character in Hanna Krall's reportage). A Polish woman from the town of Kock, who lost her life after sheltering Jews during the war. The Germans found out. All the Jews were executed and Apolonia and her father were given a choice: the one who confesses will be shot. Apolonia's father did not say one word. Apolonia died. And the most bizarre aspect of all that was that it was a Jewish woman who denounced them...

Circus drums are vibrating in the air as if to accompany Apolonia's execution, as if it was a high-wire circus act, stretched far above the ground, with no safety equipment. Ever-louder drums accompany an announcement informing us that Apolonia Machczyńska is to be awarded the medal of the Righteous Among the Nations. However, for that to

---

[33] Gr. ἀνάγκη - necessity.

[34] Gruszczyński, *(A)pollonia*, 56-57.

happen, an interrogation is required. It will be conducted by Heracles, who is now wearing macabre Joker makeup from *The Dark Knight*.[35] In Warlikowski's production, one of the most important Jewish distinctions is awarded by the justice of the Supreme Court of Israel — the fool: "Whosoever saves a single life, saves an entire universe!!!". He shouts these words as if announcing an act by a fire eater. By asking subsequent questions he is trying to discover Apolonia's true motives. He is aggressive, cynical, and provocative: "And? Did she? Can one save an entire universe?" Watchfully alert to any false note, he is the malicious trickster, who only waits for it to become common knowledge that Apolonia Machczyńska had her own axe to grind. After all, a person who is Righteous Among the Nations should not want anything in return…

The cynical interrogation, the stirring up of real, human motives is observed by Ryfka Goldfinger (Ewa Dałkowska), a Jewish woman saved by Apolonia and Apolonia's son (Marek Kalita). The hostility between them is immediately noticeable. They share the experience of war, but the two do not seem able to reach an agreement. Ryfka cannot understand Apolonia's son's resentment. After all, his mother behaved exactly how she should. What if she died… many people that Ryfka knew died during the war. Apolonia's son cannot cope with the thought that his mother was saving strangers aware of the risk of her own son having to be raised by strangers. Without a mother, with just a vague memory of her, and a meaningless medal. He resents her to this day for abandoning him and choosing death. The sorrow of an abandoned child who hates those for whom he was abandoned is smouldering inside him. Because of them, because of the Jews, he lost her presence, her love. Such a variation of anti-Semitism is also possible…

> Magdalena Cielecka (Alcestis/Apolonia): It is a dilemma which is difficult to solve. Anyway, there were plenty of similar dilemmas during the war. One wonders what should have been done. If Apolonia's father said that he was hiding Jews, in theory everything would have been resolved. Everyone would say that he was old and therefore he should die. The only thing is that we should look for emotions rather than logic in such situations: fear, attachment to life. This position is represented by Apolonia's father and it is explained by Admetus' father who says that everyone has the right to live and make a decision. Apolonia could also have said that she was not the one hiding Jews, or she could have said nothing and then, most certainly, everyone would have been executed. We do not know her or Alcestis' motifs. In that respect, both characters are identical to me. We do not know what Apolonia's life was like. We speculated about Apolonia's

[35] dir. Christopher Nolan (2008).

> life in that village. We do not know her husband — we do not know what that marriage was like. She was pregnant, but it is uncertain by whom. There is also a motif of a German who liked Apolonia a lot, which obviously allows for a whole range of associations and fantasies. Perhaps they had an affair, and perhaps it was just the price she paid for the sake of peace, and perhaps it *was* love? We also do not know what Apolonia's life in that village was like. Perhaps she was ostracised by the villagers? To me, the more such contradictory speculations appear when constructing a character, the better. (…) There have been plenty of moments of crisis, and I am sure there are many ahead, but at the same time Krzysiek's productions are alive and continue to change. I know him and his entire group, and I know that the work on *(A)pollonia* is not over. What we found new and interesting about the work was the system of rehearsals. Everyone rehearsed separately and we did not know what was going on in rehearsals of different threads. *The Oresteia* was rehearsed separately. *Alcestis* was rehearsed separately. Krall was rehearsed separately. *Costello* rehearsed separately, video recordings were made separately, musicians rehearsed separately, so we never met at all. Our curiosity and anxiety were caused by our unawareness of the common goal. What happens when we put all our threads together, what is it going to be about? We knew only an outline of the stage design and we have seen mock-ups, but everything changes anyway once you enter such a space. We wanted to satisfy our curiosity: "How's *The Oresteia*?", but we were also curious to know if we were repeating some topics. The friction of ideas was unusually interesting. In the final week we were connecting the scenes. We were terrified because the production would last three days, therefore the work began: to edit, select, connect meanings. (…) In this regard the work was exceptional: it was only at the end that we discovered what was most important to us, what we wanted to say.[36]

The scene is interrupted at the key moment, we will not know what happened next until the end of the show, how the trial developed, what the judgement was, whether it was unanimous. Elizabeth Costello (Maja Ostaszewska) comes up to the lectern on stage. She is beautiful, smart — a *glamour* vision of a scholar. She is to give a lecture on: "Everyday animal Holocaust". For the next forty minutes, Maja Ostaszewska's main acting task is to give a lecture powerful enough to keep the audience spellbound and not let their attention wander for even a single second. She talks about animal experimentation with fervour. She talks about their cruel slaughter. Sometimes it is better not to know everything; it is safer not to know about it all. Sometimes you cannot afford to know. And each of those caged

---

[36] Marta Bryś, Monika Kwaśniewska, „Spektakl jak sztafeta - rozmowa z Magdaleną Cielecką," *Didaskalia*, no. 92/93 (2009): 22-23.

animals has just one thought: where is home and how to get there? Those people never thought: what if it was me in a cattle car, what if it was me burning down to ashes. We can do literally anything and we will get away with it. Only those in camps were innocent. And places of extermination surround us all the time. Expanded by industrial powers to an unimaginable extent, even to the creators of the Holocaust. This distressing, very emotional monologue which ends the show is a master performance by Maja Ostaszewska. Her words change at times into squeals, shrieks, hysterical crying. A regular paper beginning innocently with a quantum leap of imagination, between amphibians and reptiles (since there are no fossil records of a creature linking amphibians and reptiles), becomes another one of Warlikowski's accusations addressed to the audience: "You do not reach for the Holocaust as if for Andersen's fairytales…"[37]

* In France, the board of ARTE television channel refused to air a film documenting rehearsals for the production of *(A)pollonia* in Avignon, deeming the show to be anti-Semitic. In Poland, after the premiere, the Chancellery of the President of the Republic of Poland, on behalf of the Polish Government, awarded Apolonia Machczyńska the Commander's Cross and the Order of Merit of the Republic of Poland.

3. Shakespeare
The deserts of Bohemia

On the other hand, his production of Shakespeare's *The Winter's Tale*[38] was fairytale-like. Shakespeare has become one of the main points of reference in Warlikowski's theatre. He keeps returning to his works. He looks for new ways of interpreting old verses. By reading into what is between the lines, perhaps into what Shakespeare really wanted to tell us, he uncovers some word structures and their logical arrangements. He looks for subversion. His productions attempt to keep up with the energy of the works. He tries to go against the current of classical interpretations and provide them with a radically contemporary message. His *A Midsummer Night's Dream*, produced at the Theatre National de Nice,

[37] Pawłowski, „Rzecz, która nie lubi być zabijana…," 14.
[38] Original title of the production: *Zimowa opowieść*
Date and place of premiere: April 5, 1997, The Nowy Theatre, Poznań
Direction: Krzysztof Warlikowski
Set design: Małgorzata Szczęśniak
Music: Paweł Mykietyn.

shocked subscription spectators who were not prepared to see a show inspired by Nan Goldin's photography. In *Twelfth Night* (Stadt Theater, Stuttgart) he went in the direction of *Festen* (a film directed by the creators of Dogme 95) and Sarah Kane's *Cleansed*, because in Warlikowski's opinion *Twelfth Night* is not a comedy at all. How can you laugh at a girl saved after a shipwreck who cross-dresses as her dead twin brother? She had lost all her family. She heads for the prince's court to start her life from scratch… but why did she want to start this new life as a man? Was it only because life was easier for men back then? And perhaps she was brave enough to listen to her inner voice suggesting such a solution? Obviously, conservative audiences of Shakespeare's works will be appalled by such over interpretation of the play. It was just a regular dress up… Shakespeare did not write heavy existential dramas to penetrate the dark side of the human mind. Warlikowski, however, has strong supporting arguments:

> If we are able to find so much in such a story it is difficult to believe that the person who wrote it did not intend to put it all in there. (…) It is ironic that we are still trying to tame the man who was so uncompromising, nonconforming and rebellious towards both real and unreal order and turn him into a bland common good.[39]

The above words can be used to support all Warlikowski's productions. His "Shakespeares" are certainly not a common good: the ones produced in Poland, as well as those prepared abroad, test their spectators' tolerance.

Warlikowski enclosed *The Winter's Tale* in a fairytale-like, Hans Christian Andersen glass ball. The production began with a scene of Hermione (Antonina Choroszy) and Mamilius (Dominik Górka) having a conversation (originally in the second act). They are both standing at the window hanging downstage. A gloomy winter night, perfect for staring out the window. Red floor, black wings. The stage is almost empty, with a Christmas tree at the back. Wrapped gifts are scattered around, waiting for the Christmas star. Styrofoam snow is falling from the sky. Mamilius asks his mother to tell him a story, but he wants a scary one… And so it is going to be a "winter's tale" — and this is where Warlikowski's show begins to gather momentum. The show is performed in the glow of a comet which brings madness. The general character of stage space had to combine the dramatic "now" with events which will occur in eighteen years' time. Eighteen years for which no one will be able to compensate.

[39] Piotr Gruszczyński, *Szekspir i Uzurpator, z Krzysztofem Warlikowskim rozmawia Piotr Gruszczyński* (Warsaw: Wydawnictwo W.A.B., 2007), 33.

"All these weddings have nothing to do with a happy ending. They are announcements of great, life catastrophes. In *The Winter's Tale* husband and wife find each other after eighteen years. To them it is certainly eighteen wasted years, spent on regret and a feeling of one's life's ruin. How can there be a happy ending after something like that?"[40]

The Clown (Krystyna Feldman) gives the Time monologue. She fills eighteen years of plot with it. There are two parallel dressing rooms on stage. One for the King of Bohemia (Mariusz Sabiniewicz), and one for the King of Sicily (Mirosław Konarowski). The passing of time is to seem like a dream to the audience. A hazy illusion told by a clown. Actors do not leave the stage, they put on old-age makeup, apply artificial beards and wrinkles in front of the audience. The clock of the performance is running faster as we watch. Andersen in his original form is not the most appropriate author for children. His tales are full of cruelty and nightmares which make even adult readers feel anxious. Warlikowski used such Andersen to direct his actors. From the calm, warm love of the first scene we suddenly fall into a wild, uncontrollable and inexplicable jealousy. Leontes breaks the glass ball of family happiness. Apparently, the more you love, the greater the impending hate, the hate that appears out of nowhere for irrational, nonexistent reasons. Subsequent events: death of a boy, imprisonment of a beloved woman, labour in jail, taking the baby away from its mother — the plot resembles a tabloid or a soap opera and the director provided it with fitting acting. The white bear which kills Antigonus (Jerzy Stasiuk) is an actor wearing a bear costume for tourists to take photos with at a ski resort. Dionysian shepherds are dancing over a slain hog, still steaming with hot blood. These scenes are far from a shepherd idyll and snow-white lambs. Perdita is found wearing a beautiful gown with heavy rubber boots. Warlikowski took every opportunity to provoke, to dissect the characters' emotions: "Those strange suggestions from the husband for the woman and the man of his life to live close to each other…"[41] It is a fairytale… for grownups, and critics said that no one before had understood Shakespeare like that in Poland.

With his *Taming of the Shrew*,[42] Warlikowski proved that no one had understood Shakespeare so radically and adamantly as him. After what

---

[40] Gruszczyński, *Szekspir i Uzurpator*, 14.
[41] Gruszczyński, *Szekspir i Uzurpator*, 26.
[42] Original title of the production: *Poskromienie złośnicy*
Date and place of premiere: January 3, 1998, The Dramatic Theatre, Warsaw
Direction: Krzysztof Warlikowski
Set design: Małgorzata Szczęśniak
Music: Paweł Mykietyn.

happened on the stage of the Dramatic Theatre in Warsaw his name became familiar to everyone in Poland. The performance began as the audience were entering. The usherette (Danuta Stenka) does not want to admit a drunken spectator (Adam Ferency). She tussles with him, tries to stop him, and he pushes through between other spectators to get to his seat in the audience. “Stop pulling me!”, “We have not shared a bed!”, “A woman is not going to give me orders!”, “Go home and do your husband’s laundry!” In a moment they will both appear on stage as Kate and Petruchio. A drunken spectator climbs the stage and goes behind the curtain where he will be found sleeping by Earl (Marcin Troński). The start of the performance is taken from Shakespeare. There is a scene of hunting: half-naked, yapping men are held by servants on tight leashes. There is disturbing aggression, darkness and impetuosity in this clamour. After all, the beginning of the play is about woman-hunting… The parts of Lord and Baptista Minola are played by the same actor. Earl is talking to the servants about the dogs ready to set off in pursuit. The same actors who play mad dogs will be Bianca’s wooers. Like dogs in a kennel, they will be carefully evaluated for speed, character, grip and, most importantly, obedience. Hounding and constant feelings of insecurity fill the entire play — performed on a stage planned like a circus arena, and directed with drastic allusions to the taming of a wild predator.

The doubled spectators (real ones in the audience and extra ones composed of actors) add dynamism to the whole performance. After all, both the taming and the hounding require adequate scenery. After each scene the actors do not go behind the wings but merely move to the side. They sit in loge and, on sofas. They carefully watch the action unfold. They make comments on subsequent characters’ statements, and when an open conflict between Kate and Petruchio breaks out they will cheer them, as if they were witnessing a boxing match. Petruchio is everyone’s favourite: this is the order of things that has not changed in ages. According to the universal law of nature, he should put Kate in her place. However, in this play men and women are equal opponents, and when both of them are on the attack, neither will surrender. The director consciously made his actors wear historic eighteenth-century costumes, just as their characters were forced to live by social rules and conventions. He intentionally restrained their moves and completely limited their room for manoeuvre. They can nod their head, fan themselves, make one step forward… but throwing a man a right hook might be somewhat problematic. When angry Petruchio causes Kate to fall to the ground, the metal construction supporting her dress makes it impossible for her to get back on her feet on her own. She is like a grotesque beetle knocked on its back desperately attempting to gain a foothold in the air. How easy it is to rape an opponent disarmed like this… How easy it is to savour such victory.

The story told by Warlikowski's actors is "a gradual breaking of bones and, eventually, the neck".[43] Kate, the shrew who has so far chased away all wooers, is an obstacle great enough for Petruchio who, as any common male, wants to prove to his buddies that no woman can resist him. As soon as he has broken her, humiliated her, when he has proved his strength, he will lose interest. Danuta Stenka, cast in the main part, is a beautiful woman with a strong stage-presence. Would Shakespeare want to show us a rough, sharp-tongued tomboy, who does not want to get married out of spite? Having seen Warlikowski's production we might argue otherwise. Danuta Stenka's Kate is a very attractive woman in her thirties, aware of the strength of her personality: when her father sends her off to crochet in her room the audience bursts out laughing — women like her come home late, and always go where they like. They most definitely do not spend their spare time on needlework.

Małgorzata Kożuchowska, who played the polite and good-natured Bianca, is the opposite of demonic Kate. She is the epitome of Slavic beauty. Warlikowski put two ideals of feminine appearance together on stage. Their joint presence highlights and affirms the differences between them; each of them implements her own scenario of managing men. Bianca is a sweet little girl coquettishly lifting the rim of her habit (in fact this garment is not much of a cover). Consciously, and without reservations, she is using the fact that men, naïve and dumbfounded by her beauty, believe in her sweetness and affability — until the wedding… Up to then she is going to display traditional attitudes and behaviour.

The scene of the wedding is clearly another act in Kate's humiliation. The photographer lines up all the guests in front of the audience, but the bridegroom is not there. The waiting begins — in a pose, prolonged, and uncomfortable. At this point, Warlikowski inserts a pause. The image on stage lasts another few minutes, as if in a freeze-frame, as if the photographer had pushed the shutter but not released it. And when Petruchio does appear, he is riding a moped, wearing a white wedding dress and a long train on his bald head. A bride leading her spouse to a wedding reception in some dive. Dirty, filled with cigar smoke, sticky with spilt alcohol. We can subconsciously smell the sour odour of male dominance. Petruchio among his buddies is like a mafia boss, he could be Sicilian, or he could be from Warsaw. The wedding guests are mobsters

---

[43] Gruszczyński, *Szekspir i Uzurpator*, 103.

playing a game of cards. Biting their cigars and drinking strong spirits they set their women against one other to have an arm-wrestling competition.

It becomes apparent that Petruchio's behaviour during the wedding was not only for show. When he takes Kate to his house, they have their first dinner together. They are sitting at a long and empty table. Strange, cold, lonely, and quiet. Eventually a servant arrives and takes a raw chicken out of a mouldy, dirty fridge. He throws it ostentatiously on Kate's plate. Where Petruchio should be showing off with Ovid's *Ars amatoria*, in Warlikowski's play he is simply watching porn. The models of love in this production are very dramatic. Petruchio calls in dressmakers to prepare garments for his beautiful wife. Three transvestites, introduced straight from a film by Pedro Almodovar, enter the stage. Their task is to make her look as unattractive as possible. To humiliate her and give her a brutal makeover, vulgar and degrading. The men will be teaching her how to walk, how to sway her hips. They dress her to look like a stereotypical prostitute. A black leather mini dress, heavy makeup, a faux fur jacket which is bright orange, and too short. High heels that are too high — keeping one's balance defies gravity. Making each step requires effort and concentration, and Kate is no longer strong. She gives up, becomes similar to them, her femininity exaggerated… What is most interesting is that the transvestites are actually her husband's good friends. Only a moment ago we saw him parading on stage in a white wedding dress. The question is where he had been loitering if he is now receiving his guests in a smart suit highlighting his masculinity. He is a *macho* from a gangster film, drinking with his buddies, while Kate is pushed away to the sidelines of a stage ramp and begins her final monologue. Even today, when Danuta Stenka speaks in interviews about working on that scene, even though it has been almost twenty years, the emotions return. Unrestrained tears once again fill her eyes… Defeated, too weak to stand on her own feet, she gathered the strength to make the final effort and go out towards the audience. To stand at the edge of the stage precipice. Words get stuck in her throat. They are suffocating her. She makes assurances of her love, obedience and devotion. Her final monologue is a culmination of emotions. She is too weak to oppose, her body begins to tremble as her defences are running out. The words of the monologue are still resonating in the air as if refusing to take responsibility for the state she found herself in and for what has to be said, testified to. A defeated and downtrodden person needs to be defined. Huge tears are falling down her cheeks. Hysteria creeps in, taking away control of reason, articulation and reflexes. She is shattered — just two hours earlier, beautiful, strong, aware of her worth, laughing at every man in the face — and how did it end? It seems that the actress is not going to be able to finish the scene, that she will fall into the abyss to escape it. Petruchio is listening to her words carefully. There is a cold fascination with the observed phenomenon in his eyes, but he is already embracing another woman: "There is no such thing as a way to happiness. And marriage is most certainly not one! Marriage can lead to hell, to crime, to great harm but not to happiness. It is a terrible social institution".[44] Warlikowski deconstructed the comedy and with the elements he retrieved he created a show which tears spectators apart. It is, however, equally probable that Shakespeare never wrote a comedy…

When Warlikowski was preparing the script he observed that there are numerous statements throughout the play which make it possible to question the entire piece. Shakespeare time and time again made provisions for himself by putting the presented reality in inverted commas, as if he himself was anxious about the dormant strength in his writing. Therefore, what Warlikowski did first was to remove all the inverted commas. He let out the text with no conventionality. He removed the entire coating of comedy which in a classical interpretation created a safety margin for the play. He produced a strong show, advancing bold theses about the need for domination, the battle between patriarchy and matriarchy. By firmly directing his actors he brought up feminist criticism and issues related to the definition of gender. With the characters he presented he posed questions about the classically-adopted models of masculinity and femininity and about the social conditioning of our definitions. During the show, he dismantled interpersonal relationships and dependencies just as he exposed all the theatre's innards, the scaffolding and engine room. He would unexpectedly turn on the light in the auditorium. While actors from a previous scene were still on stage, others had already begun the next one. He allowed the lobby door to slam. He disassembled the text and all the tools he needed to stage it. He let musicians on stage to parade between the actors and play probably the most magnetic piece ever written for Polish theatre on two instruments, the saxophone and the accordion.[45] The music is persistent, monotonous with a relentlessly repeated melodic line, and dangerously seductive, even aggressive at times. The irritating saxophone: unreal, sexual. The accordion is disturbing from the first notes, tugging at the senses with strongly articulated accents. The music enchanted all:

> Later I saw *The Taming of the Shrew* in the Dramatic Theatre, and I became completely intoxicated with the hypnotically endearing ambiguity,

[44] Gruszczyński, *Szekspir i Uzurpator*, 16.

[45] Paweł Mykietyn, *The Taming of the Shrew*.

> those excesses of concealed associations… Later, when I lived in Stalin's loge facing the stage,[46] when they played *The Taming of the Shrew*, I liked to lie down on the bed in the dark, with the door half open, and take in the air of the production, the capricious animal vitality, the joy and longing… There is one scene — two actors suddenly stop acting… and they dance, like you dance when you are alone, to your thoughts, to your own body, which at that point you love and accept. I adore that scene. When the saxophone solo began — I would tip-toe to the loge and watch. I wanted to cry, I do not know why. There was a peculiar feeling of longing and happiness. One day I wrote a long text about that scene. I do not know why but my computer deleted it… Anyway… And critics and respectable spectators still dragged it through the mud. Warlikowski was dragged through all kinds of mud.[47]

He was accused of unjustified vulgarity and lack of taste. And when next year he let out a naked *Hamlet* on stage another scandal erupted.[48] The audience and critics were upset with the amount of sexuality, gender and Freud present in that Shakespeare of his… Yet again, as in the case of *The Winter's Tale* and *The Taming of the Shrew*, his thinking of the production was directed by a carefully planned method safeguarded by cultural references:

> Do you remember the demonic chef from *Festen* — a Dogme film based on the framework from *Hamlet*? And the kitchen where the disastrous course of action is manipulated? And a couple of dishwashers with Down syndrome who know all the secrets behind the heinous events in Lars von Trier's *The Kingdom*? Warlikowski probably also has a kitchen like that somewhere, a place of low rank, where the secrets of *Hamlet's* events are known. The only thing is that no one has access to it, not even the director himself.[49]

---

[46] The mysterious "Stalin's loge" is a special loge located to the right of the stage of the Dramatic Theatre in Warsaw. A separate staircase leads to it and it is connected to a private suite. The loge allowed one to sneak out of a performance unnoticed which was often appreciated by Communist dignitaries, who used the small rooms for unofficial meetings covered up with official visits at the theatre.

[47] Lupa, „Krzysztof W….," 38.

[48] Original title of the production: *Hamlet*
Date and place of premiere: October 22, 1999, The Dramatic Theatre, Warsaw
Direction: Krzysztof Warlikowski
Set design: Małgorzata Szczęśniak
Music: Paweł Mykietyn.

[49] Gruszczyński, *Ojcobójcy*, 125.

Warlikowski has read Shakespeare's tragedy from Aeschylus' perspective. He combined ancient Greek and Old Testament thinking by presenting on stage a myth in which crime motivates the need for family vengeance. The text of the play was edited to make the characters' statements sound as close to colloquial speech as possible. It was not a production of a tragedy at a royal court but an intimate "family *Hamlet*" with a small group of actors and limited staging solutions. A simple playing space was set between two banks of seating for the audience. The emotional void of such a solution left no room to escape, to hide, to take cover behind imitation, when the narration got out of hand. In such a merciless space each false note hits twice as hard, it becomes an irritating creak in the audience's perception.

Warlikowski sought motivation in the characters' inner experiences rather than historical contexts or long-established conventions at the royal court. He completely removed any political threads. He constructed his show with contrasted emotions and an atmosphere of individual events which shed light on the characters' actions. He did not want to stage *Hamlet*, but to touch upon the people in it.[50] This is why his Hamlet (Jacek Poniedziałek) was not reading a book… Warlikowski was more interested in his complexes, and his psychological limitations which made him unfit for revenge. His Hamlet is a textbook example of neurosis. He is unable to make any decision. He cannot cope with emotions attracting him in opposite directions simultaneously. He is aggressive, but terrified at the same time. He cannot tune his assessment of reality to actual situations. The ones that made him feel ecstatic only a moment ago suddenly give him a panic attack. Going from one extreme to the other, he cannot see the problem within him. It is the world that is evil. He thinks it is his duty to make the people surrounding him reveal the darkness and wickedness within them. He dismisses the need for bloody vengeance as he believes that by taking it he will become just like those he loathes. By not fulfilling his obligations he tries to remain on the sidelines of the court's responsibilities where everyone has a role to play which defines their "to be or not to be". Each character joining him on stage brings out a different feature in him. Each one provokes a different type of behaviour, and different levels of openness and sensitivity are revealed, though it may seem that Hamlet can only hurt his close ones. When in the presence of Ophelia (Magdalena Cielecka) he talks to Horatio (Omar Sangare), he sends direct messages which are aimed at humiliating his loved one:

---

[50] Joanna Targoń, „Grzech pierworodny – rozmowa z Małgorzatą Szczęśniak, Krzysztofem Warlikowskim i Jackiem Poniedziałkiem," *Didaskalia*, no. 34 (1999): 8-11.

"Horatio, thou art the only pure man." His relationships with Rosencrantz, Horatio and Ophelia are so different that his homosexuality in this production is not obvious, stereotypical, or imbued with coarse interpretations. Even Hamlet does not know many things about himself. In Warlikowski's show, Rosencrantz and Guildenstern are played by women (Maria Seweryn, Jolanta Fraszyńska). Their relationship was very strongly emphasised, and Hamlet watched it fascinated, as if they remained in some region unattainable to him.

The scene of a double performance is played with lights dimmed, just bordering on visibility. It was a perfect space for events which should have remained covered. When they were working on *The Murder of Gonzago*, Hamlet drew an actor's face towards his, reciting the speech on rugged, all clad in black armour, as if he was trying to put a spell on reality so that the reality of the production could become one with facts. When Claudius stops the performance and calls for light, the interval begins. After it is over, Warlikowski returns to the narration as if he were giving a recapitulation of the previous episode. Once again we see *The Murder of Gonzago*, but now when the king demands the lights everything is plunged into darkness. We can only hear Hamlet's voice: "Tis now the very witching time of night…" Hamlet's madness infects his close ones. At the end of the show all the characters will be dead.

To all, the scene of Gertrude's (Stanisława Celińska) conversation with her son was the most shocking. A mother wearing a tight wedding dress, using the vulgar eroticism of her ageing body to shock and provoke the much younger Claudius, at the same time cruelly ridiculing Hamlet's undefined sexuality. The son entered her bedroom naked. Critics looked for Freud, Oedipus or cheap provocation in that gesture, but the scene in which two people are desperately trying to save their feelings was in fact created by accident: before one rehearsal of the scene, Poniedziałek had had a huge argument with Celińska in the dressing room. When the rehearsal began, completely unexpectedly, he came on stage naked to demonstrate his helplessness to her. The scene proved so intense that it was left in the production:

> He entered naked and young people, I do not know, either could not take it, or were simply looking for some scandal. In any case — there were giggles. Since this scene — between mother and son — is very dramatic, and performed deeply, with intimate gazing, in dimmed light, such reactions were terribly difficult to us. Jacek was heroic, he looked at me, saw my composure and was looking for support. I gave it to him. (…) I remember when I said "Enough now, Hamlet," and explained to him that he was touching on matters which were extremely painful to me and that I

> had dark spots in my heart which I could never wash off — I was using these tricks of mine to control the audience. I would make a pause, speak very suggestively, and they did not know what would happen next. Slowly, slowly they went quiet and towards the end we got hold of them.[51]

Madness flooded the stage. Polonius' dead body, which lay between them throughout the entire scene, will forever divide the mother and the son. Wounded by Gertrude's rejection, he rejects Ophelia by raping her brutally. He is hurt and can no longer trust any woman. They all lie, they all deceive… There will be no violets, no rosemary for remembrance. Madness is articulated by a desperate sound of the accordion which Ophelia hung around her neck. At one point, carrying the heavy instrument, which with her petite figure seemed colossal, she fell to the ground. She froze, like a Clockwork toy that has run down.

The end of the whole performance is just as sudden as Ophelia's death. The lights go on in the auditorium when Hamlet, as if leaning towards another opportunity outside the stage, asks himself the question: "What compell'd me?" It was the first big role for Jacek Poniedziałek: no one at that point expected him to become the greatest star in Warlikowski's ensemble. Especially, since the production was unanimously laughed at by reviewers. They did not like the soldiers throwing snowballs during night watch, they did not like the fact that heavy, mediaeval swords were used in the duel. They collectively accused Warlikowski of incompetence, an inability to direct actors and lack of a leading idea to bind the entire production together.

Apparently *The Tempest* is Shakespeare's most difficult play because it continues to resist easy attempts at modernisation.[52] It is fairytale-like, extremely unreal. References to the Kingdoms of Milan and Naples mean nothing to the audience. It seems that the perfect setting for this story does not exist. Contexts for the situation on Prospero's (Adam Ferency) island are foggy; they can be arranged into any constellation. Prospero does not have a magic coat or a magic wand, just a simple black sweater:

> I was wondering for a long time whether there are any actors at all who could play Prospero. What kind of an actor would it have to be? Certainly,

---

[51] Teresa Wilniewczyc, „Dzień wcześniej skończyłam pięćdziesiąt lat - rozmowa ze Stanisławą Celińską," *Notatnik teatralny*, no. 28-29 (2003): 18.

[52] Original title of the production: *Burza*
Date and place of premiere: January 4, 2003, The Dramatic Theatre, Warsaw
Direction: Krzysztof Warlikowski
Set design: Małgorzata Szczęśniak
Music: Paweł Mykietyn.

> someone who at one point would not care about his actor's face, about the ending of his theatre life. It would have to be someone who suddenly chooses life, leaves the theatre and already on the sidelines of mainstream theatre events, gracefully accepts such an offer. He should be an outsider who maintains a distance from life and is bitter towards theatre, not attached to anything. Only someone like that can play this part, because what matters in *The Tempest* is that Shakespeare is already retired, and returns to the life he escaped, once again drawn by someone into the standards of middle-class life. It is Shakespeare running out of money, once an author, a king of life, a homosexual, an admired personality who was rapidly sidetracked. Afflicted by disease and old age. The selflessness of *The Tempest* can only be revealed by someone who is like that himself.[53]

Miranda (Małgorzata Hajewska-Krzysztofik), unkempt, wearing old sneakers, a worn-out pink cardigan, is no longer a teenager but a grown woman. A little savage, unmannered, unaccustomed to the company of people other than her father. A tomboy. She walks round-shouldered, moves clumsily and heavily. Nothing has been happening on her father's island for years. It would also be difficult to assume that it would ever change, so for days on end she cuts figures out of white paper, thus increasing her circle of friends. And when eventually, after so many years (!), good fortune brings about a storm, and with it a ship with real living people on board, her dad sinks it in the depths. Miranda is inconsolable, like a little girl. It might have been her only chance for something to change…

The performance obviously begins with Prospero's conversation with Miranda about their past in Milan. The storm started by Ariel (Magdalena Cielecka) rages in the background. Prospero is bitter. How can one not remember the past? He asks her about her memories from the royal court but the images imprinted in her mind are her father's stories rather than real memories. She skilfully reconstructs the stories she has heard. She creates semblances of images recovered from oblivion by the child she used to be.

In the tempest created by Ariel, the whistle of the windstorm transforms into an uneven, coarse rattle of a broken aircraft engine. An aeroplane crashes in the raging storm, because the narrative time in the performance has been blurred. It is Ariel who directs all events. Wearing a flight attendant's uniform he presents a full choreography of actions which passengers have to perform when there is a loss of cabin pressure. He demonstrates how to put on oxygen mask and life jacket. Prospero's persecutors are rulers on the scale of the twenty-first century. They are

[53] Gruszczyński, *Szekspir i Uzurpator*, 151.

CEOs of international corporations on business trips. When they regain consciousness after the catastrophe, they light up their cigars and turn on their laptops to check the emails they received in the meantime.

Ariel, dressed in a well-worn track suit, is a tragic character in the story, like the play. He is hopelessly in love with his master, trying his best to work his way to regaining freedom. He is the perfect servant. He appears as soon as Prospero thinks his name. But it is perfection against will. He reads his master's mind and immediately puts his thoughts into action. He undergoes a constant metamorphosis, he is constantly on the move in between tasks. He always speaks about his perfectly performed duties with sorrow, presenting the results of his work he gives Prospero an insolent look — will this do?

Caliban remains a similar creature. Half-fish and half-man, played by the petite Renate Jett, who transformed the part into a meticulously sculpted marvel. She is wearing oversized overalls, a knitted cap, and her delicate face is tattooed. A little savage. A dangerous savage. A malicious animal. A nasty creature. She spits out a flow of words with disgust. Caliban is struggling with the language of humans. The Austrian actress's grappling with the challenge of barbaric sounds of the Polish language worked out perfectly. Precise chiselling of frills and diacritic hooks of declinations, depicted with the tip of the tongue like arabesques of communication. Miranda taught Caliban their language out of pity, she taught him to speak, and he, in turn, tried to rape her, to supply the earth with little Calibans.

In this show, everyone is deadly dangerous. Ariel, Caliban… as well as Trinculo (Stanisława Celińska) and Stephano (Jacek Poniedziałek). The two servants who escaped the power of a force of nature are sitting at a long bar, as if in a second-rate pub. Trinculo is wearing a chemise, a messed up curly blond wig, and heavily overdone makeup. In Warlikowski's adaptation it is a woman with a past, who has experienced much, seen much and is not afraid to take on any job. She likes to hit the bottle and drinks like a fish. She enjoys reminiscing, but the good things have already happened. Stephano, her drinking companion, is a self-obsessed bruiser. A simpleton. He has gelled hair, a smart jacket and shoes, but he is sitting there with no trousers on. Caliban appears out of nowhere. A funny animal looking at their emptied bottle inquisitively. Stephano pours alcohol from the bottle straight into Caliban's mouth, as if feeding a thirsty calf, and indeed refers to him by the affectionate name "moon-calf". Caliban drinks greedily. He clearly enjoys the situation. He is enchanted with his new friend. Just as with any new friend… he is not even remotely suspicious after what other people did to him. He idolises

Stephano. He adores him indiscriminately and Stephano clearly enjoys another being that only has eyes for him. He gets Caliban drunk and dependable. When Caliban takes off his shoe and kisses his foot — the feeling of divinity fuddles Stephano's brain more than the alcohol. "Oh, shit…" is the only reaction he is able to articulate. He begins to feel what real power means. It appears that servants are as susceptible to its dangers as the masters they serve. They listen carefully to invisible Ariel's suggestions and set out to kill Prospero. "Freedom" yelled out by Caliban in a thickening darkness sounds more and more ominous.

Miranda and Ferdinand (Redbad Klynstra) are played by the same couple of actors who, exactly one year earlier, played a brother and sister in Sarah Kane's *Cleansed.* Warlikowski placed them in a new context and a new relationship, which had to be sieved through the memory of their previous acting experience. This love story in Warlikowski's show is not tacky. There is no puppy love. Prospero, with his resentment of the world of people, did not teach his daughter to wheel and deal, plot and manipulate. She enters relationships pure. When she and Ferdinand shake hands, she does it so firmly that his fingers almost get crushed. Warlikowski will immerse the presentation of their wedding in the tradition of Polish rustic wedding customs. Three elderly women wearing traditional folk costumes will be introduced instead of the three Roman goddesses. Lights in the auditorium go on. By returning to the world of civilisation we return to tradition. There is a huge loaf of bread and vodka in shot glasses. Traditional folk wishes for the newlyweds are inserted instead of Shakespeare's verse. It seems that after everything we have seen so far, the voices of these three women are the first honest declaration giving hope that a (brave?) new world is still possible.

But it will not neutralise the feeling of overwhelming dread throughout the performance. The stage design was poetically aesthetisized. Floor mirrors flickered in the intense the light, at once romantic, magical, at once transforming into trails of cold steel. Disturbing music by Paweł Mykietyn seemed to cut through spotlight beams. Following the original, the show ends with the scene of reconciliation. Older spectators interpreted it with references to Poland after the fall of Communism — to the reconciliation between executioners and victims of the former system. To them, Prospero was a political emigrant who had to leave his country because of his activity in the opposition. The marriage of the children of former enemies integrates the story. Trinculo in a black evening gown, like a singer in a live music bar, sings Louis Armstrong's *What a Wonderful World.* Antonio (Andrzej Chyra) quickly drinks a glass of champagne and leaves Prospero's lavish banquet humiliated. Warlikowski, as he did in *The Taming of the Shrew*, tears Shakespeare's optimistic ending to pieces. In the real world, whose structure and rules determine human emotions and grievances, true forgiveness will never be possible. There are things one never forgets nor forgives. If someone hurt you, there will come a time when they ask for your help. Help them: revenge is always most important.

> Miranda utters the words: "brave new world", which in fact evokes embarrassment and pity. That sentence announces some tragedy for Miranda: we can already see that she cannot understand the world of people. She will definitely collapse because of it; there will be no happy ending. When I was working on *The Tempest*, we translated the story of Miranda and Ferdinand into a Jewish-German story. A high school student falls in love with a German. Her grandfather does not want to forgive her and rejects his granddaughter. There is the question of forgiveness. Are we able to forget, fix what happened in the past? Can Miranda, who belongs to the world of nature, and Ferdinand — actually a completely uninteresting, big city boy — can they communicate? Their meeting is like an experiment: they were let in the same cage and instinct proved infallible, they fell in love. But perhaps one day they will realise how they were deceived and used? That they come from two different worlds, different orders? When we start adding stories of their background, even the way Shakespeare did; Naples and Milan, we see the sources of conflict immediately. Separatist, prosperous Milan, which does not want to provide for the poor South, will never come to an understanding with Naples. They had to be two strange countries hating each other; even if it was just Shakespeare's fantasy, it is meaningful anyway.[54]

In a sense, Shakespeare in Warlikowski's interpretation becomes an impossible author. He is the author dissected by the director and placed in opposition to the reality presented. The title *The African Tales by Shakespeare*, which refers to the book by Doris Lessing, suggests to the spectators interpretations leading to the (so-far) unsettled colonialism and inability to have an honest, intercultural dialogue (especially in the relationship between an oppressor and a conquered victim).[55]

---

[54] Gruszczyński, *Szekspir i Uzurpator*, 15.

[55] Original title of the production: *Opowieści Afrykańskie według Szekspira*
Date and place of premiere: October 5, 2011, The Dramatic Theatre, Warsaw
Direction: Krzysztof Warlikowski
Set design: Małgorzata Szczęśniak
Music: Paweł Mykietyn.
The text of the production was created based on plays by William Shakespeare: *King Lear*, *The Merchant of Venice*, *Otello*, short stories by John Maxwell

> Behold, I will send you Elijah the prophet before the coming of the great and dreadful day of the LORD:
> And he shall turn the heart of the fathers to the children, and the heart of the children to their fathers, lest I come and smite the earth with a curse.
> (*Malachi 4:5-6, King James Version*)

Warlikowski begins his performance with a reciprocity postulate without which communication is impossible. Bringing up the Biblical idea of Christian-Jewish reconciliation, he translates it into relationships within families: between fathers and sons, fathers and daughters, daughters and fathers. Loving fathers often cannot give their little princesses away to strange men. Their selfish love, which at some point does not have enough driving force to prevent their children from leaving, transforms into directly proportional hatred.

While directing the show, Warlikowski methodically implemented his idea from the time of his work on *Cleansed:* Sarah Kane has to be turned into Shakespeare, and Shakespeare into Sarah Kane. By combining: Renaissance plays with the writings of Coetzee, Cleaver, Littell and Mouawad, he created a "Trilogy of the excluded". He presented three men from Shakespeare's plays: Lear, Shylock and Othello (all played by Adam Ferency), whose age, religion and race have turned them into social outcasts. Ostracism can be easily explained by a brainless crowd's refusal to accept someone who is different from them. But does exclusion simultaneously make a character positive? One you sympathise with and whose reasons you defend? Sometimes we ask to be thrown out where it is cold and uncomfortable to stand alone. Our cultural areas of exclusion resemble old white spots on maps of Africa. We fill them in with our imagination, fears, concerns, and, very rarely, hopes. Warlikowski extracted moments from the texts which most clearly explain the characters' motifs. Even if they are very different characters, the same actor unified all issues, as if bringing them to a common archetypal denominator. We see them in different situations, in contact with other people. But the really trying moments are those when Warlikowski leads Adam Ferency to confront women: Lear and Cordelia (Maja Ostaszewska), Shylock and Portia (Małgorzata Hajewska-Krzysztofik), Othello and Desdemona (Magdalena Popławska).

> Some decisions regarding the text were made very quickly: Wajdi Mouawad, with whom Krzysztof collaborated on the adaptation of *A*

Coetzee: *Summertime*, *In the Heart of the Country*, *Slow Man* as well as writings by Eldridge Cleaver, Jonathan Littell and Wajdi Mouawad.

> *Streetcar*,[56] was commissioned to write three monologues presenting the state of mind of three Shakespearian women: Cordelia, Portia and Desdemona. In the structure of the plays they do not have the floor very often. Meanwhile, it is they who become a prism that focuses results of actions of men: fathers, husbands and fiancés, whose whims always have fatal results. Even if there is no murder or suicide, each time there is exclusion from the world death is the best-case scenario. Wajdi is a poetic writer through and through, balancing on the verge of post-traumatic delirium, and his task was to create accounts from within three minds which are burning and falling apart. In an early stage of the work *Summertime*, a novel by J. M. Coetzee, also appeared. The author, so important to Krzysztof for some years now (first used in *(A)pollonia*), in the process of rubbing one text against another, creates a counterbalance of time, by introducing the energy of passion comparable to Shakespeare's in contemporary times, but also a counterbalance of reason. Anglo-Saxon discipline of thought devoid of sentimentality and easy compassion leads to a certain objectification of relationships between those who love and those who hate. A model of a relationship between a father dying of cancer and his son forced to care for the increasingly vegetative old man becomes a possible contemporary relationship between Cordelia and Lear. It was a suggestion given to Wajdi Mouawad, a suggestion (which found a strong resonance in his dark head) that human existence leads inevitably to disaster.[57]

Old and crippled, Lear dies in hospital of laryngeal cancer. That is it, he does not have much time, therefore he decides to divide up his wealth and distribute it, naturally, between his loving daughters who visit him in hospital every day. Clearly, they do it out of a sense of obligation. Years of experience have taught them how to talk to him to make him feel content. They are perfectly aware of how valuable their father's happiness is. However, they do not try one bit to make him truly part of their lives. He is more of a burden ruining their best years with his obtrusive presence. The distribution of assets is not a pleasant situation to any of them. The daughters fidget impatiently, anxious to see if their previous actions are going to be adequately evaluated. They recite precisely designed expressions of love and devotion. Only Cordelia (as usual) creates problems. The one who truly loved her father, reproaches him for his toxic love which transformed into sexual harassment. She stands up to him for no good reason, she reopens old wounds as if she could not understand

[56] *A Streetcar*, based on *A Streetcar Named Desire* by Tennessee Williams (Date and place of premiere: February 4, 2010, Theatre de l'Odeon Paris).

[57] Piotr Gruszczyński, *Opowieści afrykańskie według Szekspira – program do spektaklu* (Warsaw: Teatr Nowy, 2011), 13.

that in this game you only nod in agreement with the dying one. Creators of the show discovered the daughter's emotionality in the text of Coetzee's short story *In the Heart of the Country*:

> It constitutes an almost hallucinatory record of the madness of a daughter in love with her father and bitterly jealous of him. A desperately lonely spinster, fantasising about murdering her father, begins to hear men's voices from planes flying over her house. She begins to collect stones and paint them with whitewash to spell out messages, poems by a schizophrenic lover addressed to gods flying over her head (...) It is different for Lear's other two daughters: Goneril and Regan. They also get their story from Coetzee. *Summertime* contains several interviews conducted by a young biographer of the late Coetzee. He is collecting information on the subject of his book. He mainly meets "the women of his life", who tell bitter things about Coetzee and very cruelly judge his sexuality, lack of passion and skills which would make him good lover material. In the course of interviews, however, they reveal situations and behaviours which make those relationships impossible to classify in a straightforward and unambiguous way.[58]

The whole situation is observed by a fool — a patient in the same room. It is possible that the essence of the question was not Lear's pride but fear at the end of his life — has he even been a person in their lives whom they could love at least to some extent? We have learnt to react with disgust towards elder sisters lying shamelessly to achieve their goals. Perhaps, however, we should be disgusted with the old man who terrorises them with his old age and by threatening them with eternal qualms of conscience forces them to humbly assure him of their endless love?

During one rehearsal, the director shouted:

> I would like to make a scene which does not hide behind theatre. To detach myself from the situation and be left alone with the father, with my father. After all, our relationships with our parents are something inconceivable and unfathomable. And in this scene the father suddenly requires what is inconceivable from us. That is scandalous![59]

Love cannot be forced, and neither is mercy at anyone's beck and call, especially if previous attempts at it had been preceded by humiliation. Young men who come to borrow money from Shylock are a gay couple of hustlers who, by "borrowing from a Jew" and marrying well want to get

---

[58] Gruszczyński, *Opowieści afrykańskie według Szekspira*, 14.
[59] Gruszczyński, *Opowieści afrykańskie według Szekspira*, 17.

out of debt. The girl does not matter. She also realises that she will not stand a chance against the other man. She also understands Shylock in this situation. (Characteristically, Małgorzata Hajewska-Krzysztofik, who plays Portia, is going to play the part of a judge in a moment.) Shylock, in Warlikowski's show, is presented as an experienced butcher, methodically quartering meat with a huge butcher knife. The deposit he suggests is revenge for the general contempt he receives. So far he has been humiliated, spat at, kicked, and today they come, as if nothing has happened and want to borrow money…

Scenes from *The Merchant of Venice* were presented in reference to a comic book *Maus. A Survivor's Tale*, by Art Spiegelman. It is a graphic novel set in World War II, in which the Jews are represented as mice, the Germans as cats, and the Poles as pigs. When new clients come to see Shylock they are wearing demonic pig masks. They slap him with their jokes:

> - What do you call a Jew hammered to a door? A Judas hole.
> - What was the inscription at the entrance to the gas chamber? "Mind the step."

The Merchant of Venice, although so distant, renders the entire horror of Nazi crimes. These scenes are Warlikowski's very strong stand against anti-Semitism in view of the uncomfortable questions which upset the Polish people: about their co-responsibility for the Holocaust. It is convenient to depict a Jew, whose bloodthirsty desires will never be completely fulfilled. Such a Jew is easy to stigmatise as guilty. The judge (Małgorzata Hajewska-Krzysztofik) defending Antonio (Jacek Poniedziałek) returns home after a trial, takes of her wig and clothes, takes a pound of raw meat out of a briefcase and eats it. Bit by bit. This scene requires heroic sacrifice from the actress, but her body revolts and she throws up on stage.

A video is screened over the blacked out stage. A white woman is caught having sex in a toilet with a black man. They are both smartly dressed; it is probably a gala reception or a ministerial banquet. They are charged with engaging in sexual intercourse in a public place. Obviously it is a red herring to cover up the real problem which is that a white girl is giving a black guy a blowjob, that a black guy had strayed into forbidden regions. *Othello* is a phenomenon of a relationship between a white woman and a black man. When we watch Desdemona's wedding to Othello, she chokes with laughter, she cannot yet see her stigmatisation. She cannot feel the social exclusion she has sentenced herself to by engaging in a relationship with a black man. Othello is a rare example of a lucky man. Driven by a streak of successes he has managed to distinguish himself, to achieve the unachievable and marry a white woman. He does not sense that one day fortune will change and he will have to pay a high price for crossing that boundary. Fate will be assisted by Iago (Marek Kalita), who is racist and has feelings for Cassio, who rejected his advances. He does not like the fact that Othello enjoys privileges reserved for white people. Driven by hatred he will destroy Othello, Cassio, and the innocent Desdemona. As Othello's private doctor he has direct access to him and can infect his mind with suspicion. When they watch TV together, during a massage or a game of chess, he shares his thoughts and casual remarks, words which make accidental connections and equally accidentally fade away… To voice a suspicion out loud is to make it possible. Desdemona's actions involuntarily confirm the suspicions. She cannot adapt to her husband's barrack manners and withdraws from cohabitation. She spends her days lying in bed and watching films on her laptop. She is resigned and reconciled to the fact that she was merely a conqueror's reward: in the patriarchal system in to which she willingly entered by marriage, she only has the right to listen to insults and accept death at her husband's hand.

Having worked on the author for over twenty years Warlikowski learnt to read Shakespeare with his non-standard associations:

> That really is a partner! The kind of partner whom — I discover it as I work — I will never match. He always opens up a path for me, further than I am able to go. And I need that. To put it firmly: I am not interested in authors worse than me, who do not continue to put forward new demands. (…) He is simply a master who taught me how to think about theatre. All I needed to do was to trust his intuition in defining the contemporary man very deeply. (…) Shakespeare constitutes a compendium of knowledge about man and the world — he says everything we so badly need today. Not long ago everything was described, named, defined. We had the Church as a place of shelter, combated by a specific ideology, therefore, out of necessity, it was unambiguous. The ideology painted everything one colour, the Church another: it was easy to make a choice. And today the Church is not monochromatic, nor is any ideology strong enough to control us. We are faced with ambiguity; therefore we are very lost people. (…) And on the other hand, Shakespeare can be treated almost as a creator of pop culture. English Renaissance theatre combined various stories and various registers to create a melting pot, an ant colony. When we read *The Taming of the Shrew* we can feel the author is almost like a journalist, an employee of modern media, who finds a hot topic, puts together various viewpoints and provokes. Please look at Shakespeare from the perspective of the three works: *The Taming of the Shrew*, *Othello* and *The Merchant of Venice*. How much violence! How much denial of any political correctness

regarding the problems of the Jews, women and race. These issues continue to tear us apart. Political correctness is an attempt at softening them in an elegant way, and Shakespeare turns them into scandals, speaks against the rules, against the patterns. This is the power.[60]

His strength became Warlikowski's faithful ally. Hiding behind productions of the classic he knocks his spectators out of their comfortable, weekend complacency. The greatest power of these productions, total derailments of our previous certainties on Shakespeare, is the fact that having watched a production by Warlikowski we no longer accept any other interpretation as appropriate. We watch safe productions, presented in line with textbook understanding, with compassion. But inside we feel that such a concept of Elizabethan theatre is a waste of time. After all we have seen we simply have to agree with the director's words:

If we are able to find so much in such a story it is difficult to believe that the person who wrote it did not intend to put it all in there.[61]

4. Sarah Kane
The Song of Songs

And I want to play hide-and-seek and give you my clothes and tell you I like your shoes and sit on the steps while you take a bath and massage your neck and kiss your feet and hold your hand and go for a meal and not mind when you eat my food and meet you at Rudy's and talk about the day and type your letters and carry your boxes and laugh at your paranoia and give you tapes you don't listen to and watch great films and watch terrible films and complain about the radio and take pictures of you when you're sleeping and get up to fetch you coffee and bagels and Danish and go to Florent and drink coffee at midnight and have you steal my cigarettes and never be able to find a match and tell you about the tv programme I saw the night before and take you to the eye hospital and not laugh at your jokes and want you in the morning but let you sleep for a while and kiss your back and stroke your skin and tell you how much I love your hair your eyes your lips your neck your breasts your arse and sit on the steps smoking till your neighbour comes home and sit on the steps smoking till you come home and worry when you're late and be amazed when you're early and give you sunflowers and go to your party and dance till I'm black and be sorry when I'm wrong and happy when you forgive me and look at your photos and wish I'd known you forever (…) get cold when you take

[60] Agnieszka Celeda, „To rzeczywistość jest skandaliczna - rozmowa z Krzysztofem Warlikowskim," *Polityka*, November 4, 2009: 58-60.
[61] Gruszczyński, *Szekspir i Uzurpator*, 33.

> the blanket and hot when you don't and melt when you smile and dissolve when you laugh and not understand why you think I'm rejecting you when I'm not rejecting you and wonder how you could think I'd ever reject you and wonder who you are but accept you anyway and tell you about the tree angel enchanted forest boy who flew across the ocean because he loved you and write poems for you and wonder why you don't believe me and have a feeling so deep I can't find words for it and want to buy you a kitten I'd get jealous of because it would get more attention than me and keep you in bed when you have to go and cry like a baby when you finally do and get rid of the roaches and buy you presents you don't want and take them away again and ask you to marry me and you say no again but keep on asking because though you think I don't mean it I do always have from the first time I asked you and wander the city thinking it's empty without you and want you and think I'm losing myself but know I'm safe with you and tell you the worst of me and try to give you the best of me because you don't deserve any less and answer your questions when I'd rather not and tell you the truth when I really don't want to and try to be honest because I know you prefer it and think it's all over but hang on in for just ten more minutes before you throw me out of your life and forget who I am and try to get closer to you because it's a beautiful learning to know you and well worth the effort and speak German to you badly and Hebrew to you worse and make love with you at three in the morning and somehow somehow somehow communicate some of the overwhelming undying overpowering unconditional all-encompassing heart-enriching mind-expanding on-going never-ending love I have for you.[62]

There is a quiet voice coming from the darkened stage.[63] A petite woman is sitting on a stool. She is reciting an excerpt from *Crave* by Sarah Kane. A monologue which became the postmodernist *Song of Songs*. Renate Jett is speaking timidly. She stumbles over the sound of the foreign language. When she was working on the monologue she did not know Polish. Jacek Poniedziałek read out the whole text to her and she wrote it down phonetically without understanding. She memorised sounds, not meanings.

---

[62] Sarah Kane, *Complete Plays: Blasted; Phaedra's Love; Cleansed; Crave; 4.48 Psychosis; Skin*, (London: Methuen Drama, 2000), 169.

[63] Original title of the production: *Oczyszczeni*
Date and place of premiere: January 9, 2002, The Polski Theatre, Poznań/The Rozmaitości Theatre, Warsaw
Direction: Krzysztof Warlikowski
Set design: Małgorzata Szczęśniak
Music: Paweł Mykietyn.

> The text is like a thread of light in Warlikowski's show, introduced in intense darkness of death and suffering, sadistic madness and sacrifices. And it must be remembered about until the end because only that thread of light can show the way out of Kane's labyrinth. Otherwise, affected by the heart of darkness, we may remain in darkness forever.[64]

In the darkness of a huge stage space. We do not know where we are. At the back we can see showers, tiled walls, old metal beds, a punching bag and a gymnastic horse. A sports hall? Hospital? Slaughterhouse? Intense light from spotlights highlights the clear simplicity of the entire space. It may be Tinker's or Dr. Mengele's research facility. Who is Tinker? For some unknown reason he has full power over all the residents. He administers punishments and offers rewards. He might be the evil god of that place. He has the ability to trigger the worst in people. He does not allow anyone to love because he himself is not loved. He rages sadistically at his victims and there does not seem to be an alternative of an outside world. The space of stage is a finite universe to which the door opens only one way.

> Mariusz Bonaszewski (Tinker): Initially I asked him [Warlikowski] if he was aware that when reading Kane people become disgusted and no longer wanted to finish. It was particularly the case with the bits in which I was to participate. I did not know how to play it. He replied that he was looking for something close to the cruelty of a fairytale. (…) I do not want to look for easy comparisons. Tinker has nothing in common with the completely fake — though because of that, strongly effective — nurse Ratched from *One Flew Over The Cuckoo's Nest*. I was not looking for inspiration in accounts about a smiling Dr. Mengele, beautifully describing his criminal experiments to his assistants. Stating that Tinker is running a concentration camp at a university and cuts people's legs leads nowhere. What seems important is the status of his relationship with Grace and why in the first scene shuts her brother Graham up after he announced her arrival. (…) Sometimes Tinker seems to me the embodiment of the characters' doom. We can assume he only exists in their minds. He does not really exist and there is nothing terrible happening there. The characters take drugs and this is when the worst experience imaginable to each of them appears. For a homosexual couple it is disbelief in love. Everyone is afraid that who they are will turn out not to be true. Tinker asks basic questions and administers severe punishments for lying. (…) An oppressor-victim comparison means nothing here as a clichéd, stereotypical notion. A foreign reviewer wrote that Tinker, who had imagined them all, is the truly unfortunate one. He is trying to punish them and prove that they lie in love. If we can say that

[64] Gruszczyński, *Ojcobójcy*, 136.

> Tinker is in their heads, the opposite is just as possible. This is a conclusion drawn from Kane's descriptions: Tinker as the only living character who tells his story.[65]

When he appears on stage, a previously prepared lemon, syringe and spoon are ready for use. While he heats the drug, Graham (Redbad Klynstra) appears behind his back. They argue in narcotic hunger; Tinker does not want to provide him with a deadly dose but Graham grabs the syringe and injects the entire content into his eye. We are still hoping to be able to explain it, to place it in a familiar reality and believe that it was only a hallucination, a narcotic vision. But Graham falls to the floor dead and the nightmare continues. His sister (Małgorzata Hajewska-Krzysztofik) arrives. She wants to become her own brother. She wants to retain his presence in her body. She undergoes surgery, but Graham does not come back to life in her body. Severed breasts and a sewn-on penis did not change her personality. Graham came to see her at night. He taught her everything: how to move and how to behave. In deafening silence they touch one another in awe of the physicality of being. She has become one of Shakespeare's twins, but when she looked in the mirror wounded, wrapped up in post-surgery bandages — a thunder did not strike. No transformation occurred. Her metamorphosis into Graham was an unfulfilled dream of androgyny to satisfy the need of the other half of the subconscious. Grace dared to realise a dream many of us barely sense.

> Shakespeare's nightmare-dream of a sex-change has suddenly become a fact, and it is a painful one. (…) Shakespeare's hunch, expectation, became a possibility. It is a new kind of Copernican revolution. (…) Our civilisation more and more deprives us of illusion, the feeling of order and constancy. Would it not be better to continue thinking the Earth is an immobile centre of the universe, with the Sun revolving around it? How fearless it would make us…[66]

By her actions, Grace answers the question which aroused so much dismay in *(A)pollonia* — by getting rid of her own personality she dies for her brother. She hoped she could transplant him into herself. That it would be possible to descend into Hades for someone. The motif of Carl (Thomas Schweiberer) and Rod (Jacek Poniedziałek) is the recurring question of how much we are willing to do for a loved one. Carl expresses his love,

---

[65] Maria Hepel, „Nie ma przepisu - rozmowa z Mariuszem Bonaszewskim," *Notatnik teatralny*, no. 28-29 (2003): 149-150.

[66] Agnieszka Fryz-Więcek, „Skondensowany strach – rozmowa z Krzysztofem Warlikowskim," *Didaskalia*, no. 47 (2002): 7.

proposes, wants to get married and wear a wedding band. He has made up his mind. Rod treats his declarations with cynicism. As if throwing down the gauntlet, he asks Carl if he would be ready to die for him. Carl, who is committed, obviously says yes. Unfortunately, Tinker eavesdropped on these declarations and a sadistic game began. Tinker literally commits hyperbole in expressing love. Since Carl offered to die — he will. Tinker's bandits torture him during interrogation. They ask him about his relationship with Rod. They bring up everything that has ever been said in ecstasy. In a carelessly overheated fantasy. Promises taken out of intimate inverted commas, when materialised, become ghastly. Carl's physical endurance is not enough to carry everything he has promised to the other man. And since he lied, Tinker cuts his tongue off. Mutilated, Carl writes a request to Rod on the floor: "Say you forgive me." For that enormity, Tinker cuts off his hands. A love scene between two men is performed with their front to the audience. Rod and Carl are sitting naked in chairs. Rod touches his groin with one hand and Carl's with the other. After such a long and unimaginable suffering Carl hears the longed-for declaration: "I will always love you. I will never lie to you. I will never betray you. On my life." Tinker emerges from the dark: "You or him?" Rod, so cynical in accepting Carl's declarations will die for his loved one. Tinker will cut his throat right away.

The sound of a falling coin triggers a peep show. Intense, red light marks the limits of stage space. A dancing older woman (Stanisława Celińska) is significantly overweight. She emulates an erotic dancer and has clearly become tired. Her moves are mechanical. She is not going to seduce anyone, this is not a profession for her "assets". In the entire production, actors are cast against their predispositions, against their age, against their acting experience. However, there was certain stubbornness in her dance. Staring in the dark audience she was waiting, as if for the end of her shift, for the time when she would be able to change and go home to spend the rest of the day in front of a television. Tinker will look for fulfilment of his love for Grace in her. They will become friends. And the love scene between them will be played out completely beyond literality. In tension, in emotion. They will sit next to each other, facing the audience, providing merely a verbal layer of the narrative.

Stanisława Celińska:
I have different burdens. I am a woman of a certain age, I have made a name for myself, I have a position which I do not want to lose, different anxieties. I was afraid that perhaps that literature was not worth taking such a risk for. I also did not want to touch certain sides of life which I have put behind me, I was embarrassed about my looks. In order to do it I

> had to believe in Sarah. Obviously, I believed in Warlikowski as well, although not entirely, because we are all a little bit sceptical, Doubting Thomases. We want to save our own skin, frankly speaking. There was a rehearsal with Mariusz Bonaszewski. Krzysiu put two chairs on a piece of rag and said: this is your stage, act. In Sarah's play it is a stage in a peep show window. They are to make love. The whole act. Yet, here we are, in those chairs. Just that. (…) Then I showed a breast and — what next? What next? This is it, the end, I do not know what to do next. Next, in the play, Tinker takes her right breast into his mouth. Mariusz had a problem, eventually, gently, he did it. But what next? So far, we can say I knew what to do, but further than that, I do not know anything. I was like a little girl, utterly terrified. And Krzysiu said: "What do you mean what's next? Sit next to each other and act. Let the text speak through you." I felt a big load fall off my chest. I calmed down… I was afraid something might go wrong later. Too literally. (…) Several times during rehearsals I ran away from the show. Krzysztof asked me then: "And where will we go without you? It is you who leads us. The young ones are looking to you." My name and courage were what sealed the show. He knew what he was betting on. Besides, he also knew that people love me. At the time, I was afraid to expose myself, as well as touch what I have already ended in my life. The need for physical, mental love (…) Today we are using limited language, we hide our emotions. A woman says: "Fuck me, fuck me," but inside she has the soul of Tatiana from *Onegin* (…) When I finally decided to take the part and understood that *Cleansed* is also about me, I think I also became more truthful in real life. More honest, open to people, to love, to suffering, I do not participate in lemming-like rushes, I behave more authentically. (…) At the beginning of the work I was afraid of the subject matter. So far I had been a character actress. I could be funny, witty, cheerful, and fat. And it was fine. I have been through drama in life, perhaps I had had enough and did not want to go back to certain things. (…) this text has made me open up to people.[67]

"In order for a performance to work like thunder, it has to strike a sensitive cord in each of us."[68] Warlikowski's wish is coming true. This show will not make you feel good. In the cold beauty of the stage design and images you will be following the scenes one after another in shock, not knowing what else you can expect. It is a show about love which opens with one of the most moving monologues ever put down on insensitive paper. It is about how limitless love is reduced to extreme cruelty which accepts no metaphors. Here one really has to sacrifice one's life to authenticate one's words. Everything is played out in a very intense

---

[67] Wilniewczyc, „Dzień wcześniej skończyłam pięćdziesiąt lat…," 21-24.

[68] Gruszczyński, *Szekspir i Uzurpator*, 145.

way. With words finely carved by Kane. In hermetically clean colours of stage lights. In a focused presence of actors who created the rhythm of the show. By engaging in a difficult dialogue with his spectators Warlikowski crossed boundaries in every way. One could reject this show, negate it, say that Kane's text is naive in reducing human relationships to the banality of words — if you continue lying to me, I will cut your tongue off. But Kane worked on this play for three years, and she did not waste a single word. She created a juicy work worthy of best Greek tragedies. Like a model student, she precisely implemented the mechanism of *katharsis* described in Aristotle's *Poetics*: we sympathise with that character who is similar to us, neither better, nor worse… exactly like us. Therefore, there are only two ways, either we accept it and filter it through our sensitivity, or we negate it and go home slamming the door to the audience, where for the next several days we will feed our middle class indignation.

The production obviously raised a storm and almost national discussion. To many, such a radical show was a deep shock. Such an uncompromised crossing of all boundaries which had so far created the tradition of Polish theatre once again made Warlikowski's name the talk of the town. He shocked with the ugliness of the human body. He completely rejected the inverted commas of character, performance and theatre. Hysterical critics described it as the disowning of theatre metaphor. This show was in fact like thunder in a Polish spectator's theatre experience. The shock was greater still because it was inflicted by a director previously perceived as a harmless artsy dreamer.

5. *I expect and I look for truthfulness*[69]

> Krystian said he didn't know if what I was doing was theatre, but that I should give it a chance — that is, not to think through theatre, but through myself. One should meet someone like him as early as possible.[70]

From the very beginning Warlikowski has leaned towards Western European theatre. The list of artists whose work he follows particularly closely includes: Karin Beier, Peter Stein, Roberto Ciulli, Martin Kušej and Frank Castorf. Such lavish display of foreign names for some critics is a perfect occasion for an accusation of intellectual snobbery. Interestingly, Warlikowski is perceived abroad as a revelation: a perfect example of

[69] Gruszczyński, *Ojcobójcy*, 90.
[70] Mieszkowski, „Do jutra…," 235-238.

individual Polish style, whereas in Poland he is discredited as a slave of Western models.

"Quant à l'action qui va commencer, elle se passe en Pologne, c'est-à-dire nulle part"[71]. The same can be said about locations in Warlikowski's productions. Such spaces of higher risk, where spectators are deprived of the comfort of a safety belt, could be found anywhere. The director does not spare his audience. He throws furious accusations at them. He whips them with stories exceeding the limits of human sensitivity and turns on all the lights in the audience so that everyone can see each other in that situation of vulnerability. All the elements of the show are so tightly closed that its intensity, flowing from actors to audience, reaches as far as the technicians' desks. Sometimes even they surrender to the strange energy oozing from the fictional universe. In such events mistakes in music or light direction occur. Such situations would be a disaster to a different director, and to Warlikowski they are manifestations of the production's life:

> There were shows which did not want to end. I left it to the audience, turned on all the lights but actors seemed not to stop acting, and I checked to see at which point it would end. Instead of finishing a show I prefer to blow it out, I often make a prolonged finale. (…) The end has to be a soft landing, slow exit from the space. The point is to change the reality by not changing the world or space, i.e. leave but stay in the same place. (…) The point is to abandon the exhausted models: the bell rings three times, the light goes off, the curtain falls, the show is over. Established moments, well-defined, act one, two, three, ice cream break. Those are inventions of middle class theatre. Let us forget about those bad habits. Theatre always differs from what is standard.[72]

People mentally whipped like that often feel the need for further contact with actors. They make conversations, smoke cigarettes by the stage door. Warlikowski, as well as the actors working with him, whether they wanted it or not, became a part of the Warsaw establishment. They are guests on morning television shows, they feature in magazines. They are cast in romantic comedies and soap operas. Their ensemble is often referred to as "Noah's Ark", and the director himself compares working on new productions to a trek in the Himalayas. With each succeeding show, the group becomes more and more in sync, they trust each other more and more:

---

[71] "As to the action which is about to begin, it takes place in Poland - that is to say, nowhere." Alfred Jarry, *Ubu Roi* (Paris: Editions Chemins de tr@verse, 2011), 9.
[72] Gruszczyński, *Szekspir i Uzurpator*, 36.

> When we are together we feel completely safe. Actors sometimes behave like special needs kids, get lost, drink, do things. Those husbands, fathers and mothers would never act like that if not for the feeling of security. They know that as a group we take care of one another. Everyone does what they want, there is no pressure, but we observe each other. We notice each other. People no longer notice each other. In fact, it is probably the great success of our group — the feeling that we can do anything. The best as well as the worst. No one shuts off their emotions from another person. I remember Jacek arguing with Renate and calling her a "Nazi nightingale"...[73]

Warlikowski never controls his actors. He never tells them how to play. He allows their imagination and sensitivity to construct a part. His way of working on productions lies at the opposite pole from the system of work represented by Krystian Lupa who always follows his actors very intensely. He is fully tuned to his production and becomes angry when his actors begin to act like "celebrities", because of premieres, festivals or performances abroad. At such times they are accused of betraying their common cause, which is the performance. Whereas his most talented student says:

> I do not have such bad suspicions about actors, or the need to interfere with their rhythm of a day to follow them around and change things. If something is not working out I understand that there is lack of energy, that you cannot fulfil every intention every night. It is a hard job. My productions are often very long. Like very long journeys, during which spectators also become tired.[74]

Tiredness, and often also mental exhaustion. For in these productions there is the unbelievable, simple beauty of presentation but also very intense emotionality. Warlikowski is not sentimental, he does not pick broken dreams with a stick. With all his sensitivity to other people's moods, his productions are extremely cold. The stage images he creates emanate bitter cold. Małgorzata Szczęśniak (who has been preparing stage designs for him from the very beginning — see start of chapter) uses very simple materials: plastic foil, mirrors, metal sheets, ceramic tiles. The stage places they create are mainly post-industrial spaces in which people are left on their own. However, the objects introduced in productions are borrowed from life, there is a real floor from an old cinema theatre, wooden doors from a dilapidated barn. Even a mug cannot be random

---

[73] Skwarczyńska, „Wolność wyboru...," 45.
[74] Gruszczyński, *Szekspir i Uzurpator*, 91.

because actors play differently with props which have the pulse of real life brought in from the outside. Such asceticism, combined with sophisticated, poetic language allows them to discuss the darkest regions. Sometimes we might get the feeling that these productions invoke evil spirits which can sense the blood of a person who is torn inside. Warlikowski always goes very deep into the structure of the texts he stages. He derails their obvious interpretations, shifts accents and points of support. He scratches the surface to look for meanings which had been covered by piles of academic analyses. He laughs at artists who safely touch only the surface of events. He believes there is always something beneath, that there are meanings which could not have been presented directly, and that no interpretation, no way of reading a text is permanently fixed forever.

CHAPTER FOUR

JAN KLATA

1. *Desperation can conquer the world*[1]

Probably the greatest value of Krystian Lupa's work as educator is that he has shown the ropes to artists who are fundamentally different. This obviously pertains to the most talented ones who, remembering their teacher's words, follow their own path. They look in places no one has looked in before. They ask questions never before asked. Additionally, they have the courage to disregard the consequences. They unceremoniously destroy systems of beliefs, and often have to pay a high price for it.

In the discussion about the theatre of Jan Klata, the term "Catholic Postmodernism"[2] is often used. He has a strong Christian background provided by his family home, but he is not favoured by conservative circles, perhaps because in his creative work he deals the blows in equal measure. When a situation or a subject he discusses calls for it, he leans left but keeps his rosary in his pocket. The shows he directs explode with multi-coloured, Catholic, right-wing views, mixed with references to mass culture. He is interested in the man against his historical background. He has a definite character of a commentator and is particularly sensitive to conservative, historical propaganda, which he refers to as "patriotic meta-Disneyland"[3].

Jan Klata was the first theatre director in Poland to be promoted as a celebrity of pop culture. As one reviewer wrote, he is a completely unrivalled director. There is no other artist in contemporary Polish theatre that would be able to join the discussion on the topics picked by Klata. It has its good as well as bad sides: "In the long run the sole absolute ruler

[1] Jan Klata, „O prawdzie i nieprawdzie, etyce i estetyce," *Notatnik teatralny*, no. 32-33 (2004): 76.

[2] Rafał Węgrzyniak, „Niepoprawny. Kontrowersje wokół wymowy ideowej przedstawień Klaty," *Notatnik teatralny*, no. 38 (2005): 25.

[3] Karolina Błaszkiewicz, „Wkurwili się ludzie na butną władzę, chcieli jej pokazać faka i pokazali," *naTemat*, December 6, 2015.

himself will become fed up with it (…) with being stroked to death exactly because there is no one else to stroke."[4]

He was born on 24 February 1973 in Warsaw. He comes from a good, well-educated family (his father was active in the underground Solidarity movement). He graduated from one of the best Warsaw high schools. As one actress described him, he is "A very knowledgeable rebel".[5] He began studying at the Directing Department of the National Academy of Dramatic Art in Warsaw, but after the second year moved to study in Krakow. He changed much in his life to be able to learn from Krystian Lupa. It is said that he went to see his production of *The Sleepwalkers* (based on the writings of Herman Broch) over twenty times. During his studies he became Lupa's assistant working on *Platonov* after Anton Chekhov, produced by students to complete a semester. Other students approached Lupa asking for advice, Klata from the very beginning wanted to be left alone. He has always worked alone.

> Krystian Lupa:
> I had mixed feelings about Klata. There was something distinct smouldering in him from the beginning. He had very sharp vision, was observant, with a special sense of humour. But sometimes he seemed like a nitwit or a con artist. I did not know him as well as the others. We did not meet in the first term when I dissect, recognise my students. (…) What he had to offer was extraordinary. It was a ready scene which could be pasted into the show right away. I did not change a thing, although — perhaps — the way I would have made the act would be different, maybe worse. (…) Janek was one of the people who definitely did not speak the language of cause and effect. You know, if we know someone longer we finally grow to like their illogicality, their intellectual absent-mindedness. However, if you know someone briefly, such behaviour is simply distressing and irritating. It impedes communication. You listen to what someone is telling you. You do not understand a thing and feel old, downtrodden (…) I had similar nasty thoughts after my conversations with Janek Klata. However, indeed, he blew me away with what he did with *Platonov*. It was the breakthrough in our relationship.
> - A breakthrough, but inefficient one. You first took Klata under your wing and then forgot all about him.
> - (silence)
> - Did I upset you with that question?

---

[4] Jacek Sieradzki, „Jan Klata, czyli pasja," *Notatnik teatralny*, no. 38 (2005): 110.

[5] Natalia Ligarzewska, „Relacje - rozmowa z Joanną Bogacką, Marcinem Czarnikiem, Grzegorzem Gzylem i Martą Kalmus," *Notatnik teatralny*, no. 38 (2005): 74.

> - No, I am just thinking. If you say something like that, perhaps it is true? (…) Perhaps I do have a vaguely guilty conscience regarding Janek, some regret. You provoked me to think strange thoughts. Now I realised that whenever I see a text published about Klata, I read it immediately. He interests me, annoys me, I expect something from him. I am counting on something.[6]

Today, Klata tends to stand in opposition to his teacher and rarely speaks about the early fascination with his theatre. Disappointment with Krakow, despite studying in the legendary Drama School and the long-awaited meeting with Krystian Lupa, proved enormous. Klata finished his studies in 1997. Unable to find a job in his profession he worked as a copywriter, music journalist and director of television talk-shows. He was frustrated when more and more of his peers left Poland looking for a job. He continued applying to theatres, to no effect. His only job offer was a as a porn director. His name did not appear on a playbill until the theatre season 2002/2003. He was offered the job of preparing a production in provincial Wałbrzych: he did not have much to lose, but he was aware that that might be his last chance. Therefore, he went to war, to fight for himself. He staged Gogol's *The Government Inspector*, transferring it into the reality of Communist Poland and drew everyone's attention.[7] Soon enough, Klata proved to be a star of Polish theatre which unexpectedly rose away from the great theatre centres of Krakow and Warsaw. The media eagerly promoted him as a destroyer of the *status quo* and an uncompromising patricide, one who has talent and his own opinions, one who carefully observes the reality around him, by listening, thinking, and filtering. In each of his productions there is a problem to consider, sometimes to ridicule it. He is committed when talking about what pains him in contemporary Poland. In *The Government Inspector* he presented the corruption-ridden times of Communism. In *H.* (after William Shakespeare's *Hamlet*), staged in the devastated Gdańsk Shipyard, he referred to the "abandoned" history of Poland, its opportunities and potential which were thoughtlessly thwarted by the introduction of capitalism. He is avidly interested in Polish history and politics, but does not produce allusive shows, ending with a wink to the audience.

---

[6] Łukasz Maciejewski, „Dziwny dynamit - rozmowa z Krystianem Lupą," *Notatnik teatralny*, no. 28 (2005): 6.
[7] The production was recorded and broadcast by the Polish Television.

> His strategy is to preach on stage about Poland.[8]

> Everything with the general slogan: to present contemporary Poland without illusion. Klata sees his Fatherland as a vast dumping ground of discredited values, from flashy nationalism to middle class hypocrisy, from primitive religious wars to the ambiguity of the European Community. He has been proclaimed almost a saviour of theatre, the righteous one, an unrivalled leader of the new generation who broke into high society with no mercy for anyone or anything.[9]

Klata openly criticises the Polish reality but does not enforce any ideology. He practices socially involved theatre, although after the system transformation of 1989 it has become unfashionable, to say the least. Participation in elections among Klata's generation is below average, whereas he has been at war from the very beginning: he is fighting to activate his audience, to raise issues of real importance to society. He makes it clear what he thinks about spectators who treat theatre as safe, Sunday entertainment:

> I do not invite such spectators to my performance, I think they should not come, and if they are already there, I think they should get out. We always have a few controversial scenes for them in the first 30 minutes. They can painlessly leave the venue and get some sleep elsewhere (...) They are people who do not want to change. They do not want to talk. And it is a problem for an artist. There is no communication between one hardliner and another hardliner. So we say goodbye, farewell Pamela. And we look for those for whom it is not too late. In everyone's life there are periods of *Sturm und Drang* which foster questions. Let us say you are eighteen, or almost forty, and you are still not satisfied with something mediocre. The period of stability comes later, when you begin to understand what it means to pay instalments: for a TV set, furniture, a Fiat 126. There are people who reach the final phase as early as before leaving high school. (...) If someone says that theatre is a temple of art, because we start a serious discussion with spectators, and that if we invite them to cake or to tea we cannot serve them with bad language or slap them in the face, then I disagree. Because I do not invite theatre spectators to tea. If you treat someone seriously, you talk to them also about what hurts. And if you

[8] Łukasz Drewniak, „Tsunami młodości," in *Strategie publiczne, strategie prywatne. Teatr polski 1990-2005*, edited by Tomasz Plata, 109. Izabelin: Świat literacki, 2006.

[9] Tadeusz Nyczek, „Teatr Klaty - rewolucja na niby," *Gazeta Wyborcza*, December 17, (2005): 18-19.

want to deceive someone, you do not tell them everything, let's not worry grandma, right?[10]

One of the reviewers compared him to "edukators" from the film by Hans Weingartner,[11] in which young people break into luxurious mansions, but do not steal anything. They simply rearrange the interior, for instance, by throwing a grand piano into the pool. Causing anxiety is simply more effective than causing bloodshed in the streets…[12]

When Klata comes to a rehearsal he knows exactly what he wants. Everyone agrees that he is not an easy collaborator. On the other hand, they stay with him, and bring his visions to life with curiosity. When he takes the rehearsals on stage he has a ready vision of the entire performance. He defines acting tasks precisely. He wants nothing more than their accurate implementation. He is not an experimenting director who collaborates with his actors in the creative process.

Ryszard Węgrzyn (assistant director):
On principle, he does not welcome objections to his ideas. What he does is brilliant, and protests evoke anxiety. In private conversations he also always has an opinion on every subject and is ready to voice it authoritatively. Privately, when he is wrong, he simply changes the subject or leaves off in mid-sentence. At work it is slightly different — if someone dares to continue a dispute, he begins to listen and eventually says "yes" or "no". Usually it is "no". (…) He is one of the people who educates by yelling and lashing.[13]

Marta Kalmus (Ophelia in *H.*):
Klata is busy with other issues and does not get involved in the meticulous work with actors. He does not want to participate in all the tiny acting problems. He expects us to come to him with a final result. That result is crystallised at the third stage, at the stage of final rehearsals. We often begin them with a feeling of helplessness and panic, because actors working with Klata do not mature to a part gradually but in leaps, from table work to the first situation, from the first situation to the first dress-rehearsal. I even sometimes comfort myself with the thought that there is

[10] Łukasz Drewniak, „W oku salonu – rozmowa z Janem Klatą," *Przekrój*, February 17, (2005): 48-51.
[11] *The Edukators*, 2004.
[12] Jolanta Kowalska, „Egzorcysta," *Notatnik teatralny*, no. 38 (2005): 85.
[13] Katarzyna Migdałowska, „Do Timbuktu - rozmowa z Danutą Marosz, Ryszardem Węgrzynem, Dariuszem Majem, Andrzejem Szubskim," *Notatnik teatralny*, no. 38 (2005): 56.

no need to panic because I will not achieve the final result until the dress-rehearsal.[14]

Marcin Czarnik (Hamlet in *H.*):
Klata deals with actors mainly at the start of the project. He looks for as much material as possible in the smallest acting tasks. What is more, he brings blood and humanity to many "paper" characters. Working with Klata, at one point of rehearsals, I experienced the same thing I did working with Lupa. A terrible need to go on stage and rehearse. To test what we have discussed at the table. That tension disappears at some point, obviously. Janek deals with other matters. Like Lupa, he is first and foremost a director of shows. For both of them rhythms, images, music and set design are important. In fact, at some point Klata leaves his actors on their own. (…) Everything we do with him, so hectic, is what is most creative! By the way, what Klata does is nothing. If you could see Lupa bawling us out…[15]

Joanna Bogacka (Gertrude in *H.*):
What do I think about the young man? Klata is a brilliant boy, young enough to be my child. Sometimes when I look at him and watch his reactions I have a feeling that he has not gone through adolescence. But perhaps it is his asset, because eventually every artist has to have a child and a certain naïveté within. It is certainly a very interesting theatre personality. Obviously, I can see some flaws in him. For instance, he is impatient with actors. He expects a result right away, now. Like a child. (…) You have to work for a result. And he does not understand it and simply becomes angry. I ask him, for example, where an emotion should come from, and he starts yelling: "Don't worry where it comes from! It has to be there! It has to be there and that's it!" I suspect that when Klata speaks to us he knows what he wants to say. He just cannot communicate it. So I collect all his sentences thrown away over a few weeks and gather them to make a whole. Later I go on stage and he shouts overjoyed: "Yes, yes, that's exactly it!"[16]

He draws extensively on pop culture, graphic novels and music videos. In his production of Aeschylus' *The Oresteia*, Apollo was presented as Robbie Williams. He filtered *King Lear* through TV series *The Borgias*, and King Ubu sat on a throne resembling the one in *Game of Thrones*. He builds his narrations dynamically, as if he were trying to shorten the distance between spectators' synapses. In interviews, he always emphasises that music is the most important element of his productions, and actors

[14] Ligarzewska, „Relacje…," 70.
[15] Ligarzewska, „Relacje…," 70-74.
[16] Ligarzewska, „Relacje…," 74.

who work with him say that it is a very rare thing for a theatre artist to have such vast knowledge of music. He often constructs the meaning of an entire scene around a carefully selected piece. Often, the piece's original context and circumstances surrounding its creation define the meaning of a situation between characters on stage. The production of *To Damascus* by August Strindberg began with David Bowie's *Space Oddity*. A chorus of children who performed it replaced the church choir from Strindberg's play. Klata directed associations against the religious context. He mainly wanted his spectators to listen to the meaning of Bowie's lyrics, written about human loneliness. Klata long ago admitted that as a teenager he preferred going to rock concerts than to the theatre. In line with the theatre tradition of "great predecessors" he lists directors he had assisted (Jerzy Grzegorzewski, Krystian Lupa, Jerzy Jarocki), but in doing that always emphasises that his masters are not people who create theatre, but rather Glenn Gould, Charles Mingus, Captain Beefheart, The Velvet Underground, Frank Zappa, Can or Robert Wyatt:

> Because they were doing something unusual, they were honest with themselves, and at the same time had the courage to destroy something and create something new. Their first expectations were of themselves. (…) I think one needs to be ruthless about oneself, and about what one wants to achieve. The bar must be set high and perhaps in a different place than others set theirs (…) This kind of honesty with oneself should be absolute. The main condition is: if you have nothing to say, don't bug me.[17]

> My parents made sure I also received an education in this field but, alas, I turned out to be stupidly insubordinate (which was the case in many other fields) and I ended my musical education after a few years of playing the piano. I also refused to practice music at the time of *Sturm und Drang* — during the first year of high school I was invited to sing in a death metal band, Last Crusade, but I was no longer interested in that, and it is a shame — because perhaps I could have experienced initiation as an active musician. I regret it, it would have been an interesting experience. I did not manage to do that, and perhaps that is why I became a director. I am simply too shy to stand on stage on my own and be the one who plucks the strings or sings, so I cast others in that role… I have never dreamt of becoming an actor, but I envy musicians, and I feel much closer to them than to theatre creators. But regarding that obsession with sounds, I do not know where it came from. It had already started by the end of primary school. On Polskie Radio's "Trójka" and "Dwójka" channels, journalists would broadcast full albums and tell us what tape we needed to buy to

[17] Dorota Kardasińska, „Dorosnąć do widowni - rozmowa z Janem Klatą," *Notatnik teatralny*, no. 32-33 (2004): 64-65.

> record them, as well as after how many minutes we had to turn the tape over. I asked my parents not to turn the light on when they came into the room, because the switch would be heard in the recording… I terrorised my family this way a few nights a week. (…) I waited so impatiently, with my ear to the radio, to nervously press "record", and it was a real tragedy if the tape got stuck or I did not make it in time to turn the tape and half a piece was not recorded… (…) I will never throw away those hundreds of carefully hand-labelled, original Sony and TDK cassettes: title, band, year of release, all pieces in order, with duration time — the time was not always given, but I always wrote it down, precisely to the second. I had to write it, I do not know why; it took a lot of time. I probably had nothing better to do. (…) The advantage was that we appreciated that music. Today, you can go online, find the website of any radio station, define the mood, pace, enter "artists similar to"… and twenty-five suggestions pop up. When we can see five hundred best records from Mali with one key stroke, we no longer appreciate it. I will probably sound like an old fart, who says that there were good sides to Communism, but it is a fact that we could get a lot of good music on the radio then, but not any more. Everything is becoming homogenous, which is particularly noticeable when we go abroad. When we went to Buenos Aires with *The Danton Case*, there were few shops or bars which did not play the latest hit by Shakira. In Düsseldorf everywhere they play smooth jazz versions of classic rock pieces — sometimes the most penetrating and dramatic ones. I am waiting for a soft rendering of U2's *Sunday Bloody Sunday*… There is total inflation.[18]

In the archives of the Internet we can find many photographs of Jan Klata. In one of them, taken by Andrzej Banaś, Klata is sitting on the back of a stuffed deer, wearing a bright pink jacket and sunglasses, and has the typical mohawk hairstyle. Only a few years before he was throwing accusations at journalists preying on the death of the Polish Pope.[19] Soon, he became one of the most important creators in Polish theatre. At the time the photograph was taken he had been acting director of the National Stary Theatre in Krakow. That photograph perfectly captures the phenomenon of Jan Klata as an artistic personality, and at the same time refutes all

---

[18] Anna Róża Burzyńska, „Druga strona singla – rozmowa z Janem Klatą," *Didaskalia*, no. 97-98 (2010): 2-3.

[19] He even devoted to them a play which he wrote and staged. *Grapfruit's Smile* (premiere: 6 June 2003, The Polski Theatre, Wrocław) was inspired by a press note about a terrace in Rome overlooking St. Peter's Square, rented by a television station well in advance in anticipation of a life coverage of Pope John Paul II's death.

stereotypical images of Polish Catholic mentality: "This is me, Jan Klata the Ambivalent. What am I to do, move to some mental Düsseldorf?"[20]

2. A long, not such a long, time ago… Polish history in the productions by Jan Klata

In any interview or any artistic statement of Jan Klata we can see that we are dealing with someone uncompromising who strongly defends his opinions. He is a very critical observer of the times he lives and creates in. In his productions he likes to provoke and point to painful areas omitted by the history books, and easily turned away from and quickly forgotten. He mercilessly deals with Polish martyrology and national heroes who treated dying for their country as if they were immortal characters in a computer game:

> Newsweek: Do you feel robbed of your patriotism?
> Jan Klata: I am not that stupidly perverse to reply: "No, not at all". Yes, I do feel robbed because patriotism has been appropriated by followers of the cult of the dead, and I am not one of them.
> Newsweek: They say Poland is governed by coffins.
> Jan Klata: They govern our discussion. They enforce their sacrificial visions, constantly force us to refer to them, define ourselves with them, pay homage. Our history is an account of wrong-doings. Our community are the dead and the fallen. It is catastrophically sad (…) We keep making the same mistakes. As if we were intentionally collecting heroes for the Pantheon of the national dead. Thanks to our sacrifices we can feel the best. Polish patriotism is constructed around messianism. Around suffering. Christ also failed, after all. He had to die, so we should die as well. Perhaps after that the world would fall to its knees before us, and not be indifferent towards us. Our patriotism continues to be pompous and detached from reality. Based on myths and messianic fantasies.[21]

Observing the issues which appear in Jan Klata's productions we could venture writing a "short history of Poland" based on them. That is why in this chapter I will stray from the chronology of premieres and adopt a "historical" order of events presented in his shows. This will allow us to see what image of Poland is created by one of our most talented Polish directors.

---

[20] Joanna Derkaczew, „Żądam dostępu do włazu – rozmowa z Janem Klatą," *Gazeta Wyborcza*, November 21, 2011.

[21] Aleksandra Pawlicka, „Kibolski patriotyzm – rozmowa z Janem Klatą," *Newsweek*, August 25, (2015): 16-20.

Well then, from the top…

The Trilogy: 3 parts, 6 volumes, 2603 pages — 1 show.[22] *The Trilogy* is a historical novel by Henryk Sienkiewicz. It was written at the time of Poland's partition.[23] By reminding people of the heroic times in Poland's history, Sienkiewicz wanted to strengthen his fellow countrymen's national awareness. For many Polish people it is a compulsory element of their home library; however, just as many have not managed to read past the first chapter…[24] As compulsory school reading it has haunted Polish youth for generations. One of the main obstacles is the novel's dated language. Additionally (as it was written at a very specific time and historical context), it is irritating to the contemporary reader because of its intrusive, right-wing vision of Polish tradition and history.

It is set in the seventeenth century during the First Polish Republic. It spans the Khmelnytsky Uprising (1648), through the Polish-Swedish wars (1655-1660), to the beginning of the war between Poland and Turkey (ending with the victorious battle of Khotyn in 1673). The plots in all three parts are similar in character. A beautiful woman in love with a heroic Polish knight is captured by his rival traitor to the homeland, obviously.[25] Dramatic lives of the characters, filled with kidnappings, duels and impasses, always have a happy ending (although sometimes the main character is forced to make a tragic choice, between love of a woman and love of his country).

The beginning of the show is the beginning of war. The Turks are invading Poland. They burn everything in sight, murdering people and turning churches into mosques. There are old hospital beds on stage with blankets and dirty pillows scattered around. A field hospital? The characters are not wearing historical costumes. The costumes they are wearing are not uniforms; they look as if they come from a charity shop.

---

[22] Original title of the production: *Trylogia*
Date and place of premiere: February 21, 2009, The Helena Modrzejewska Stary Theatre, Krakow
Direction: Jan Klata
Set design: Justyna Łagowska
Music (music arrangement): Jan Klata.

[23] Sienkiewicz wrote his oeuvre in the years 1884-1888.

[24] Even the production dramaturge (Sebastian Majewski) admitted in one interview that he had not read *The Trilogy* before he began working on its adaptation for the stage.

[25] The characters are fictitious; however, they were constructed around historic figures.

Among them is she — the beautiful Helena (Małgorzata Gałkowska) — and he — Skrzetuski (Jerzy Grałek). Klata went against the grain in casting. Against the actors' looks and Polish people's idealistic visions of their favourite characters. The young and handsome Skrzetuski in Klata's production is played by a 60-year-old actor. The whole scene is depicted lightly, with no trace of a tacky love story. The director consistently led his actors "parallelly" to the narrative of the novel. Texts of their dialogues were interwoven with descriptive elements, which is why in the conversation between Helena and Skrzetuski, the actress keeps interrupting herself to add: "Again the princess raised her eyes, and her glance met the manly and noble face of the young soldier..."[26] The director and actors' intelligent sense of humour created a distance from the "archnovel". When Skrzetuski asked cuckoos to tell him the good fortune of how many sons he and Helena would have, the entire forest filled with song... and Helena, not sure what to believe, tried counting the birds' calls on her fingers, constantly losing track and having to start over. Even two hours later she will enter the stage still counting: one, two, three, four, five... But the idyllic story of lovers must be interrupted. Helena is kidnapped by Bohun (Zbigniew Kaleta) a young Cossack, secretly in love with the beautiful girl. The kidnapping scene is a directing masterpiece. The dynamics of a stage situation, borrowed from action films, is based mainly on music: loud sirens are coming from speakers above the stage (*Anastasia* by Laibach was used in this scene as a music background), spotlights cut through the darkness so that even the audience can feel branches strike their faces as the main characters' horses are racing through the storm at full gallop.

Settings change as easily as hospital beds are moved. When Helena was in Bohun's captivity, Skrzetuski took part in the defence of Zbarazh (which in fact took place during the Khmelnytsky uprising between 10 July and 22 August 1649. Zbarazh was defended by approximately 9,000 soldiers of the Polish-German army, and joint armies of Cossacks and Tatars, approximately 110,000 men in all). In Zbarazh, barricades are built of beds and mattresses. Pillows jump high in the air every time there is an explosion. The wind of history carries sheets over the heads of defenders. The visual side of that scene brings to mind the images of barricades built during the Warsaw Uprising. To emphasise this association, an actress dressed in a costume typical of girls who were liaison officers in the uprising appears crawling between the beds. In Sienkiewicz's plot half a

---

[26] Henryk Sienkiewicz, *With Fire and Sword: An Historical Novel of Poland and Russia* (Boston: 1894), 39.

million enemy soldiers were to collect at the walls of Zbarazh. The defenders were "an island against the sea…" The characters, looking over bed frames, count each enemy separately, on their fingers. They lose count, start over. Once again sirens are heard above the stage. We can hear the speakers play *Fortress Europe* by Asian Dub Foundation, a British band. After all, Poland at the time was referred to as *Antemurale Christianitatis*… The director plays with the convention of theatre. The entire image is a convention but the words of his actors describing the armies coming to the walls are moving and even though the scene looks like great fun, no one in the audience is laughing.

Klata promised to place some provocative motifs in the first 30 minutes of his shows, to scare away those who came to his performance "by accident". In that scene those spectators merely began to fidget with anxiety. The whole scene was commentated upon by the Black Madonna of Częstochowa, Our Lady from the most iconic Polish religious painting, and in fact an actress (Ewa Kolasińska) who put her head in the picture. At the premiere, spectators did not begin ostentatiously leaving until the scene in which the Madonna grabbed one of the "prodigal sons of Polish history" by the hair. And the creators only wanted to portray the particular belief of the Polish people that Our Lady treats them in a special way. She leans out of the picture to grab Kmicic (Krzysztof Globisz), the troublemaker, with a mother's affection, like a son who has come back home with his trousers ripped.

In *The Trilogy* Islam, Orthodoxy, Catholicism, Evangelicalism and Judaism constantly interact. The world of Sarmatians at the time was a great rich and colourful mosaic of nations and religions. Just as Bohun earlier on, also the son of the Tatar leader, Azya Tughai Bey (played by the same actor), is another interference with the Polish macrocosm. He appears on stage as a dervish. His gown is whirling in the air. There is beauty and majesty, but also growing dread in his dance moves. Azya gives a long monologue in Tatar. He might even be right, but who is going to understand him? Brought up among the Poles he switched sides to join the Turks and commit a bloody massacre of Polish commanders. Everything happened methodically on stage. Azya killed each character with a shot in the back of the head fired with a finger gun. Actors come and stand before him like Polish officers during the Katyn massacre in World War II. Everyone kneels down awaiting death, but in the show their faces are bright with ecstatic joy. We could even say that they are eager to give up their lives. Klata mercilessly points out our national, idiotic idealisations of death for the country. The sequence (accompanied by a religious song from the speakers: *Bless Our Free Homeland, Lord*) lasts for quite a while, as all the dead get up a second after they are shot and stand in line "for the next death". They are like computer-game heroes. They can be attributed with an indefinite number of lives. It is not difficult to cause scandal by directing a scene referencing the Katyn massacre, obvious to Polish spectators, especially among right-wing spectators: because national martyrology and memory of Polish heroes is tarnished.

After references to Katyn and the Warsaw Rising, the scene of Azya Tughai Bey's execution is the most appalling moment in the entire show. All the lights go off on stage and in the auditorium. The description is read out off stage, a long, graphic, horrific description. Imagination begins to work and present everything more clearly in the dark. There is time in the dark for each word to resonate. There is enough time for every adjective to be followed by a realistic image. We feel that there is a smell of leather straps and horse sweat in the air:

> The horses moved: the straightened ropes pulled Azya's legs. In a twinkle, his body was drawn along the earth and met the point of the stake. Then the point commenced to sink in him, and something dreadful began, something repugnant to nature and the feelings of man! The bones of the unfortunate moved apart from one another; his body gave way in two directions; pain indescribable, so awful that it almost bounds on some monstrous delight, penetrated his being. The stake sank more and more deeply. Azya fixed his jaws, but he could not endure; his teeth were bared in a ghastly grin, and out of his throat came the cry, "A! a! a!" like the croaking of a raven.[27]

Sienkiewicz's prose is like an endless Bayeux tapestry. The novel is dated, touching on issues of patriotism, honour and fidelity, issues which have to be defined by each generation separately according to their appropriate contexts. The novel is filled with a great number of events, characters and the entire historical background of seventeenth century Poland, which all had to be fitted onto the stage. The process of editing and stitching began. Jan Klata, and Sebastian Majewski who worked with him as dramaturge, created a modern play, daringly performed. The dynamic narrative suddenly burst out of a depressing school text. Assumptions that all spectators must know the novel led to a certain amount of theatrical shorthand… Duels acted out with imaginary weapons, swishes of blades heard only because of actors' whistling; a prison merely hinted at by a rhythmical light from a guard tower; a metal bed from the

[27] Henryk Sienkiewicz, *Pan Michael: An Historical Novel of Poland, the Ukraine, and Turkey* (Boston: 1889), 426-427.

field hospital, used for building barricades which in another scene will serve as a sleigh in which a young nobleman will be trying to seduce a girl. There is an American western aesthetic, with a pinch of Monty Python (because it would be difficult to introduce the entire Polish cavalry on stage). Klata, by venturing to stage this work, created a perfect show about mortals who are forced by their experiences to realise the heroic myth.

In *The Trilogy*, through references to the Katyn massacre and the Warsaw Rising, a particular problem appeared in Jan Klata's creative work: World War II. To describe the complicated Polish-German relationship, funny stereotypes, and still-open wounds, Klata chose Shakespeare's bloodiest tragedy: *Titus Andronicus*.[28] He invited actors from the Staatsschauspiel in Dresden[29] to cooperate, and thus the production was simultaneously performed in Polish and German. The characters were clearly divided from the very start of work on the show: the Germans become the Romans, because of the Holy Roman Empire of the German Nation, eagles, processions with torches, and because it was a cruel and very ambitious empire. It was a nation which mercilessly killed its slaves. It builds endless motorways in order to use them to perform *blitzkrieg* on entire Eastern Europe/Land of the Goths: the source of a cheap and dumb work force, the "Potato Land", in which someone ought finally to carry out a civilising mission.

What was taken from Shakespeare was mainly the clash of two cultures. A clash of their visions of themselves. Stereotypical, German discipline clashed with cavalryman's flair of cunning Polacks. "The Polish-German Manual" enclosed in the production brochure introduced popular Polish-German stereotypes. Is every Polish woman a nurse going to Germany to find work, and was every German man a member of the *Hitlerjugend*? The Germans are perceived in Poland as thoroughly organised, lacking sense of humour and drinking gallons of beer during the Oktoberfest. Poland is associated by the Germans with a tacky imitation of Italian religiousness, nice babysitters and cheap labour working on German building sites. Romans in Klata's production are wearing white T-shirts with military emblems and shiny leather riding boots. The Poles/Goths are running

---

[28] Original title of the production: *Titus Andronikus*
Date and place of premiere: September 15, 2012, The Polski Theatre, Wrocław
Direction: Jan Klata
Set design: Justyna Łagowska
Music (music arrangement): Jan Klata.

[29] Dresden premiere: September 28, 2012.

around wearing unbuttoned Hawaiian shirts (bringing to mind “a chav dream holiday”).

The main axis of the show is the cruelty of war, in accordance with Shakespeare’s concept: the Goths all die one by one. However, Klata makes the point that the Goth army was simply cleverly used by strategically thinking Romans. The Goths fulfilled their task and were sent back to their own, savage land. In this way, Klata was trying to provoke his audience: is this to be the fate of all new member states of the European Union?

Klata did not bother making any post-dramatic reinterpretations of Shakespeare’s concept. He left the main thread unchanged and connected it to additional ones. The story of Titus Andronicus is most of all a parable about the cruelty of war crimes. It is the year 1939 on stage. After the “September campaign” ended, Titus returns to Berlin with his troops. The song *Over Fire and the Void* by the death metal band Behemoth attacking from the speakers creates an atmosphere of ongoing war. We are in for a long sequence in which all 21 coffins with Titus’s sons are carried on stage. A perfect organisation of statehood is created with the bodies of fallen soldiers. Their coffins are arranged so as to create a part of the playing space for the actors. Throughout the play they will silently remind us about their existence, because our dead participate in all Polish-German conversations…

Titus (Wolfgang Michalek) and Tamora (Ewa Skibińska) are two opposites. Tamora, an uncompromising, proud Queen of the Goths, a frantic mother who lost her child, but also a woman aware of her sexual attractiveness. Her pain frees aggression and a need for bloody vengeance. We do not know which force dominates, which pain provokes her to act most: a defeated queen, a mother who lost a child, or a rejected lover? At one point, however, she reaches her limit. She is no longer able to make a level-headed assessment of her own actions. Emotions win over her carefully prepared intrigue. Private vengeance becomes her only goal. There is suicidal determination in her. Facing her stands Titus, a man going through a mid-life crisis, who has lost it all. A workaholic who lost his family because he lost himself in what his profession required. When he felt burnt out and wanted to go back to the family, there was no longer anyone around. He is left with only a daughter. In view of the events which take place, his only salvation is in madness. In such circumstances, a final settlement between neighbours will never be possible. Especially since all the strings of events are pulled by the diabolic Aaron the Moor (Wojciech Ziemiański) — a force that obeys no one.

The story of Titus did not exhaust Klata's attempts to tackle the subject of war which claimed many thousands more victims. He prepared a multimedia project: *Triumph of the Will*, which was presented to the public on 1 August 2007 at the Warsaw Rising Museum in Warsaw. The work was skilfully attuned to the characteristic interior of the Museum. The audience was placed under the replica of a B-24 Liberator bomber hanging from the ceiling. Three screens were hung on side walls, showing the screenings simultaneously. Dead bodies of Wehrmacht soldiers were lying right beneath them.

The show began with a red light imitating fire glow. Wagner's music accompanied fragments of newsreels showing the demolition of Warsaw, a ceremonial parade, when German army entered the Polish capital and fragments of the film *Triumph des Willens* directed by Leni Riefenstahl. The show did not have a linear plot or specific characters. A collage of images and music was combined with texts of memoirs and letters of German soldiers. Klata, preparing for the project, read hundreds of documents from the Museum collection. Eventually he decided to present the Rising from the Nazi perspective. When he read letters of German officers he was surprised how enthusiastic they were about the act of destruction, which they directly caused. They were filled with ecstatic delight. As well-grounded intellectuals, they looked at the reality around them from the perspective of art, music, literature… One of the officers in a letter to his family wrote that he found a collection of poems by Heine and Goethe at the house of a Polish professor. With delight he described the night he watched the burning city looking up from the book. It was with those poems that he observed the entire horror of the extermination: the smoke, fires, explosions and a sunset over burning Warsaw. He did not notice that faced with such unbelievable carnage poetry, even of the greatest kind, becomes merely naive talentless writing. But this is one conclusion by contemporary people, who watch newsreels showing the burning city and listen to his words.

When Adolf Hitler first learned of the rising in Warsaw he ordered all its citizens to be murdered and the city destroyed. Part of that large-scale extermination was the so-called "Wola Massacre" by General Heinrich Reinefarth as main commander. Between 5-10 August 1944, fifty thousand citizens of the Wola area were murdered (the number can be compared to the number of victims murdered in Treblinka during 1942). There are Reinefarth's reports in which he helplessly admitted having more prisoners than ammunition to shoot them with… Klata showed his computer animated face on screen together with extensive quotes from an interview. After the war, a Polish journalist managed to find Reinefarth, who was considered not guilty (after a trial lasting many years). He patiently listened to the confession of an old man convinced of his innocence, and who was clearly repressing the memory of the crime he committed. At the same time, he was complaining about the "unimaginable" trauma he and his family suffered throughout the twenty years of investigation. (He never served any punishment for the crimes in Warsaw. He received a large general's pension until his death in 1979.) One of the most shocking fragments of the interview was the moment in which he told how in the city ruins he suddenly heard a German colonel play a miraculously saved grand piano. He immediately had his aide bring his violin…

The show ended with an image of a girl with her arm extended in the "Heil Hitler" salute. There were computer animated red butterflies flying from her hand. After a while, swastikas appeared on their wings. Memories of the Poles who survived the rising were read out off-screen, fragments of memories about stains of human blood in streets and children burnt alive…

Triumph of the Will is mainly associated with the film by Leni Riefenstahl. What constituted the triumph of the will was the total war initiated by a man who became leader of Nazi Germany. What also constituted the triumph of the will was the hopeless resistance against the invader which remains controversial to this day:

> Cezary Kosiński: You said: "We should commemorate the end of the rising not its beginning."
> Jan Klata: Yes. October 3, the day of surrender. If we want to treat our history in a responsible and honest way it is obvious that we should venerate the memory of involuntary victims and not honour the commanding officers responsible for the death of the city and its people. How many times can we repeat that the Warsaw Rising was an absolute embarrassment in terms of tactics and strategy? The greatest catastrophe in the history of our nation, offered to my countrymen in the hope that the world would not remain indifferent. Only one in twenty-five freedom fighters had a gun, there were only food reserves for three days, tops, and the commanders were well aware of that. But the names of the commanders are commemorated on squares and streets, whereas for what they did, they should have been hanged. It is high time to finally acknowledge that certain things we worship have a second, usually very painful, shameful and unwanted side.
> Cezary Kosiński: In 2007 you directed a show at the Warsaw Rising Museum entitled *The Triumph of the Will*.
> Jan Klata: It was exactly about the enormously high price we had to pay for the rising. However, the experience of the following years proved that we are unable to draw conclusions from the past. It is beautiful and sweet to be exploded for one's homeland, because later there are dead heroes to

> be mourned. Admiral Nelson also died at Trafalgar, but at least he won the battle and saved his country. But us? We worship defeats and failures. The greater the hecatomb, the better. A massacre of children and civilians marks the peak of our patriotic pride. And we will not be cured of this paranoia, because we continue to tread in the same blood-stained rut. We are building our patriotism on the foundation of great sacrifice, which hides an assumption very harmful to the Poles that we are simply not good enough for anything else. Every sensitive person would fall for that. I am from Warsaw, I know the drill. I as well, when I go for walks with my children, can hear the crying from beneath the asphalt road, of those people who died here. (…) what are they crying? "Be like us!", or "Be smarter than us!"?[30]

The Polish people like to boast that they never collaborated with the Nazis. It is not entirely true. Not many Polish people have heard of "Goralenvolk". This part of the history of German occupation was effectively repressed from Polish history books. People do not discuss that subject in the Podhale region. It is never mentioned. In early September 1939, when the army of the Third Reich occupied the entire area of the Tatra mountains (including Podhale), the Gorals (Górale) who lived there were separated from the Polish nation, as the so-called "East Aryans" — a nation of German origins. On 12 November 1939 Hans Frank arrived in Zakopane, and the visit was to officially confirm "the liberation of the Gorals from the oppression of Polish authorities". The Gorals' national autonomy was acknowledged. Separate kennkarten were issued for them and they were allowed to form an autonomous administration (an SS battalion was even created). A "Goralenvolk state" existed and collaborated with the Nazis until 1944, when the approaching troops of the Red Army forced the leaders of the newly-formed state to flee to Germany. (They never had the courage to return to Podhale.)

Jan Klata together with dramaturge Sebastian Majewski prepared a radio play based on that story (often referred to as "the disgrace of Podhale"). Combining threads from Tadeusz Miciński's novel, *Nietota. The Mystery Book of the Tatra Mountains*, and the history of the Gorals' collaboration with the Nazi Germans, they created a "sound séance" entitled *Nietotas (Non-beings)*.[31] They touched on a problem which had not been discussed in Poland, and which has not been touched by a deeper historical debate. However, the creators' intention was not to bring back

---

[30] Cezary Michalski, "Guślarz w mundurze Jungera – rozmowa z Janem Klatą," *Newsweek*, September 20, 2008.

[31] The play was first broadcast on 16 December 2013 at 9:05 p.m. by Radio Krakow.

uncomfortable facts and names, but rather to think about the mechanisms which lead to the tabooisation of uncomfortable events in nations' histories. How a community is developed around omitted facts. How our memory moderates our history. How two people can have two different memories of the same event and interpret it differently. After all sweeping uncomfortable facts under the carpet is not only a Polish speciality.

There was therefore no judgement or stigmatising, just "figure skating around historical facts", as one reviewer wrote,[32] presented in such a way as not to describe the story from the perspective of the twenty-first century or the year 1939 (because the latter is simply impossible: We cannot understand those people and their choices, just as we can never fully understand why they ventured a Rising which was bound to fail). The creators began with a documentary and moved on to an artistic form to create a surreal story, a little grotesque, a little fairytale like.

Radio Krakow made a live broadcast, as if straight from the mind of Witalis Wieder (Roman Gancarczyk), one of the Goralenvolk commanders. He was hanged in a mountain pass from a butcher's hook — he did not even merit a bullet from the Polish Underground State activists. They hung a note around his neck stating that this is the way each traitor ends. And the spruces growing round about stand ready to hang his comrades who managed to escape to Germany. The wind howls in radio sets. Wieder gives an account of his past, even as his life escapes him. However, Free Electrone (Katarzyna Krzanowska) appears, liberated as the result of a chemical reaction caused by fear and the iron of the hook upon which Witalis had been hanged. Her appearance in the ether of the radio play opens a metaphysical space. Witalis dies and next to him appears the spirit of the dead Włodek (Adam Nawojczyk) — Vladimir Ilyich Lenin. His life is just being completed. His image on a red flag is moving West, together with the Red Army troops. The NKVD has installed its administration on Polish ground, but they are still a "work in progress": all in all there is not yet much to talk about…

Our heroes await eternal damnation. Witalis will hang from the butcher's hook till the end of the world, and Lenin will be eternally torn by wind and rain pulling the flag with his image (after all, as he complains to other characters and listeners, he does not like wind or cold and had always wanted to be a hot Italian lover…). They are the *nietotas* of the title, heroes who did not make it. They both have to repent for their sins so that Witalis can rest peacefully underground and Vladimir can move to the

[32] Łukasz Drewniak, "Nietoty," *Radio Krakow*, December 17, 2013, http://web1.radiokrakow.pl/kultura/nietoty-recenzja-lukasza-drewniaka/.

Mausoleum. They have to do something useful for humanity, which is why they set up a "Company of universal collaborators". The company will offer group disclosure of sins, debate and redemption. As universal collaborators they will be available for rent, spitting, humiliation and spectacular punishment. The offer is addressed to all nations that had ever chosen collaboration, betrayal or other disgraceful actions which with time became traumas or taboos. Now, every community will get a chance at redemption and liberation. Such a highly ethical and humane mission surely deserves a Nobel Peace Prize.

Within two minutes of the advert's appearing online the first potential clients appear: Norwegians, who would finally like to be reconciled with the fact that their country collaborated with the Nazis. Following soon after them, Croats came to rent a "universal collaborator" to make amends for the faults of Ante Pavelić. Our heroes set off on international tour. They allow crowds to enjoy executions which will let them forget their nation's guilt. There is also a commission from Poland. The Poles want to wash away the blame of collaboration with the Soviet invader, crowned by the introduction of martial law in 1981. They want to get rid of the collaborator, General Wojciech Jaruzelski, the betrayer of the nation who was never prosecuted by a court or a tribunal. This is why the Polish nation is begging to rent a "universal collaborator". In return they offer a really impressive execution tree — a palm tree in the centre of their capital city,[33] and a marble plaque commemorating the whole event. However, it is winter in Poland. It is grey and sad; therefore, our heroes decide to remain in warm Cambodia (which receives redemption for Pol Pot's activity from Lenin himself). Unfortunately, they have to regretably decline: "Dear Poles, you are on your own."

The text of the play, written by Sebastian Majewski, provided actors with plenty of opportunities. The intensely metaphorical language opened the imagination allowing every association. Klata, on the other hand, had unlimited room for experimenting in constructing a sound space: mountain winds, howling, piercing, ominous; echoes, polyphonies, splinters and reflexions of sounds were rolling throughout the entire impossible historical journey. A play prepared for radio was transformed into a "sound séance", a mixture of forgotten history with fictitious images unrestrained by any rules of probability.

Towards the end of World War II everyone was well aware that to go back to the pre 1 September 1939 situation would be impossible. From 4 -

[33] An allusion to an art project by Joanna Rajkowska, "Greetings from Jerusalem Avenue", which involved an artificial date palm planted on the Charles de Gaulle roundabout in Warsaw.

11 February 1945 there was a conference in Yalta of an anti-Hitler coalition, the so-called Big Three (Stalin, Roosevelt and Churchill), to discuss Europe's post-war reorganisation. One of the problems discussed was the shape of new borders. They were established using three symbolic matches, which could be easily moved over the map of Europe. None of the leaders making those decisions at the time were reflective enough to consider that the people who lived in the areas under discussion could not be as easily relocated. Still, the lives of two million people were simply moved to a "more convenient" location.[34] Alluding to the contemporary practice of selling football players between clubs, Jan Klata created a show, *Transfer*, describing the consequences of those decisions.[35]

Because (like *Titus Andronicus*) we are dealing with a problem between two nations, the production was created in collaboration with the Berlin Hebbel-am-Ufer Theatre.[36] In addition to the professional actors who played Joseph Stalin (Wojciech Ziemiański), Franklin D. Roosevelt (Zdzisław Kuźniar) and Winston Churchill (Wiesław Cichy), original participants of those events were invited to co-create the show: Ilse Bode, Angela Hubrich, Karolina Kozak, Hanne-Lore Pretzsch, Jan Charewicz, Matthias Goeritz, Jan Kruczkowski, Guenther Linke, Zygmunt Sobolewski, Andrzej Ursyn Szantyr — five Poles from the Eastern Borderlands and five Germans from Silesia… 10 victims of the post-war resettlement of 1945.

The historical part of the production takes place in Yalta, at the "Hades Riviera". The completely bare stage is covered with a thick layer of ploughed land. There is a high, metal platform set in the middle of the stage. On it, the three frontmen of Europe are playing *Days of the Lords* by Joy Division. At the back of the stage, beneath the platform there are 10 chairs. The Big Three cannot see the expelled. Entering the stage they start talking. The audience hear an incomprehensible buzz of Polish-German voices. They are silenced by Stalin: "Quiet! Out!" His demographic engineering is in full force. He can afford to be in a good mood, as seen in

[34] Poland lost its eastern territory (Kresy) to the Soviet Union, for which it was "territorially compensated" with the previously German territories of Lubusz Land, Western Pomerania, East Prussia, Silesia and the former Free City of Danzig.

[35] Original title of the production: *Transfer*
Date and place of premiere: November 18, 2006, The Edmund Wierciński Contemporary Theatre in Wrocław
Direction: Jan Klata
Set design: Mirek Kaczmarek
Music (music arrangement): Jan Klata.

[36] Berlin premiere: January 18, 2007.

archive photographs, because he knew very well that both Churchill and Roosevelt were prepared to make far-reaching concessions regarding his demands. In the production, they even agree to Stalin's ironic toast the Führer's health. They are content, present official smiles, and say yes to all Stalin's suggestions, completely unreflective of the decisions they are making, as long as they gain what they could for themselves. The problems of the countries absent from the conference are marginalised (for example, matters regarding Poland and the establishment of Polish borders were agreed without the presence of the Polish delegation.) Klata picks our allies to pieces. He does not get involved in the politically-correct smoothing out of the creases European history:

> Churchill: The sovereignty of Poland is a matter of honour for Great Britain. Blah blah blah…

Roosevelt cared about the votes of the Polish community, whereas Churchill cared about several thousand Polish soldiers. After the borders were established (significantly different, compared to the pre-war ones), the politicians were considering what to say to the Poles, how to explain…

> Churchill: There's nothing you can do to satisfy the Polish…

Everything happens over the heads of the most interested parties. The layered acting space is a perfect illustration of the problem discussed in the play. The top and bottom will never meet. Klata shows, how a "historically" anonymous individual clashes with a situation they cannot control. After all, we did not want these lands, and those ones… had been ours for centuries… Victims of expulsion get up and one by one walk towards the audience. They talk, in Polish and in German, about the fates of their families. Nothing here is a metaphor or skilfully written literature. We are presented with authentic lives of people who once lived peacefully in Ukraine, Lithuania or Silesia, who have been blown far from home by the winds of history. These people, old today, have never got over the feeling of being uprooted:

> My family arrived in Lithuania from Pomerania in the sixteenth century…
> On 1 September 1939…
> I remember my father went to the village library every night to read *The Trilogy*…
> We had a Jewish neighbour…
> The Germans returning from the Eastern Front were no longer elegant…
> I pushed the dolls under the bed, so the Russians would not find them…
> Actually, they were nice lads…

> War is not a symphony…
> War is tragic, that is why I do not like to talk about it. And I will not.
> The Germans, as poor as us…

Talking about the character of work on this production Klata said that it was most important to remain careful and not objectify any person, and not use one's tragic memories for something young creators are eager to say. In the scenes in which our heroes walk towards the audience and recount the worst memories of their lives, director was careful to switch off the spotlight on a character's face before they began to cry, to make sure they did not unintentionally create emotional porn.

In opposition to those stories, a young German man (Matthias Goeritz) enters the stage carrying a smart overnight bag. Stuck in another transfer to the airport, he lists his destinations: New York, Moscow, Barcelona, and Shanghai. He opens the bag, revealing the contents: "This is my Homeland." He lists the things he always brings along: a yoga DVD, headphones, a pack of condoms, a tie, a toothbrush, a calendar, and a charger. The twenty-first century has become another era of nomadic people who are constantly on the move between destinations. His parents were expelled from Lower Silesia and even if the young man feels deracinated in the new, contemporary way, he will always carry along a series of associations and memories anyway. He must face the history of the country he keeps leaving behind on his own.

At the end of the show Stalin (still in great spirits) tells everyone a joke:

> Stalin, Churchill and Roosevelt go hunting. They shoot a bear and are dividing their kill:
> Churchill: I will take the skin; you and Stalin can share the meat.
> Roosevelt: I will take the skin, and you and Stalin can share the meat.
> Stalin: the bear is mine, after all I killed it.

Reviewers called *Transfer* "*The Dead Class* of the twenty-first century".[37] Just as Tadeusz Kantor in his production described the experience of World War I, Jan Klata found a way to describe World War II. The madness of history, the drama of uprooting, and the fact that such history can repeat itself. He did not want to argue about which nation suffered most. If someone felt offended by the production it would most definitely have been the Russians because it was the inhuman cruelty of their army

---

[37] Roman Pawłowski, „Umarła klasa XXI wieku," *Gazeta Wyborcza*, November 20, (2006): 14.

that both Polish and German witnesses remember most vividly. When the production was played at the Meyerhold Centre in Moscow half the audience expressed their gratitude to the artists; however, the other half left their seats offended by the apparent typically Western distortion of history: "If it were not for my grandfather, a soldier of the Red Army, the Germans would have wiped Krakow off the map," said a dark-haired woman already at the door, and who refused to stay for discussion.[38]

Transfer was subliminally asking the question about the possibility of formulating "objective history". It did not make interpretations, or pose historical diagnoses; it did not justify, nor defend anyone.

During the Yalta conference it was also established that the Soviet Union would gain "sovereignty" over Poland and a part of Germany. With Churchill's and Roosevelt's consent, Stalin annihilated the Polish Home Army and National Armed Forces. At the same time, Roosevelt assured Stalin, that the US would never endorse any provisional Polish authorities whose activity infringed the interests of the Soviet Union. Thus Communism was installed on Polish ground, and endured until 1989.

The staging of *The Government Inspector* by Nikolai Gogol in a provincial theatre in Wałbrzych was Jan Klata's debut.[39] Later on, directors of the theatre openly admitted having initial doubts:

> The mohawk. An image of a weird person and an association that such people can be dangerous. Seeing a man like that I am not sure whether he is about freedom, tolerance, culture, whether he can use a knife and fork, whether he will say "hallo", or "excuse me", and whether he is safe and is ready to be a partner.[40]

Still, they wanted to reform their theatre, they hired new staff and changed the repertoire. They did not have much to lose and therefore decided to take a risk and give Klata a chance. He instantly became the talk of the town (the production was recorded and broadcast by Polish Television). With this production the director kicked open the door to his

---

[38] Anna Żebrowska, „*Transfer* Klaty zdenerwował Rosjan," *Gazeta Wyborcza*, September 24, (2008): 17.

[39] Original title of the production: *Rewizor*
Date and place of premiere: March 30, 2003, The Jerzy Szaniawski Dramatic Theatre, Wałbrzych
Direction: Jan Klata
Set design: Justyna Łagowska
Music (music arrangement): Jan Klata.

[40] Migdałowska, „Do Timbuktu…," 52.

own theatre success. He was soon referred to as the "Polish Frank Castorf".[41]

Klata transferred *The Government Inspector*, a play ridiculing the Russian, tsarist administration, to the Poland of the 1970s, i.e. the era of deep-seated Communism. The transfer was blunt, and to the point. The Governor (Wiesław Cichy) is a mediocre Communist Party activist somewhere in the armpit of the world. At a dance in a local youth club he is dancing enthusiastically to *Rasputin* by the then iconic band Boney M. The heritage park Klata created on stage was strikingly veristic. On the wall: orange wooden panels typical of Poland of the Communist era; centrally on stage: a portrait of Edward Gierek (First Secretary of the Party's Central Committee), and the ubiquitous ferns which were the most popular decorative item at the time. In his interpretation, Klata merely changed the time and place, while keeping Gogol's classic text:

> Gentlemen, I have bad news. A government inspector is on his way.[42]

Therefore, we must immediately interrupt the disco and summon an extraordinary meeting of the Party's Committee. It reflects the popular vision of the structure and mechanisms of the Communist system. Klata made the characters in the play stand out: the doctor, a drunk; the teacher, a coward; the inspector, a denunciator; the judge, a seducer, just like in a classic morality play with multicoloured allegories of various human vices.

The scene changes take place in front of the audience, and we are transported from the dance hall to the Party meeting hall and to the Governor's apartment which might as well be a museum of memories of the style of interior decoration at the time of the Polish People's Republic. It has all the features of a typical Polish Communist apartment. The phenomenon of Communist design was that everyone's apartments looked virtually the same: furniture was provided by national factories (and there was never enough, so everyone bought what was available at the store (if it was available) and they would never even dream of criticizing the appearance or workmanship of a miraculously captured wardrobe or bed).

---

[41] Frank Castorf — German theatre director. Till 2017 he was the artistic director of Berlin's Volksbühne. Famous for his "political shows", he was working "against mainstream conformity" and treated Volksbühne as the last bastion of defence against the pervading materialism of the Western consumer society.

[42] Nikolai Gogol, *The Government Inspector* (New York: Oberon books, 2005), Act One.

The same furniture, the same lamps and the same carpets (with ubiquitous "Turkish" motifs) could be therefore seen in all homes.

Khlestakov (Piotr Kondrat) the Inspector, who has arrived incognito, is a real playboy of those Communist times, with a thick layer of pomade in his hair, wearing a leather jacket, jeans (which were then inaccessible in Poland), and an Adidas bag. He even has his own car (at the time it was yet another luxury product, besides a telephone, a TV set and a washing machine). He quickly realises the situation and talks about his connections in the capital city: how he plays cards every week with the Cuban ambassador and Soviet minister of foreign affairs, and how movie stars accompany him to parties. He tries to persuade the officials that "Karl Marx" is his pen name and that he wrote it all… including *Capital…*

Even the act of seduction, showing sexual attraction to a man (as Khlestakov is a perfect candidate for a son in law for those times) happens in the aesthetic of "liberated" Communism. The Governor's daughter (Karolina Adamczyk) obviously cannot openly throw herself at the guest, so she plays a record with the dance *Guantanamera* — an imported commodity from the friendly country of Cuba. The suitor, too, is hitting on his beloved one in Aesopian language… by quoting from compulsory school readings (and thus the poem *Bayonets Ready* by Władysław Broniewski suddenly assumes an Aristophanean quality).

Khlestakov is one of the best scoundrels to have appeared on the Polish stage in recent years. There are distinct ideological echoes in his character as well. Instead of merchants (who appear in the play by Gogol), factory woman workers come to see him. They complain about working conditions. They show him photographs of their sons and husbands murdered by the Communist regime. Klata was accused of blurring the line between Communist and democratic Poland… and he wanted to show that there has never been true decommunisation in Poland, that many people who are in power now have very strong Communist roots. In that context the premiere of the show taking place on World Theatre Day was particularly problematic. All the important politicians of the region were gathered together for the occasion:

> We were all a little afraid of the reaction. I mean, I was not, but the management were and rightly so, because their job as managers is to foresee the consequences of what happens if you let someone look into a mirror, because this production might not have been pleasant to the authorities. (…) So they had every right to take offence, they had a reason to feel offended and I think they did feel a little insulted. They watched the show, later there were speeches, with all the pompous ceremonies and carnations handed out on the occasion of Theatre Day. (…) And every one

of them praised the production but pretended it was not about their political formation but about the political formation of their opponents.[43]

The famous ending by the Governor: "What are you laughing at? You are laughing at yourself." is performed to the tune of *Come On and Sing Along* (one of the most popular party hits of that time[44]). This coda ends the entire show by Klata, who ironically demonstrated that the political objective of "maximum power, minimum responsibility" is universal.

In 1929, Stanisława Przybyszewska wrote *The Danton Case*, a play devoted to the French Revolution, depicting the power struggle between Robespierre and Danton. The author's personal sympathies are clearly noticeable. She clearly defended the character of Robespierre. She did not agree with the one-sided presentation of his character as a bloody dictator. In her play, the Revolution is a special moment in history which allows outstanding individuals (such as Robespierre) to spread their wings. The author justified even some radical moves, often bloody ones, aimed at the objective of fulfilling revolutionary ideals.

What is most important, in Klata's production: "It was not the people who barged into palaces, but distinguished ideologists who descended to the bottom of existence. Into the innards of fledgling capitalism".[45] There is no room at all for the people of France in this production. The fight for power is limited only to selected, outstanding individuals. The location, on the other hand, was the back of some filthy warehouse, garages, perhaps slums? So the Revolution can be a thing for the few chosen ones, but it happens at the very bottom. It resembles a gang war. Wearing accurately reconstructed eighteenth century costumes the heroes seem to impersonate their historical prototypes, rather than really be them.

When Andrzej Wajda staged *The Danton Case* in 1975 in the Warsaw Powszechny Theatre, everyone knew that he was using it as a metaphor for the October Revolution.[46] After thirty years the pendulum of history swung back through the same trajectory. Reviewers writing about Klata's production looked for references to the system transformation of 1989, stories about a revolution which, once initiated and let loose, started to live its own life. In the production, we are in the most unstable moment of the revolution, when it is beginning to lose momentum, when it is time to decide what has to be done next. Merely starting a revolution is never

---

[43] Kardasińska, „Dorosnąć do widowni…," 60.

[44] Original title: *Cała sala śpiewa z nami*.

[45] Łukasz Drewniak, „Marzenia ściętej głowy," *Dziennik*, April 4, (2008): 14.

[46] In 1982 Andrzej Wajda also directed a film based on the same play, starring Gérard Depardieu in the title role.

enough (just as Lech Wałęsa's jump over the fence of the Gdańsk shipyard or the demolition of the Berlin Wall were not enough). There needs to be an idea of what happens after the state of revolution becomes ordinary. There will have to be a new order built on that new reality. However, it is good to have a specific idea about it. Danton wants to stop at what they had already achieved. Robespierre wants to continue fighting for more, and thus the conflict begins.

In Przybyszewska's play there is a clash of two world views: the rational and the idealist. Danton in the production is approximately twenty years older than Robespierre. He is already bitter; his ideals have long been ridiculed and refuted. We can see him playing with a remote-control toy tank. He is cynical, and no longer believes in anything, and only cares about his own business. In this comparison, one is experienced, while the other is driven, but Robespierre is too young and too ill to take full power. In the opening scene we see him in a bathtub, in the same pose as Marat in Jacques-Louis David's *The Death of Marat. Requiem for a Jerk* by Placebo can be heard from the speakers. The song becomes a requiem for Robespierre. His youthful drive and enthusiasm will have to be reconciled with the necessity to introduce terror, a solution which Robespierre fears the most. He tries to protect Danton who, instead of switching to his side, tries to subordinate the stronger Robespierre. It will be most clearly demonstrated in the scene of Danton's trial which will seem like a part of a huge electoral campaign. The conflict between them will be presented as a duel of *La Marseillaise.* Danton performs it like a gospel song. In turn, Robespierre and his men start their chainsaws (yes, *La Marseillaise* can be performed on those). By the way, in Klata's production heads are cut off by chainsaws…

After *Requiem for a Jerk*, Klata employed the whole revolutionary repertoire of popular radio stations. *Children of the Revolution* by T-Rex, which is the main theme of the Jacobin Club, is in opposition to Frederic Chopin's *Revolutionary Etude*, characteristic of Danton's moderate programme. In the scene where revolutionaries are discussing the strategy of their further actions, the speakers play Tracy Chapman's *Talkin' bout a Revolution.* After Danton's beheading, we can hear The Beatles' *Revolution.* By mixing the motif of revolution with its reflections in pop culture, Klata showed how quickly all revolutions become commercialised. In liberal Europe it is very fashionable to be a "Friday night rebel", but not many will decide to wear trainers to a corporate office on Monday morning. Revolution in capitalist countries has been trivialised. It fell into the trap of easy clichés and behaviours. Revolution proved to be a great selling product, too. We could resent the fact that the references he used are not subtle enough and that they are too obvious. Yet, thanks to such a selection of music, Klata demonstrated the sophistication with which he directs his works and how, with carefully selected motifs, he directs the dynamics of his actors' work as well as the audience's attention.

While Poland was undergoing political transformation Klata was finishing high school. He was old enough to remember Communism well, and had enough social awareness to understand what was happening when democracy was established. Klata, unlike the author of the play, takes neither the side of the Jacobins, nor the Girondins. There is no black or white here. He does, however, demonstrate how revolution brings to life new social awareness. Yet, there is always the problem of what to do with that awareness and how to use it constructively.[47]

Jan Klata gave the "revolution" of 1989 a bitter judgement. Stanisław Wyspiański (one of the most outstanding playwrights of Polish modernism), in his interpretation of *Hamlet* wrote that "*Hamlet* is what there is in Poland to think about". In his production, Jan Klata directly referred to that most famous sentence of Polish theatre studies and moved the action of *H.* to the Gdańsk Shipyard,[48] the place where "Solidarity" was born. It was here that gradual decomposition of Communism began; it was here that Lech Wałęsa was employed as a shipyard electrician. But that is history now. The Gdańsk Shipyard has become a symbolic space, with a scary post-industrial character, somewhat embarrassing as it declared bankruptcy years ago and is now slowly falling into ruin. The wind is blowing in empty assembly halls. There are piles of rubble, broken windows, the walls are about to collapse. Dangerous-looking constructions suspended from the ceiling are being slowly damaged by corrosion. There are rusty hulls of abandoned ships in the shipyard canal. The smell of rust and old grease is in the air. The decomposing shipyard is Klata's decomposing Poland which did not use the full potential of system transformation, and thus lost. In Klata's opinion, the fall of Communism was not necessarily a change for the better.

---

[47] The production was perceived as one of Jan Klata's greatest stage achievements, and received the most awards in the history of the Polski Theatre in Wrocław. The *Polityka* weekly classified it as one of the ten most important productions of the previous 25 years.

[48] Original title of the production: *H.*
Date and place of premiere: July 2, 2004, The Wybrzeże Theatre, Gdańsk
Direction: Jan Klata
Set design: Justyna Łagowska
Music (music arrangement): Jan Klata.

The setting for the production is Hall No. 42, where "Solidarity" legend Anna Walentynowicz used to work. This is where, under the huge gantry crane, the story of the Danish prince will play out. Picturesque, post-apocalyptic spaces. Wild greenery growing from the groundwork. Enormous cranes resembling sleeping, blind monsters. Spectators are led through subsequent "locations" of the Shipyard, through halls, workers' changing rooms, and over the port canal, where Ophelia is going to drown. Stage spaces are marked off with red and white warning tape, used by the police in accident areas. Horatio (Cezary Rybiński) is our guide through the show, telling a story which will transform into a myth before the spectators' eyes.

There are two figures approaching from the distance wearing snow-white fencing gear. One of them, wearing a black, mourning band on his sleeve, is Hamlet (Marcin Czarnik). They carry golf clubs and a silver CD player. They are listening to *Seven Nations Army* by The White Stripes:

> I'm gonna fight 'em off
> A seven nation army couldn't hold me back
> They're gonna rip it off
> Taking their time right behind my back
>
> And I'm talking to myself at night
> Because I can't forget…

"*Hamlet* to me is a story about rebellion against the older generation which betrayed its ideals once it assumed power".[49] Hamlet is not a neurotic intellectual, but a furious youngster who does not agree with the people in his closest environment, yielding to comfortable amnesia. He is a regular boy, who goes to concerts, reads graphic novels and plays computer games (and who probably does not go the theatre, discouraged by his humanities teacher). To kill time he plays turbo-golf with Horatio, but their goals are not defined. They aim for the window, or for the bushes — a nice metaphor to underline the uselessness of all Hamlet's acts of rebellion.

Their white fencing gear is ready for the final duel scene. Klata heavily edited Shakespeare's text. The director allowed the character of the location to dramatise and provoke the entire show. There is nothing natural or realistic here. The Ghost of Hamlet's father appears, a huge heavy door opens and a hussar (Igor Michalski) riding a galloping grey horse enters

---

[49] Roman Pawłowski, "Gdański Hamlet postindustrialny," *Gazeta Wyborcza*, July 2, (2004): 13.

the shipyard hall. The hoofbeat is audible all over the hall, reflected by an ominous, growing echo. The scene is rather anachronistic. The spectators' minds begin to mix historical orders. What happened hundreds years ago is galloping into the present. The spirit of the nation and reality falling on our heads. The ghost of the father is the history of Poland. It is a mythology of pathos, demanding bloody vengeance from a white horse. The thing is that in this show, Hamlet's revenge will lead the country to ultimate disaster…

A council of war is in progress. All the people gathered are wearing fencing gear: after all, we are at war with Norway… Discussing military strategy resembles a meeting of a company's supervisory board. Papers, files, handshakes. Closing a deal crowned with a wine tasting. Claudius (Grzegorz Gzyl) pronounces French wine names like a *nouveau riche*. He articulates the sounds with delight, but Hamlet kills everyone's buzz. He breaks his glass with a golf club. He is not going to pretend in front of everyone that he is having fun. Red wine is spilt on white garments. They will be wearing visible blood stains until the end of the show; everyone has blood on their hands in this play.

Klata is juggling the text and its intertextual potentiality. Instead of Hamlet's monologue, the spectators listen to *Heroes* by David Bowie with the meaningful: "We can be Heroes just for one day". The entire meaning of the scene is expressed through music. When Polonius (Sławomir Sulej) asks Hamlet what he is reading… "words, words, words"… Hamlet reads out an excerpt from a prayer book about the necessity to forgive one's enemies.

The scene of returned letters is a dangerous mixture of mawkishness and the sound of broken glass. Hamlet and Ophelia bring each other's letters. They are tacky melody cards. They open them one by one and arrange them in a row. A nasty cacophony can be heard. The actress playing Ophelia (Marta Kalmus) brought a box with her high school memorabilia — letters, postcards, hearts, and shells to one of the rehearsals. She mentioned in an interview that, during the rehearsals with Klata, for the first time ever she felt like doodling over the script, and decorating it with photographs evoking the right associations necessary to construct the part.[50] The letters are closed in bottles. Returning them, they break them against a wall. One letter, one memory.

Rosencrantz and Guildenstern (Wojciech Kalarus and Rafał Kronenberger) who have arrived in Elsinore are entertaining guys. They organise a theatre show for something to finally happen in the sad and

[50] Ligarzewska, „Relacje…," 70.

mouldy court. They organise an audition, with an obvious "to be or not to be" as a challenge for amateurs. There is a lot of sweet trashiness on stage, as everyone wants to do their best. The famous line from *Hamlet* will be given a tone of philosophy, classroom, pathos, sexuality… Amateur efforts will bring the meaning of the line to an absurdity. Klata also questions Shakespeare's trick: the mousetrap is not working. Claudius falls asleep during the show. He misses the main scene:

> If you do it as God intended, letter by letter, then a tragedy company from the capital city theatre should make a moving, emotional show which would deeply shake the audience. Only then would we believe it moved Claudius too. If Claudius only *acts* as if he were very deeply moved, and the audience remains unmoved, it is going to be a classic theatrical embarrassment. And today I am convinced, though perhaps in several dozen years I may not be, that a person such as Claudius cannot be moved by any theatre.[51]

In Klata's production, Gertrude (Joanna Bogacka) does not know what had happened. If Hamlet the king had lived, she would most probably have left him for the younger Claudius anyway. This means that Hamlet the prince has a slightly bigger problem. When he leaves Gertrude's bedroom he is ironically humming a pilgrims' song: *Mother Who Understands All…* He is a hurt boy who cares more about his late father than his living mother. Such a father, who overshadows everything, is a good excuse for any negligence. While Hamlet is thinking what to do next, warning sirens go off in the shipyard. There is an ambulance driving fast from hall to hall: Ophelia has drowned in the port canal; the police are surrounding the coast like a crime scene. Divers retrieve her body and put it in a plastic bag. The spectators, like a mob of bystanders are watching everything from the shore: the rescue action, the young people jumping into the water to save the girl; the scene of despair.

Everyone is continuously dressed in fencing gear. The épées have already been commissioned… When Hamlet is sitting in the changing room, a messenger with news of a bet arrives. Klata slows down the pace of his show. He leads it to the scene of the duel which ends with Nirvana's *Smells Like Teen Spirit*, played on an out-of-tune piano to the rhythm of ragtime music. You cannot start new fire with broken dreams… When everyone is lying dead on a dusty floor of the assembly hall, there is a

---

[51] Piotr Gruszczyński, „Wawel na mnie nie działa – rozmowa z Janem Klatą," *Didaskalia*, no. 63 (2004): 19.

shadow of a hussar riding by the window. We can hear the sound of hoof beats dying away.

Janulka, Daughter of Fizdejko is a 1923 play by Stanisław Ignacy Witkiewicz, about the Neo-Teutonic Knights who raided and colonised pagan Lithuania. The axis of the play was a collision between the civilised West with the wild, untamed East, which ended with a massacre of all participants. Klata used the play to talk about Poland's accession to the European Union.[52] Our joining the EU, in Klata's stage metaphor, was another invasion by the Teutonic Knights. A huge copy of one of the most famous Polish historical paintings, Jan Matejko's *The Battle of Grunwald*, is hanging in the upstage area, as a background to all events. Grunwald was one of the greatest victories in the history of Poland. Joined armies of Poland and Lithuania defeated the knights of the Teutonic Order. The stopping of the Teutonic Knights (who were officially to Christianise the area of Lithuania, while practically wanted to subdue it), was used in the show as a symbol of blocking a brutal expansion of Western (German) culture in the East.

Several unemployed men from Wałbrzych, a former coal town in which many were plunged into poverty after the mines were closed, impersonated Lithuanian boyars from Witkiewicz's play. Indeed, Poland's accession to the European Union was presented from the perspective of the citizens of the provincial town. In such places, many people looked forward to Poland joining the European structures in hope of a new order. It would, however, be too easy if the production described only our expectations regarding the transformation. Our accession to the EU was accompanied by a heated historical debate. It turned out that our traumas had not disappeared even fifty years after the war. It is, therefore, also a show about the Polish-German relationship, "about two nations closed in one closet together with their skeletons".[53]

Lithuanian prince Fizdejko (Wiesław Cichy) together with his unemployed subjects awaits the arrival of a delegation of EU Commissioners, Neo-Teutonic Knights, who are to capture Polish lands and civilise them. The master of ceremony, responsible for the right scenery for the event is

---

[52] Original title of the production: *...córka Fizdejki*
Date and place of premiere: December 18, 2004, The Jerzy Szaniawski Dramatic Theatre, Wałbrzych
Direction: Jan Klata
Set design: Mirek Kaczmarek
Music (music arrangement): Jan Klata.

[53] Roman Pawłowski, „*...córka Fizdejki* – współcześni niewolnicy historii i stereotypów," *Gazeta Wyborcza*, December 21, 2004.

Director of Séances der Zipfel (Andrzej Szubski) made up to look like the dwarf from the graphic novel *Achtung Zelig!* Typically for a wizard he is wearing a pointed hat and a long dark coat, decorated not with stars but with swastikas.

The EU delegation arrives, headed by Gottfried von und zu Berchtoldingen (Hubert Zduniak). Foreign visitors are portrayed as representatives of some different, higher race, as some Nietzschean Übermenschen, wearing perfectly fitted suits with ostentatiously shiny Swiss watches. They stand in strong contrast to the friendly, badly dressed prince Fizdejko. At a meeting, the officials take out boards with printed slogans to present the locals with achievements of a higher civilisation: Siemens, Mercedes, Bosch, Dürer, Kant, Goethe… But with them come unwanted demons of the historical past. The stage is lit by a strong, red light resembling hell's fire (or perhaps that of a crematorium?). Ashes of Auschwitz are still blowing over Europe… Prisoners of concentration camps run to the stage. Klata throws strong accusations, that the European Union's historical policy is sugar-coating the past. All members are obligated to observe unanimous political correctness. There are idealistic shared history school books which omit places of bloody massacres. Meetings in Brussels are only concerned with "positive programmes" for the European Union.

Puzzled EU Commissioners, willing to change their negative image, start to show off their knowledge of Polish swear words. Prince Fizdejko, who does not speak any foreign languages, communicates with them using elaborate miming. He acts out great events from Polish history: the charge of the hussar cavalry, the Prussian tribute, Wałęsa jumping over the fence… He makes every effort to demonstrate that Poland is about more than the unemployed on social benefits, but also about struggle and heroic tradition. After all, there is Grunwald in the background… which no one in Europe remembers any more (besides the Poles).

Something which the EU Commissioners did not foresee happens in that drastic situation of political incoherence: Berchtoldingen falls in love with Janulka, daughter of Fizdejko. At the beginning it was nothing serious, casual sex with a pagan princess… Berchtoldingen does not even notice when his actions start resembling those of his beloved's countrymen. His arrogance and German precision slowly disappear. He drops his Teutonic Knight's cape and is eating *bigos* straight from the pot in an old worn out jacket. The Western high culture does not last in confrontation with barbarians. Berchtoldingen commits suicide because he cannot cope with the power of the Slavic spirit, just as, in Matejko's painting, The Grand Master of the Teutonic Order dies at the hands of servants.

Klata puts strong emphasis on the subordinate aspect of Poland's accession to the European Union. After all, it is well known that Western countries looked not only for a new market in Poland, but also cheap labour. When Fizdejko's subjects hoist an EU flag on a flagpole in the hope of a better future, it disappears somewhere over the stage. It is so high it cannot be seen. A chorus of the unemployed sings *Ode to joy*, but they are still wearing the striped uniforms of the camps. They stand in a row, as if during a penal roll call in a concentration camp. They chant Friedrich Schiller's words, as if counting off, and Janulka is providing a light flute accompaniment.

At the very end Klata, transfers us to a non-existent Walbrzych Airport. Halogen lights, modern architecture, an international airport from which one can escape anywhere: Berlin, London, Rome… There is no arrivals to Wałbrzych. Such is the future of Polish people in the European Union — to go abroad. "Ladies and Gentlemen you are very much welcome on board this Ryanair flight" — this is the fabulous prospect for our youth. For the wealthy members of the community, poorer countries are a source of cheap labour, a natural, renewable resource, with growing deposits.

Klata was accused of making anti-EU propaganda, but having watched the show it would be difficult to firmly declare which political option the director really supports. He is definitely a Eurosceptic. He sharply attacks the policy of Western European countries, but also laughs at Poland. In his show, even martyrology becomes grotesque. One of the most notable Polish theatre critics Piotr Gruszczyński wrote that *Daughter of Fizdejko* is the "most condensed concentrate of political incorrectness imaginable in contemporary Polish theatre".[54] Klata said something important out loud. He demonstrated how flexible Polish national symbols can be: historical paintings; Chopin's *polonaises*; Wałęsa; how many ideologies can easily employ them. Both left and right wing parties can use them for their own purposes. These symbols have become clichés. It becomes apparent that they are more of a burden than actual help in integration with other nations. Klata invited actual unemployed men, real victims of the new capitalist system, on stage. This is why his production had an even deeper meaning than if the characters had been portrayed by regular actors. The Wałbrzych unemployed did not reap the benefits of the system's

[54] Piotr Gruszczyński, „Pochwała niepoprawności," *Tygodnik Powszechny*, February 9, (2005): 20.

transformation. Just a few months after Poland joined the European Union, amid general Euro-enthusiasm, one person had had the courage to come up with a very moving, bold and uncomfortable show.

3. An ending in an atmosphere of scandal

Jan Klata is often criticised for intellectual clichés and aesthetic primitivism. Reviewers often have a problem deciding whether he is a cunning deceiver, or an intelligent iconoclast. After the spectacular debut in provincial Wałbrzych he quickly became a theatre celebrity. Journalists liked to tease him with the prophecy that one day he would become a conservative classic who would buy a suit and become managing director of the National Theatre.

On 1 January 2013, ten years after his theatre debut, Klata was nominated for the position of managing director of the Helena Modrzejewska National Stary Theatre in Krakow, but not everyone supported the choice of the rebellious individual with a mohawk and a skull T-shirt. Electing him as director involved obvious controversies. However, they wanted someone who would have the courage to take an independent step forward with the foundation of the tradition of the Stary Theatre in the background. They were looking for a strong personality who would be able to face the legend of the theatre. Krakow (known for its conservative character and specific middle–class, with roots reaching as far back as the nineteenth century) is a difficult place for creative work. There was therefore much hope invested in Klata, and he started his managerial duties unhesitatingly. He refreshed the repertoire. He started experimenting by checking whether this legendary giant had any unused potential. Many considered his forceful actions too intrusive. He was accused of using revolution to cover up his lack of ideas for running the theatre.

His execution of the job was particularly frowned upon in conservative circles. They criticised the fact that he allowed a left-oriented duo — Monika Strzępka (direction) and Paweł Demirski (dramaturgy) — to stage the *Battle of Warsaw 1920*. With the production, the creators queried the real result of the Battle of Warsaw. Did Poland win by defeating the Bolsheviks, or did it lose in the international arena? The show was attacked by the right wing media for glorifying Felix Dzerzhinsky and Soviet Russia. One of the right wing journalists openly wrote about the "theatre of national betrayal", offended by the fact that such creative work should not be subsidised by the state. Not even six months after he took over the management of the theatre, conservative circles openly advocated Klata's dismissal from the post.

In the atmosphere of conflict with a city which finds it difficult to accept change, Klata tried to continue his own artistic work. He staged Alfred Jarry's *Ubu Roi*,[55] starting with the controversial sentence for the Polish people: "Set in Poland, that is to say, nowhere."[56] He was wondering what contemporary Poland is actually like. It is under constant construction. The stage looks like it is under permanent renovation conducted without a plan. In Klata's show, a toilet brush becomes a consecrated aspergill, and we can communicate with God (after all, we are the Chosen People) via satellite. The Poles get rid of their consecutive kings by popping their balloon crown. It is also an easily pleased nation, just bread and circuses, and sack races to the epic soundtrack of *Chariots of Fire*. The director-manager, possibly tired with countless documents to sign, went a little wild with his production. His intertextual references spanned the band Metallica, through popular Polish history shows, to *Game of Thrones*. The impetus Klata employed to beat the postmodernist drum was a bit off-putting. There had not been another show in his career in which he would use such unrefined metaphors. As usual, Klata's diagnosis is painfully honest. Our romantic dreams of greatness are caught with their fly down, and the new allegory of Poland is the following *pieta*: Conchita Wurst mourning over the body of King Ubu in her arms.

Right after *Ubu Roi*, Klata staged *King Lear* and once again got into trouble.[57] Let us not forget that for many people Krakow is mainly the city of the Polish Pope. Klata, however, staged Shakespeare's play with references to a popular TV series, *The Borgias.* The location is a monumental audience hall in Vatican City. Lear (Jerzy Grałek), like Pope Benedict

---

[55] Original title of the production: *Król Ubu*
Date and place of premiere: October 16, 2014, The Helena Modrzejewska Stary Theatre, Krakow
Direction: Jan Klata
Set design: Justyna Łagowska
Music (music arrangement): Jan Klata.

[56] In fact, Poles have no rational reason for finding this offensive. In 1888, when Jarry wrote his play, Poland was partitioned and did not exist as a state on the map of Europe.

[57] Original title of the production: *Król Lear*
Date and place of premiere: December 19, 2014, The Helena Modrzejewska Stary Theatre, Krakow
Direction: Jan Klata
Set design: Justyna Łagowska
Music (music arrangement): Jan Klata.

XVI, resigns from the office and divides his possessions among his daughters. The daughters (or rather sisters in faith?), are priests from the pope's closest circles who, assuring him of their love, are trying to woo him. They are young, they want to distinguish themselves and make a career in the Vatican City. At times we are not sure whether it is still the Holy See or a mafia-type association. If so, what is Cordelia (Jaśmina Polak) supposed to say? Her love for her father, the leader of the Catholic Church, becomes love for her profession, her mission. Only with Lear absent will she be able to admit that it is in fact no different from any other job. The sisters' scheming occurs within the Church's structure. The pope, on the other hand, wants to continue enjoying the power he willingly renounced. He is typically accompanied by the fool (Jaśmina Polak), a playful imp wearing a bishop's mitre and climbing behind the papal throne and whispering words of madness in Lear's ear… However, contrary to the strongly staged *Ubu Roi*, we had the impression that many staging ideas, which certainly called for greater emphasis, were merely hinted by Klata, as if he was afraid to pinpoint the meanings and possibilities.

This withdrawal is probably a result of the general atmosphere around his managerial responsibilities. *To Damascus* (the first production directed by him after he took the post), was almost never mentioned in the media because of its artistic qualities, but merely because of the scandal surrounding the director, and overblown by conservative circles.[58] One of the shows was stopped because some spectators did not appreciate the "pornographic character" of one of the scenes (which is quite amusing, since the actors were not even undressed). The audience began whistling and booing. There were harsh words addressed to the actors and the director, who entered the stage to ask those who interrupted the show to leave. According to the organisers of the incident, it was supposed to be an expression of protest against "ultra-leftism and the tarnishing of the sanctity of theatre and nation by director Jan Klata". A video showing a group of spectators ostentatiously leaving the theatre was soon uploaded to YouTube. Most reviewers, however, wondered why that provocation and aggressive protest against the director did not take place during some

[58] Original title of the production: *Do Damaszku*
Date and place of premiere: October 5, 2013, The Helena Modrzejewska Stary Theatre, Krakow
Direction: Jan Klata
Set design: Mirek Kaczmarek
Music (music arrangement): Jan Klata.

really iconoclastic production.[59] The right-wing circles, on the other hand, took their demands so far that they not only wanted Klata's dismissal from the managing director's position, but they also demanded that the Minister of Culture step down:

> After the scandal — says Klata — we were afraid they would interrupt every performance. And they made threats: "We will come every night." So I went to the shows and we were trying to figure out what to do if someone protested. During *Being Steve Jobs* I went up to Wiktor, who played a young priest and wore a clerical collar. We decided that when they start protesting he would come up to the audience and call: "Make some noise for Jesus! Make some noise for Jesus!" And he was on standby for two hours. He played his scenes, went backstage and followed the play on monitors to see if his colleagues needed to be saved. We had to hire outside security to escort potential aggressive members of the audience out. The bouncers got hooked on the play. They asked if they could bring their wives to see it.[60]

The attack was also launched from a completely unexpected source. Klata still had not accepted the nomination from the Minister of Culture, and Krystian Lupa had already criticised him for being despotic and self-centred, and simply unfit to run such an institution. The problem was that Lupa (who had thus far been unofficially in charge of the Stary Theatre), had his own favourites, his "more beloved" disciples, whom he wanted to have appointed for the post, and he considered the defeat to be a personal failure. For a long time it was obvious that Lupa could not get over the fact that despite his unquestionable status as the most important Polish theatre creator, none of his favourite students won the competition. His interviews became impassioned. He was clearly looking for reasons to be in conflict with the new director:

> He was the first person I called to ask for a meeting after I accepted the controversial position. He came in, sat in the same armchair you are sitting in now, and demanded full power over the Small Stage. He wanted it to be, as he put it, a "Krystian Lupa Studio" under his supervision and directed

[59] Articles published after the event suggested that "the offended" went to see, for instance, *Tovianskiites. Kings of Clouds*, a show in which a naked actor is sitting in the audience from the very beginning.

[60] Anna Śmigulec, „Psy na Klacie. Dlaczego Kraków nie chce w Starym Jana Klaty," *Gazeta Wyborcza*, July 3, (2014): 22-25.

> solely according to his instructions: repertoire, artists' names, calendar etc. A bankster model of "the debt's yours, the profit's mine".[61]

Lupa was fully aware that his conditions were impossible to fulfil in a theatre of "national" status supported by state funds. However, he could continue attacking Klata for not showing good will and cooperating. All those interested in theatre in Poland lived and breathed this conflict, discussed mainly through the media:

> It is sweet of Krystian to believe it is still the mid-1990s, that he is 50 and I am 20, that he is my professor, and that I am his student at the drama school. But that was a long time ago. Times have changed.[62]

This is why in early 2015 Krystian Lupa left the National Stary Theatre. His almost thirty years of work in Krakow was the period when Polish theatre was reconstructing its identity after the ultimate collapse of Communism. That occurrence, which took place in an atmosphere of scandal and heated conflict between the master and his student, is a clear symbol closing another era: 25 years of the development of theatre in democratic Poland.

---

[61] Rafał Romanowski, „Taki już mój los; podniebne wojowanie – rozmowa z Janem Klatą," *Gazeta Wyborcza*, October 16, (2015): 8-9.

[62] Romanowski, „Taki już mój los…".

APPENDIX

CHRONOLOGY OF ALL PLAYS DIRECTED BY KRYSTIAN LUPA, KRZYSZTOF WARLIKOWSKI AND JAN KLATA

Krystian Lupa

Title of the production: *The Butchery*
Original title of the production: *Rzeźnia*
Date and place of premiere: May 8, 1976, Juliusz Słowacki Theatre in Krakow
Text by: Sławomir Mrożek
Adaptation: Krystian Lupa
Set design: Krystian Lupa
Music: Krzysztof Lipka

Title of the production: *The Life of Man*
Original title of the production: *Życie człowieka*
Date and place of premiere: July 2, 1977, Cyprian Kamil Norwid Theatre in Jelenia Góra
Text by: Leonid Nikolaievich Andreyev
Adaptation: Krystian Lupa
Set design: Krystian Lupa
Music: Bogdan Dominik

Title of the production: *Ivona*, *Princess of Burgundia*
Original title of the production: *Iwona, księżniczka Burgunda*
Date and place of premiere: January 8, 1978, The Helena Modrzejewska Stary Theatre, Krakow
Text by: Witold Gombrowicz
Set design: Krystian Lupa
Music: Krzysztof Lipka

Title of the production: *Dainty Shapes and Hairy Apes*
Original title of the production: *Nadobnisie i koczkodany, czyli Zielona pigułka*
Date and place of premiere: February 19, 1978, Cyprian Kamil Norwid Theatre, Jelenia Góra
Text by: Stanisław Ignacy Witkiewicz
Set design: Krystian Lupa

Title of the production: *Dainty Earth Spirit*
Original title of the production: *Demon ziemi*
Date and place of premiere: June 25, 1978, Cyprian Kamil Norwid Theatre, Jelenia Góra
Text by: Frank Wedekind
Adaptation: Krystian Lupa
Set design: Krystian Lupa

Title of the production: *The Transparent Room*
Original title of the production: *Przeźroczysty pokój*
Date and place of premiere: February 17, 1979, Cyprian Kamil Norwid Theatre, Jelenia Góra
Text by: Krystian Lupa
Set design: Krystian Lupa

Title of the production: *Mother*
Original title of the production: *Matka*
Date and place of premiere: November 4, 1979, Cyprian Kamil Norwid Theatre, Jelenia Góra
Text by: Stanisław Przybyszewski
Set design: Krystian Lupa

Title of the production: *The Supper*
Original title of the production: *Kolacja*
Date and place of premiere: April 27, 1980, Cyprian Kamil Norwid Theatre, Jelenia Góra
Text by: Krystian Lupa
Set design: Krystian Lupa

Title of the production: *Return of Odysseus*
Original title of the production: *Powrót Odysa*
Date and place of premiere: June 1, 1981, The Helena Modrzejewska Stary Theatre, Krakow

Text by: Stanisław Wyspiański
Adaptation: Krystian Lupa
Set design: Krystian Lupa
Music: Stanisław Radwan

Title of the production: *The Pragmatists*
Original title of the production: *Pragmatyści*
Date and place of premiere: October 25, 1981, Cyprian Kamil Norwid Theatre, Jelenia Góra
Text by: Stanisław Ignacy Witkiewicz
Set design: Krystian Lupa
Music: Bogdan Dominik

Title of the production: *On foot*
Original title of the production: *Pieszo*
Date and place of premiere: February 13, 1982, Cyprian Kamil Norwid Theatre, Jelenia Góra
Text by: Sławomir Mrożek
Set design: Krystian Lupa
Music: Bogdan Dominik

Title of the production: *The Anonymous Work*
Original title of the production: *Bezimienne dzieło*
Date and place of premiere: December 19, 1982, The Helena Modrzejewska Stary Theatre, Krakow
Text by: Stanisław Ignacy Witkiewicz
Set design: Krystian Lupa
Music: Krystian Lupa

Title of the production: *The Marriage*
Original title of the production: *Ślub*
Date and place of premiere: March 9, 1984, Cyprian Kamil Norwid Theatre, Jelenia Góra
Text by: Witold Gombrowicz
Set design: Krystian Lupa
Music: Krystian Lupa

Title of the production: *The City of Dream*
Original title of the production: *Miasto snu*
Date and place of premiere: May 25, 1985, The Helena Modrzejewska Stary Theatre, Krakow

Text by: based on the novel: *The Other Side* by Alfred Kubin
Adaptation: Krystian Lupa
Set design: Krystian Lupa
Music: Marcin Krzyżanowski

Title of the production: *Maciej Korbowa and Bellatrix*
Original title of the production: *Maciej Korbowa i Bellatrix*
Date and place of premiere: April 6, 1986, Cyprian Kamil Norwid Theatre, Jelenia Góra
Text by: Stanisław Ignacy Witkiewicz
Set design: Krystian Lupa
Music: Marcin Krzyżanowski

Title of the production: *The Dreamers*
Original title of the production: *Marzyciele*
Date and place of premiere: February 28, 1988, The Helena Modrzejewska Stary Theatre, Krakow
Text by: Robert Musil
Adaptation: Krystian Lupa
Set design: Krystian Lupa
Music: Marcin Krzyżanowski

Title of the production: *The Brothers Karamazov*
Original title of the production: *Bracia Karamazow*
Date and place of premiere: April 10, 1990, The Helena Modrzejewska Stary Theatre, Krakow
Text by: Fyodor Dostoyevsky
Adaptation: Krystian Lupa
Set design: Krystian Lupa
Music: Stanisław Radwan

Title of the production: *Malte, or the Prodigal Son's Triptych*
Original title of the production: *Malte, albo tryptyk marnotrawnego syna*
Date and place of premiere: December 19, 1991, The Helena Modrzejewska Stary Theatre, Krakow
Text by: Rainer Maria Rilke
Adaptation: Krystian Lupa
Set design: Krystian Lupa
Music: Stanisław Radwan

Title of the production: *Kalkwerk*
Original title of the production: *Kalkwerk*
Date and place of premiere: November 7, 1992, The Helena Modrzejewska Stary Theatre, Krakow
Text by: based on the short story: *The Lime Works* by Thomas Bernhard
Adaptation: Krystian Lupa
Set design: Krystian Lupa
Music: Jacek Ostaszewski

Title of the production: *Kalkwerk*
Original title of the production: *Kalkwerk*
Date and place of premiere: June 4, 1993, The Beer-Sheva Theatre, Beer-Sheva, (Israel)
Text by: based on the short story: *The Lime Works* by Thomas Bernhard
Adaptation: Krystian Lupa
Set design: Krystian Lupa
Music: Jacek Ostaszewski

Title of the production: *The Sleepwalkers*
Original title of the production: *Lunatycy*
Date and place of premiere: February 11, 1995, The Helena Modrzejewska Stary Theatre, Krakow
Text by: Hermann Broch
Adaptation: Krystian Lupa
Set design: Krystian Lupa
Music: Jacek Ostaszewski

Title of the production: *Immanuel Kant*
Original title of the production: *Immanuel Kant*
Date and place of premiere: January 13, 1996, The Polski Theatre, Wrocław
Text by: Thomas Bernhard
Set design: Krystian Lupa
Music: Jacek Ostaszewski

Title of the production: *The Siblings*
Original title of the production: *Rodzeństwo*
Date and place of premiere: October 19, 1996, The Helena Modrzejewska Stary Theatre, Krakow
Text by: Thomas Bernhard
Adaptation: Krystian Lupa

Set design: Krystian Lupa
Music: Jacek Ostaszewski

Title of the production: *The Lady and the Unicorn*
Original title of the production: *Dama z jednorożcem*
Date and place of premiere: May 17, 1997, The Polski Theatre, Wrocław
Text by: Hermann Broch
Adaptation: Krystian Lupa
Set design: Krystian Lupa
Music: Jacek Ostaszewski

Title of the production: *The Temptation of Quiet Veronica*
Original title of the production: *Kuszenie cichej Weroniki*
Date and place of premiere: May 17, 1997, The Polski Theatre, Wrocław
Text by: Robert Musil
Adaptation: Krystian Lupa
Set design: Krystian Lupa
Music: Jacek Ostaszewski

Title of the production: *Art*
Original title of the production: *Sztuka*
Date and place of premiere: November 16, 1997, The Helena Modrzejewska Stary Theatre, Krakow
Text by: Yasmina Reza
Set design: Krystian Lupa

Title of the production: *Return of Odysseus*
Original title of the production: *Powrót Odysa*
Date and place of premiere: February 27, 1999, The Dramatic Theatre, Warsaw
Text by: Stanisław Wyspiański
Adaptation: Krystian Lupa
Set design: Krystian Lupa
Music: Jacek Ostaszewski

Title of the production: *First Ladies*
Original title of the production: *Prezydentki*
Date and place of premiere: September 17, 1999, The Polski Theatre, Wrocław
Text by: Werner Schwab
Adaptation: Krystian Lupa

Set design: Krystian Lupa
Music: Krystian Lupa

Title of the production: *Auslöschung/Extinction*
Original title of the production: *Wymazywanie*
Date and place of premiere: March 10, 2001, The Dramatic Theatre, Warsaw
Text by: Thomas Bernhard
Adaptation: Krystian Lupa
Set design: Krystian Lupa
Music: Jacek Ostaszewski

Title of the production: *The Dreamers*
Original title of the production: *Marzyciele*
Date and place of premiere: November 23, 2001, Thalia Theatre, Hamburg (Germany)
Text by: Robert Musil
Adaptation: Krystian Lupa
Set design: Krystian Lupa
Music: Marcin Krzyżanowski

Title of the production: *The Master and Margarita*
Original title of the production: *Mistrz i Małgorzata*
Date and place of premiere: May 9, 2002, The Helena Modrzejewska Stary Theatre, Krakow
Text by: Mikhail Bulgakov
Adaptation: Krystian Lupa
Set design: Krystian Lupa
Music: Jacek Ostaszewski, Jakub Ostaszewski

Title of the production: *Refuge*
Original title of the production: *Azyl*
Date and place of premiere: January 23, 2003, The Polski Theatre, Wrocław
Text by: based on the drama: *The Lower Depths* by Maxim Gorky
Adaptation: Krystian Lupa
Set design: Krystian Lupa
Music: Jacek Ostaszewski

Title of the production: *Clara's Relations*
Original title of the production: *Stosunki Klary*

Date and place of premiere: April 5, 2003, The Rozmaitości Theatre, Warsaw
Text by: Dea Loher
Adaptation: Krystian Lupa
Set design: Krystian Lupa
Music: Jacek Ostaszewski

Title of the production: *Zarathustra*
Original title of the production: *Zarathustra*
Date and place of premiere: June 28, 2004, The Odeon of Herodes Atticus, Athens, (Greece)
Text by: Krystian Lupa
Set design: Krystian Lupa
Music: Paweł Szymański

Title of the production: *An Unfinished Piece for actor*
Original title of the production: *Niedokończony utwór na aktora*
Date and place of premiere: October 1, 2004, The Dramatic Theatre, Warsaw
Text by: Anton Chekhov
Set design: Krystian Lupa
Music: Krystian Lupa

Title of the production: *A Spanish Play*
Original title of the production: *Sztuka hiszpańska*
Date and place of premiere: October 1, 2004, The Dramatic Theatre, Warsaw
Text by: Yasmina Reza
Set design: Krystian Lupa
Music: Krystian Lupa

Title of the production: *Solaris*
Original title of the production: *Solaris*
Date and place of premiere: February 11, 2005, Düsseldorfer Schauspielhaus, Düsseldorf (Germany)
Text by: Stanisław Lem
Adaptation: Krystian Lupa
Set design: Krystian Lupa
Music: Krystian Lupa

Title of the production: *Zarathustra*
Original title of the production: *Zaratustra*
Date and place of premiere: May 7, 2005, The Helena Modrzejewska National Stary Theatre, Krakow
Adaptation: Krystian Lupa
Set design: Krystian Lupa
Music: Paweł Szymański

Title of the production: *Three Sisters*
Original title of the production: *Three Sisters*
Date and place of premiere: November 30, 2005, American Repertory Theater, Cambridge (USA)
Text by: Anton Chekhov
Adaptation: Krystian Lupa
Set design: Krystian Lupa
Music: Krystian Lupa

Title of the production: *Over All the Mountain Tops*
Original title of the production: *Na szczytach panuje cisza*
Date and place of premiere: September 23, 2006, The Dramatic Theatre, Warsaw
Text by: Thomas Bernhard
Adaptation: Krystian Lupa
Set design: Krystian Lupa
Music: Paweł Szymański

Title of the production: *The Seagull*
Original title of the production: *Чайка*
Date and place of premiere: September 15, 2007, The Alexandrinsky Theatre, Saint Petersburg (Russia)
Text by: Anton Chekhov
Adaptation: Krystian Lupa
Set design: Krystian Lupa
Music: Krystian Lupa

Title of the production: *Factory 2*
Original title of the production: *Factory 2*
Date and place of premiere: February 16, 2008, The Helena Modrzejewska National Stary Theatre, Krakow
Adaptation: Krystian Lupa
Set design: Krystian Lupa
Music: Mieczysław Mejza

Title of the production: *Persona. Marilyn*
Original title of the production: *Persona. Tryptyk/Marilyn*
Date and place of premiere: April 18, 2009, The Dramatic Theatre, Warsaw
Adaptation: Krystian Lupa
Set design: Krystian Lupa
Music: Paweł Szymański

Title of the production: *Endgame*
Original title of the production: *Final de partida*
Date and place of premiere: April 14, 2010, Teatro de la Abadía, Madrid, (Spain)
Text by: Samuel Beckett
Adaptation: Krystian Lupa
Set design: Krystian Lupa
Music: Krystian Lupa

Title of the production: *The Waiting Room*
Original title of the production: *Salle d'attente*
Date and place of premiere: June 9, 2011, Théatre de Vidy, Lausanne (Switzerland)
Adaptation: Krystian Lupa
Set design: Krystian Lupa
Music: Krystian Lupa

Title of the production: *The Waiting Room 0.*
Original title of the production: *Poczekalnia 0.*
Date and place of premiere: September 8, 2011, The Polski Theatre, Wrocław
Text by: Krystian Lupa
Set design: Krystian Lupa
Music: Krystian Lupa

Title of the production: *The City of Dream*
Original title of the production: *Miasto snu*
Date and placc of premiere: October 5, 2012, The Rozmaitości Theatre, Warsaw
Text by: based on the novel *The Other Side* by Alfred Kubin
Adaptation: Krystian Lupa
Set design: Krystian Lupa
Music: Mieczysław Mejza

Title of the production: *Woodcutters*
Original title of the production: *Wycinka,*
Date and place of premiere: October 23, 2014, The Polski Theatre, Wrocław
Text by: Thomas Bernhard
Adaptation: Krystian Lupa
Set design: Krystian Lupa
Music: Bogumił Misala

Title of the production: *Maciej Korbowa and Bellatrix*
Original title of the production: *Maciej Korbowa i Bellatrix*
Date and place of premiere: April 28, 2015, New Bath Theatre, Krakow
Text by: Stanisław Ignacy Witkiewicz
Set design: Krystian Lupa

Title of the production: *Heldenplatz*
Original title of the production: *Heldenplatz*
Date and place of premiere: March 27, 2015, Lietuvos Nationalinis Dramas Teatros, Vilnius (Lithuania)
Text by: Thomas Bernhard
Adaptation: Krystian Lupa
Set design: Krystian Lupa

Krzysztof Warlikowski

Title of the production: *The Marquise of O.*
Original title of the production: *Markiza O.*
Date and place of premiere: February 23, 1993, The Helena Modrzejewska National Stary Theatre, Krakow
Text by: Heinrich von Kleist
Adaptation: Krzysztof Warlikowski
Set design: Małgorzata Szczęśniak
Music: Jacek Ostaszewski

Title of the production: *The Venom of Theatre*
Original title of the production: *Trucizna teatru*
Date and place of premiere: December 3, 1993, The Nowy Theatre, Poznań
Text by: Rudolf Sirera
Adaptation: Krzysztof Warlikowski
Set design: Małgorzata Szczęśniak

Title of the production: *The Merchant of Venice*
Original title of the production: *Kupiec wenecki*
Date and place of premiere: September 18, 1994, Wilam Horzyca Theatre, Toruń
Text by: William Shakespeare
Adaptation: Krzysztof Warlikowski
Set design: Małgorzata Szczęśniak
Music: Jacek Ostaszewski

Title of the production: *Ludwig. Tod eines Königs*
Original title of the production: *Ludwig. Tod eines Königs*
Date and place of premiere: November 12, 1994, Kammerspiele, Hamburg (Germany)
Text by: Klaus Mann (*The Barred Window*)
Adaptation: Krzysztof Warlikowski
Set design: Małgorzata Szczęśniak

Title of the production: *Roberto Zucco*
Original title of the production: *Roberto Zucco*
Date and place of premiere: September 22, 1995, The Nowy Theatre, Poznań
Text by: Bernard-Marie Koltès
Adaptation: Krzysztof Warlikowski
Set design: Małgorzata Szczęśniak
Music: Tomasz Stańko

Title of the production: *Old Clown Wanted*
Original title of the production: *Zatrudnimy starego klauna*
Date and place of premiere: June 9, 1996, The Helena Modrzejewska National Stary Theatre , Krakow
Text by: Matei Visniec
Adaptation: Krzysztof Warlikowski
Set design: Małgorzata Szczęśniak
Music: Tomasz Stańko

Title of the production: *Electra*
Original title of the production: *Elektra*
Date and place of premiere: January 18, 1997, The Dramatic Theatre, Warsaw
Text by: Sophocles
Adaptation: Krzysztof Warlikowski

Set design: Małgorzata Szczęśniak
Music: Paweł Mykietyn

Title of the production: *The Winter's Tale*
Original title of the production: *Zimowa opowieść*
Date and place of premiere: April 5, 1997, The Nowy Theatre, Poznań
Text by: William Shakespeare
Adaptation: Krzysztof Warlikowski
Set design: Małgorzata Szczęśniak
Music: Paweł Mykietyn

Title of the production: *Lawyer Kraykowski's Dancer*
Original title of the production: *Tancerz mecenasa Kraykowskiego*
Date and place of premiere: June 11, 1997, Jan Kochanowski Theatre, Radom
Text by: Witold Gombrowicz
Adaptation: Krzysztof Warlikowski
Set design: Małgorzata Szczęśniak
Music: Paweł Mykietyn

Title of the production: *Hamlet*
Original title of the production: *Hamlet*
Date and place of premiere: July 5, 1997, School of Drama Tel Aviv (Israel)
Text by: William Shakespeare
Adaptation: Krzysztof Warlikowski
Set design: Małgorzata Szczęśniak
Music: Paweł Mykietyn

Title of the production: *The Taming of the Shrew*
Original title of the production: *Poskromienie złośnicy*
Date and place of premiere: January 3, 1998, The Dramatic Theatre, Warsaw
Text by: William Shakespeare
Adaptation: Krzysztof Warlikowski
Set design: Małgorzata Szczęśniak
Music: Paweł Mykietyn

Title of the production: *Pericles*
Original title of the production: *Pericles*

Date and place of premiere: January 27, 1998, Piccolo Teatro di Milano (Italy)
Text by: William Shakespeare
Adaptation: Krzysztof Warlikowski
Set design: Małgorzata Szczęśniak
Music: Paweł Mykietyn

Title of the production: *Quay West*
Original title of the production: *Quay West*
Date and place of premiere: April 3, 1998, Gravela Theatre, Zagreb (Croatia)
Text by: Bernard-Marie Koltès
Adaptation: Krzysztof Warlikowski
Set design: Małgorzata Szczęśniak
Music: Paweł Mykietyn

Title of the production: *Quay West*
Original title of the production: *Zachodnie wybrzeże*
Date and place of premiere: October 10, 1998, Studio Theatre, Warsaw
Text by: Bernard-Marie Koltès
Adaptation: Krzysztof Warlikowski
Set design: Małgorzata Szczęśniak
Music: Paweł Mykietyn

Title of the production: *Twelfth Night, or What You Will*
Original title of the production: *Was ihr wollt*
Date and place of premiere: February 10, 1999, Stadt Theater, Stuttgart (Germany)
Text by: William Shakespeare
Adaptation: Krzysztof Warlikowski
Set design: Małgorzata Szczęśniak
Music: Paweł Mykietyn

Title of the production: *Hamlet*
Original title of the production: *Hamlet*
Date and place of premiere: October 22, 1999, The Rozmaitości Theatre, Warsaw
Text by: William Shakespeare
Adaptation: Krzysztof Warlikowski
Set design: Małgorzata Szczęśniak
Music: Paweł Mykietyn

Title of the production: *The Tempest*
Original title of the production: *Der Sturm*
Date and place of premiere: March 17, 2000, Stadt Theater, Stuttgart (Germany)
Text by: William Shakespeare
Adaptation: Krzysztof Warlikowski
Set design: Małgorzata Szczęśniak
Music: Paweł Mykietyn

Title of the production: *The Bacchae*
Original title of the production: *Bakchantki*
Date and place of premiere: February 9, 2001, The Rozmaitości Theatre, Warsaw
Text by: Euripides
Adaptation: Krzysztof Warlikowski
Set design: Małgorzata Szczęśniak
Music: Paweł Mykietyn

Title of the production: *Cleansed*
Original title of the production: *Oczyszczeni*
Date and place of premiere: January 18, 2002, The Rozmaitości Theatre, Warsaw
Text by: Sarah Kane
Adaptation: Krzysztof Warlikowski
Set design: Małgorzata Szczęśniak
Music: Paweł Mykietyn

Title of the production: *In Search of Lost Time*
Original title of the production: *Auf der Suche nach der verlorenen Zeit*
Date and place of premiere: May 25, 2002, Stadt Theater, Bonn (Germany)
Text by: Marcel Proust
Adaptation: Krzysztof Warlikowski
Set design: Małgorzata Szczęśniak
Music: Paweł Mykietyn

Title of the production: *The Tempest*
Original title of the production: *Burza*
Date and place of premiere: January 4, 2003, The Rozmaitości Theatre, Warsaw
Text by: William Shakespeare

Adaptation: Krzysztof Warlikowski
Set design: Małgorzata Szczęśniak
Music: Paweł Mykietyn

Title of the production: *A Midsummer Night's Dream*
Original title of the production: *Le Songe d'une nuit d'été*
Date and place of premiere: March 7, 2003, Theatre National de Nice (France)
Text by: William Shakespeare
Adaptation: Krzysztof Warlikowski
Set design: Małgorzata Szczęśniak
Music: Paweł Mykietyn

Title of the production: *The Dybbuk*
Original title of the production: *Dybuk*
Date and place of premiere: October 6, 2003, The Rozmaitości Theatre, Warsaw
Text by: S. Ansky
Adaptation: Krzysztof Warlikowski
Set design: Małgorzata Szczęśniak
Music: Paweł Mykietyn

Title of the production: *Speaking in Tongues*
Original title of the production: *Speaking in Tongues*
Date and place of premiere: February 1, 2004, Toneelgroep Amsterdam, (Netherlands)
Text by: Andrew Bovell
Adaptation: Krzysztof Warlikowski
Set design: Małgorzata Szczęśniak
Music: Paweł Mykietyn

Title of the production: *Macbeth*
Original title of the production: *Macbeth*
Date and place of premiere: March 7, 2003, Schauspielhaus Hanower (Germany)
Text by: William Shakespeare
Adaptation: Krzysztof Warlikowski
Set design: Małgorzata Szczęśniak
Music: Paweł Mykietyn

Title of the production: *Krum*
Original title of the production: *Krum*
Date and place of premiere: March 3, 2005, The Helena Modrzejewska National Stary Theatre, Krakow
Text by: Hanoch Levin
Adaptation: Krzysztof Warlikowski
Set design: Małgorzata Szczęśniak
Music: Paweł Mykietyn

Title of the production: *Angels in America*
Original title of the production: *Anioły w Ameryce*
Date and place of premiere: February 17, 2007, The Rozmaitości Theatre, Warsaw
Text by: Tony Kushner
Adaptation: Krzysztof Warlikowski
Set design: Małgorzata Szczęśniak
Music: Paweł Mykietyn

Title of the production: *(A)pollonia*
Original title of the production: *(A)pollonia*
Date and place of premiere: May 16, 2009, The Nowy Theatre, Warsaw
Adaptation: Krzysztof Warlikowski, Piotr Gruszczyński, Jacek Poniedziałek
Set design: Małgorzata Szczęśniak
Music: Paweł Mykietyn

Title of the production: *A Streetcar*
Original title of the production: *Tramwaj*
Date and place of premiere: February 4, 2010, The Nowy Theatre, Warsaw
Text by: Tennessee Williams
Set design: Małgorzata Szczęśniak
Music: Paweł Mykietyn

Title of the production: *The End*
Original title of the production: *Koniec*
Date and place of premiere: September 30, 2010, The Nowy Theatre, Warsaw
Adaptation: Krzysztof Warlikowski, Piotr Gruszczyński
Set design: Małgorzata Szczęśniak
Music: Paweł Mykietyn

Title of the production: *African Tales by Shakespeare*
Original title of the production: *Opowieści afrykańskie według Szekspira*
Date and place of premiere: October 5, 2011, The Nowy Theatre, Warsaw
Text by: William Shakespeare
Adaptation: Krzysztof Warlikowski, Piotr Gruszczyński
Set design: Małgorzata Szczęśniak
Music: Paweł Mykietyn

Title of the production: *Warsaw Cabaret*
Original title of the production: *Kabaret Warszawski*
Date and place of premiere: July 3, 2013, The Nowy Theatre, Warsaw
Adaptation: Krzysztof Warlikowski, Piotr Gruszczyński, Szczepan Orłowski
Set design: Małgorzata Szczęśniak
Music: Paweł Mykietyn

Title of the production: *The French*
Original title of the production: *Francuzi*
Date and place of premiere: August 21, 2015, The Nowy Theatre, Warsaw
Text by: Marcel Proust
Adaptation: Krzysztof Warlikowski, Piotr Gruszczyński
Set design: Małgorzata Szczęśniak
Music: Paweł Mykietyn

Jan Klata

Title of the production: *The Government Inspector*
Original title of the production: *Rewizor*
Date and place of premiere: March 30, 2003, The Jerzy Szaniawski Dramatic Theatre, Wałbrzych
Text by: Nikolai Gogol
Adaptation: Jan Klata
Set design: Justyna Łagowska
Music: Jan Klata
Title of the production: *The Smile of a Grapefruit*
Original title of the production: *Uśmiech grejpfruta*
Date and place of premiere: April 6, 2003, The Polski Theatre, Wrocław
Text by: Jan Klata
Set design: Justyna Łagowska
Music: Jan Klata

Title of the production: *The Vatican Cellars*
Original title of the production: *Lochy Watykanu*
Date and place of premiere: January 9, 2004, The Edmund Wierciński Contemporary Theatre, Wrocław
Text by: Andre Gide
Adaptation: Jan Klata
Set design: Justyna Łagowska
Music: Jan Klata

Title of the production: *H.*
Original title of the production: *H.*
Date and place of premiere: July 2, 2004, The Wybrzeże Theatre, Gdańsk
Text by: William Shakespeare
Adaptation: Jan Klata
Set design: Justyna Łagowska
Music: Jan Klata

Title of the production: *Fizdejka's Daughter*
Original title of the production: *Córka Fizdejki*
Date and place of premiere: December 18, 2004, The Jerzy Szaniawski Dramatic Theatre, Wałbrzych
Text by: Stanisław Ignacy Witkiewicz
Adaptation: Jan Klata
Set design: Justyna Łagowska
Music: Jan Klata

Title of the production: *A Clockwork Orange*
Original title of the production: *Nakręcana pomarańcza*
Date and place of premiere: April 23, 2005, The Edmund Wierciński Contemporary Theatre, Wrocław
Text by: Antony Burgess
Adaptation: Jan Klata
Set design: Justyna Łagowska
Music: Jan Klata

Title of the production: *Fanta$y*
Original title of the production: *Fanta$y*
Date and place of premiere: October 16, 2005, The Wybrzeże Theatre, Gdańsk
Text by: Juliusz Słowacki
Adaptation: Jan Klata

Set design: Justyna Łagowska
Music: Jan Klata

Title of the production: *The Three Stigmata of Palmer Eldritch*
Original title of the production: *Trzy stygmaty Palmera Eldritcha*
Date and place of premiere: January 14, 2006, The Helena Modrzejewska National Stary Theatre, Krakow
Text by: Philip K. Dick
Adaptation: Jan Klata
Set design: Justyna Łagowska
Music: Jan Klata

Title of the production: *Come on, stop it*
Original title of the production: *Weź, przestań*
Date and place of premiere: April 21, 2006, The Rozmaitości Theatre, Warsaw
Text by: Jan Klata
Set design: Justyna Łagowska
Music: Jan Klata

Title of the production: *Richard III*
Original title of the production: *Ryszard III*
Date and place of premiere: October 26, 2006, Schauspielhaus Graz, (Austria)
Text by: William Shakespeare
Adaptation: Jan Klata
Set design: Justyna Łagowska
Music: Jan Klata

Title of the production: *Transfer!*
Original title of the production: *Transfer!*
Date and place of premiere: November 18, 2006, The Edmund Wierciński Contemporary Theatre, Wrocław
Text by: Jan Klata
Set design: Mirek Kaczmarek
Music: Jan Klata

Title of the production: *The Oresteia*
Original title of the production: *Oresteja*
Date and place of premiere: February 25, 2007, The Helena Modrzejewska National Stary Theatre, Krakow

Text by: Aeschylus
Adaptation: Jan Klata
Set design: Justyna Łagowska
Music: Jan Klata

Title of the production: *The Shoemakers*
Original title of the production: *Szewcy*
Date and place of premiere: November 11, 2007, The Rozmaitości Theatre, Warsaw
Text by: Stanisław Ignacy Witkiewicz
Adaptation: Jan Klata
Set design: Justyna Łagowska

Title of the production: *The Danton Case*
Original title of the production: *Sprawa Dantona*
Date and place of premiere: March 29, 2008, The Polski Theatre, Wrocław
Text by: Stanisława Przybyszewska
Adaptation: Jan Klata
Set design: Justyna Łagowska

Title of the production: *Hello/Farewell*
Original title of the production: *Witaj,Żegnaj*
Date and place of premiere: October 5, 2008, The Polski Theatre, Bydgoszcz
Text by: Suzan-Lori Parks (*365 Days/*365 Plays)
Adaptation: Jan Klata
Set design: Justyna Łagowska
Music: Jan Klata

Title of the production: *The Trilogy*
Original title of the production: *Trylogia*
Date and place of premiere: February 21, 2009, The Helena Modrzejewska National Stary Theatre, Krakow
Text by: Henryk Sienkiewicz
Adaptation: Jan Klata, Sebastian Majewski
Set design: Justyna Łagowska
Music: Jan Klata

Title of the production: *Loose Screws*
Original title of the production: *Szajba*
Date and place of premiere: May 8, 2009, The Polski Theatre, Wrocław

Text by: Małgorzata Sikorska-Miszczuk
Adaptation: Jan Klata
Set design: Mirek Kaczmarek
Music: Jan Klata

Title of the production: *The Promised Land*
Original title of the production: *Ziemia Obiecana*
Date and place of premiere: September 10, 2009, The Polski Theatre, Wrocław
Text by: Władysław Reymont
Adaptation: Jan Klata
Set design: Mirek Kaczmarek
Music: Jan Klata

Title of the production: *Shoot/Get Treasure/Repeat*
Original title of the production: *Shoot/Get Treasure/Repeat*
Date and place of premiere: January 9, 2010, Düsseldorfer Schauspielhaus, Düsseldorf (Germany)
Text by: Mark Ravenhill
Adaptation: Jan Klata
Music: Jan Klata

Title of the production: *The Wedding of Count Orgaz*
Original title of the production: *Wesele hrabiego Orgaza*
Date and place of premiere: June 11, 2010, The Helena Modrzejewska National Stary Theatre, Krakow
Text by: Roman Jaworski
Adaptation: Jan Klata
Set design: Justyna Łagowska
Music: Jan Klata

Title of the production: *Kazimierz and Karolina*
Original title of the production: *Kazimierz i Karolina*
Date and place of premiere: October 23, 2010, The Polski Theatre, Wrocław
Text by: Ödön von Horváth
Adaptation: Jan Klata
Set design: Mirek Kaczmarek
Music: Jan Klata

Title of the production: *A Piece on Mother and The Fatherland*
Original title of the production: *Utwór o Matce i Ojczyźnie*
Date and place of premiere: January 6, 2011, The Polski Theatre, Wrocław
Text by: Bożena Keff
Adaptation: Jan Klata
Set design: Justyna Łagowska
Music: Jan Klata

Title of the production: *Amerika*
Original title of the production: *Ameryka*
Date and place of premiere: April 28, 2011, Schauspielhaus Bochum, (Germany)
Text by: Franz Kafka
Adaptation: Jan Klata
Set design: Justyna Łagowska
Music: Jan Klata

Title of the production: *The Chevau-légers*
Original title of the production: *Szwoleżerowie*
Date and place of premiere: July 29, 2011, The Polski Theatre, Bydgoszcz
Text by: Artur Pałyga
Adaptation: Jan Klata
Set design: Mirek Kaczmarek
Music: Jan Klata

Title of the production: *The Robbers*
Original title of the production: *Die Räuber*
Date and place of premiere: March 3, 2012, Schauspielhaus Bochum, (Germany)
Text by: Friedrich Schiller
Adaptation: Jan Klata
Set design: Justyna Łagowska
Music: Jan Klata

Title of the production: *Jerry Springer - The Opera*
Original title of the production: *Jerry Springer - The Opera*
Date and place of premiere: March 24, 2012, The Music Theatre in Wrocław
Text by: Richard Thomas
Adaptation: Jan Klata
Set design: Justyna Łagowska

Title of the production: *Titus Andronicus*
Original title of the production: *Titus Andronicus*
Date and place of premiere: September 15, 2012, The Polski Theatre, Wrocław
Text by: William Shakespeare
Adaptation: Jan Klata
Set design: Justyna Łagowska
Music: Jan Klata

Title of the production: *Hamlet*
Original title of the production: *Hamlet*
Date and place of premiere: March 9, 2013, Schauspielhaus Bochum, (Germany)
Text by: William Shakespeare
Adaptation: Jan Klata
Set design: Justyna Łagowska
Music: Jan Klata

Title of the production: *To Damascus*
Original title of the production: *Do Damaszku*
Date and place of premiere: October 5, 2013, The Helena Modrzejewska National Stary Theatre, Krakow
Text by: August Strindberg
Adaptation: Sebastian Majewski
Set design: Mirek Kaczmarek
Music: Jan Klata

Title of the production: *Oedipus the King*
Original title of the production: *Król Edyp*
Date and place of premiere: October 17, 2013, The Helena Modrzejewska National Stary Theatre, Krakow
Text by: Sophocles
Set design: Karolina Mazur
Music: Jan Klata

Title of the production: *The Polish Thermopylae*
Original title of the production: *Termopile polskie*
Date and place of premiere: May 3, 2014, The Polski Theatre, Wrocław
Text by: Tadeusz Miciński
Adaptation: Jan Klata
Set design: Justyna Łagowska

Music: Robert Piernikowski

Title of the production: *King Ubu*
Original title of the production: *Król Ubu*
Date and place of premiere: October 16, 2014, The Helena Modrzejewska National Stary Theatre, Krakow
Text by: Alfred Jarry
Adaptation: Jan Klata
Set design: Justyna Łagowska
Music: Jan Klata

Title of the production: *King Lear*
Original title of the production: *Król Lear*
Date and place of premiere: December 19, 2014, The Helena Modrzejewska National Stary Theatre, Krakow
Text by: William Shakespeare
Adaptation: Jan Klata
Set design: Justyna Łagowska
Music: Jan Klata

Title of the production: *An Enemy of the people*
Original title of the production: *Wróg ludu*
Date and place of premiere: October 3, 2015, The Helena Modrzejewska National Stary Theatre, Krakow
Text by: Henrik Ibsen
Adaptation: Jan Klata
Set design: Justyna Łagowska
Music: Jan Klata

BIBLIOGRAPHY

Bernhard, Thomas. *Woodcutters.* Wrocław: Polski Theatre, 2014.

Błaszkiewicz, Karolina. „Wkurwili się ludzie na butną władzę, chcieli jej pokazać faka i pokazali," *naTemat*, December 6, 2015.

Boniecka, Joanna. „Ja służę demonowi – rozmowa z Krystianem Lupą." *Odra*, no. 4 (1992): 30.

Bryś, Marta, Kwaśniewska, Monika. „Spektakl jak sztafeta - rozmowa z Magdaleną Cielecką." *Didaskalia*, no. 92/93 (2009): 22-23.

Bulgakov, Mikhail. *The Master and Margarita.* Moscow: AST Moscow, 2006.

Burzyńska, Anna Róża. „Druga strona singla – rozmowa z Janem Klatą." *Didaskalia*, no. 97-98 (2010): 2-3.

Celeda, Agnieszka. „To rzeczywistość jest skandaliczna - rozmowa z Krzysztofem Warlikowskim." *Polityka*, November 4, 2009.

Derkaczew, Joanna. „Żądam dostępu do włazu – rozmowa z Janem Klatą." *Gazeta Wyborcza*, November 21, 2011.

Dobrowolski, Paweł. „Inne czasy - rozmowa z Jackiem Poniedziałkiem." *Notatnik teatralny*, no. 62/63 (2011): 63.

Dostoyevsky, Fyodor. *The Brothers Karamazov.* Krakow: Stary Theatre, 1999.

Drewniak, Łukasz. „Czy publiczność oszaleje?." *Przekrój*, no. 1 (2003).

Drewniak, Łukasz. „W oku salonu – rozmowa z Janem Klatą." *Przekrój*, February 17, 2005.

Drewniak, Łukasz. „Tsunami młodości." In *Strategie publiczne, strategie prywatne. Teatr polski 1990-2005*, edited by Tomasz Plata, 109. Izabelin: Świat literacki, 2006.

Drewniak, Łukasz. „Marzenia ściętej głowy." *Dziennik*, April 4, 2008.

Drewniak, Łukasz. „Fałszywy mag świątyni teatru – rozmowa z Krystianem Lupą." *Dziennik*, April 4-5, 2009.

Drewniak, Łukasz. "Nietoty." *Radio Krakow*, December 17, 2013.

Fazan, Katarzyna. „Tandeta w złym, czy dobrym gatunku? Antyestetyka w polskim teatrze 20-lecia." In *20-lecie. Teatr polski po 1989*, edited by Dorota Jarząbek, 347. Kraków: Korporacja Ha! Art., 2010.

Fryz-Więcek, Agnieszka. „Skondensowany strach – rozmowa z Krzysztofem Warlikowskim." *Didaskalia*, no. 47 (2002): 7.

Fryz-Więcek, Agnieszka. „Okazja czyni diabła – rozmowa z Romanem Gancarczykiem, Jackiem Romanowskim i Piotrem Skibą." *Didaskalia*, no. 49/50, (2002): 15.

Głowacki, Paweł. „Bzyk martwej muchy." *Dziennik Polski*, May 14, 2002.

Gogol, Nikolai. *The Government Inspector*. New York: Oberon books, 2005.

Gruszczyński, Piotr. „Nie wymaga wirtuozerii - rozmowa z Piotrem Skibą." *Notatnik teatralny*, no. 18-19 (1999): 90.

Gruszczyński, Piotr. *Ojcobójcy. Młodsi zdolniejsi w teatrze polskim.* Warszawa: Wydawnictwo W.A.B., 2003.

Gruszczyński, Piotr. „Pochwała niepoprawności." *Tygodnik Powszechny*, February 9, 2005.

Gruszczyński, Piotr. „Krystian Lupa: wieczne dążenie." In *Strategie publiczne, strategie prywatne. Teatr polski 1990-2005*, edited by Tomasz Plata, 41. Izabelin: Świat literacki, 2006.

Gruszczyński, Piotr. *Szekspir i Uzurpator, z Krzysztofem Warlikowskim rozmawia Piotr Gruszczyński.* Warsaw: Wydawnictwo W.A.B., 2007.

Gruszczyński, Piotr. *(A)pollonia – program do spektaklu.* Warsaw: The Nowy Theatre, 2009.

Gruszczyński, Piotr. *Opowieści afrykańskie według Szekspira – program do spektaklu.* Warsaw: Teatr Nowy, 2011.

Guczalska, Beata. „Krystian Lupa w krakowskiej PWST." In *Gry z chaosem. O teatrze Krystiana Lupy*, edited by Grzegorz Niziołek, 58. Kraków: Narodowy Teatr Stary im. Heleny Modrzejewskiej, 2005.

Guczalska, Beata. *Aktorstwo polskie. Generacje.* Krakow: The Ludwik Solski Academy for the Dramatic Arts, 2014.

Hepel, Maria. „Nie ma przepisu - rozmowa z Mariuszem Bonaszewskim." *Notatnik teatralny*, no. 28-29 (2003): 149-150.

Janowska, Katarzyna. „Inspirują mnie nie miejsca, lecz widma - rozmowa z Krzysztofem Warlikowskim." *Przekrój*, no. 28 (2010): 65.

Jarry, Alfred. *Ubu Roi.* Paris: Editions Chemins de tr@verse, 2011.

Kane, Sarah. *Complete Plays: Blasted; Phaedra's Love; Cleansed; Crave; 4.48 Psychosis; Skin.* London: Methuen Drama, 2000.

Kardasińska, Dorota. „Dorosnąć do widowni - rozmowa z Janem Klatą." *Notatnik teatralny*, no. 32-33 (2004): 64-65.

Klata, Jan. „O prawdzie i nieprawdzie, etyce i estetyce." *Notatnik teatralny*, no. 32-33 (2004): 76.

Kluzowicz, Julia. „Faktoryjka – rozmowa z aktorami." *Didaskalia*, no. 84 (2008): 17.

Koenig, Jerzy. „Jeden dzień z życia pisarza." *Teatr*, no. 12 (2006): 22.

Kowalska, Jolanta. „Egzorcysta." *Notatnik teatralny*, no. 38 (2005): 85.

Krzywicka, Dorota. *Elektra – program do spektaklu.* Warsaw: The Dramatic Theatre, 1997.

Kubikowski, Tomasz. „Pustka i forma." In *Strategie publiczne, strategie prywatne. Teatr polski 1990-2005*, edited by Tomasz Plata, 18. Izabelin: Świat literacki, 2006.

Ligarzewska, Natalia. „Relacje - rozmowa z Joanną Bogacką, Marcinem Czarnikiem, Grzegorzem Gzylem i Martą Kalmus." *Notatnik teatralny*, no. 38 (2005): 74.

Likowska, Ewa. „Ekstrawagant - rozmowa z Krystianem Lupą." *Polityka*, no. 37, (2006): 76.

Lupa, Krystian. „Kalkwerk Thomasa Bernharda." *Notatnik Teatralny*, no. 7 (1993/94): 61.

Lupa, Krystian. *Utopia 2. Penetracje.* Krakow: Wydawnictwo Literackie, 2003.

Lupa, Krystian. „Krzysztof W. – notatki z dziennika." *Notatnik teatralny*, no. 28-29, (2003): 33-35.

Lupa, Krystian. „Aktor jako centaur." In *Świadomość teatru. Polska myśl teatralna drugiej połowy XX wieku*, edited by Wojciech Dudzik, 234-235. Warszawa: Wydawnictwo Naukowe PWN, 2007.

Lupa, Krystian. *Persona.* Warszawa: Dramatic Theatre of the Capital City of Warsaw, 2010.

Łopatka, Paweł. „Przezroczysty niepokój – rozmowa z Krystianem Lupą." *Didaskalia*, no. 53 (2003): 28.

Łukosz, Jerzy. "Kant tańczy." *Teatr*, no. 4, (1996).

Łuszczyk, Katarzyna. „Podróż w siebie - rozmowa z Jackiem Poniedziałkiem." *Notatnik teatralny*, no. 28-29 (2003): 41-42.

Maciejewski, Łukasz. „Chcę - rozmowa z Michałem Czerneckim." *Notatnik Teatralny*, no. 34 (2004): 82.

Maciejewski, Łukasz. „Dziwny dynamit - rozmowa z Krystianem Lupą." *Notatnik teatralny*, no. 28 (2005): 6.

Matkowska-Święs, Beata. „Wciąż noszę te siedem dachówek – rozmowa z Krystianem Lupą." *Magazyn Gazeta*, June 1, 2000.

Matkowska-Święs, Beata. *Podróż do Nieuchwytnego. Rozmowy z Krystianem Lupą.* Krakow: Wydawnictwo Literackie, 2003.

Michalski, Cezary. "Guślarz w mundurze Jungera – rozmowa z Janem Klatą." *Newsweek*, September 20, 2008.

Mieszkowski, Krzysztof. „Do jutra - rozmowa z Krzysztofem Warlikowskim." *Notatnik teatralny*, no. 28-29 (2003): 229.

Mieszkowski, Krzysztof. „Człowiek nie jest finałem - rozmowa z Krystianem Lupą." *Notatnik Teatralny*, no. 34 (2004): 32.

Migdałowska, Katarzyna. „Do Timbuktu - rozmowa z Danutą Marosz, Ryszardem Węgrzynem, Dariuszem Majem, Andrzejem Szubskim." *Notatnik teatralny*, no. 38 (2005): 56.

Mikos, Marek. „Konrad. Bernharda, Lupy i Hudziaka." *Notatnik Teatralny*, no. 7 (1993/94): 77.

Niziołek, Grzegorz. „Aktor w obnażających sytuacjach – rozmowa z Krystianem Lupą." *Didaskalia*, no. 10 (1995): 11.

Nyczek, Tadeusz. „Teatr Klaty - rewolucja na niby." *Gazeta Wyborcza*, December 17, 2005.

Nyczek, Tadeusz. „Andy II," *Teatr*, no. 4 (2008): 15.

Pawlicka, Aleksandra. „Kibolski patriotyzm – rozmowa z Janem Klatą." *Newsweek*, August 25, 2015.

Pawłowski, Roman. „Gdański Hamlet postindustrialny." *Gazeta Wyborcza*, July 2, 2004.

Pawłowski, Roman. „... *córka Fizdejki* – współcześni niewolnicy historii i stereotypów." *Gazeta Wyborcza*, December 21, 2004.

Pawłowski, Roman. „Umarła klasa XXI wieku." *Gazeta Wyborcza*, November 20, 2006.

Pawłowski, Roman. „Rzecz, która nie lubi być zabijana – rozmowa z Hanną Krall i Krzysztofem Warlikowskim." *Gazeta Wyborcza*, May 14, 2009.

Połabińska, Izabela. „Notatki z prób." *Didaskalia*, no. 49/50 (2002): 19-25.

Rigamonti, Magdalena. „Artysta żyje krócej niż człowiek – rozmowa z Krystianem Lupą" *Newsweek*, July 24, 2010.

Romanowski, Rafał. „Taki już mój los; podniebne wojowanie – rozmowa z Janem Klatą." *Gazeta Wyborcza*, October 16, 2015.

Sienkiewicz, Henryk. *Pan Michael: An Historical Novel of Poland, the Ukraine, and Turkey.* Boston: 1889.

Sienkiewicz, Henryk. *With Fire and Sword: An Historical Novel of Poland and Russia.* Boston: 1894.

Sieradzki, Jacek. „Jan Klata, czyli pasja." *Notatnik teatralny*, no. 38 (2005): 110.

Skwarczyńska, Agata. „Wolność wyboru - rozmowa z Małgorzatą Szczęśniak." *Notatnik teatralny*, no. 62/63 (2011): 41.

Szydłowska, Aleksandra. „To nie znaczy, że jestem fryzjerem - rozmowa z Krystianem Lupą." *Notatnik Teatralny*, no. 11 (1996): 93-96.

Sugiera, Małgorzata. "Po premierze." *Didaskalia*, no. 42 (2015).

Śmigulec, Anna. „Psy na Klacie. Dlaczego Kraków nie chce w Starym Jana Klaty." *Gazeta Wyborcza*, July 3, 2014.

Targoń, Joanna. „Grzech pierworodny – rozmowa z Małgorzatą Szczęśniak, Krzysztofem Warlikowskim i Jackiem Poniedziałkiem." *Didaskalia*, no. 34 (1999): 8-11.

Tomczuk, Jacek. „Przyzwyczailiśmy się już do pokoju. I tu nagle Ukraina – rozmowa z Krystianem Lupą." *Newsweek*, March 22, 2014.

Urbaniak, Mike. „Warszawa to nie bułka z masłem – rozmowa z Krzysztofem Warlikowskim." *Przekrój*, no. 20 (2013): 6.

Węgrzyniak, Rafał. „Niepoprawny. Kontrowersje wokół wymowy ideowej przedstawień Klaty." *Notatnik teatralny*, no. 38 (2005): 25.

Wilniewczyc, Teresa. „Dzień wcześniej skończyłam pięćdziesiąt lat - rozmowa ze Stanisławą Celińską." *Notatnik teatralny*, no. 28-29 (2003): 18.

Żebrowska, Anna. „*Transfer* Klaty zdenerwował Rosjan." *Gazeta Wyborcza*, September 24, 2008.

INDEX

E

F

G

H

I

J

K

L

Ł

M

S

Ś

T

V

W

Z